Logic as Grammar

⊣L Bradford Books

Edward C. T. Walker, Editor. Explorations in THE BIOLOGY OF LANGUAGE. 1979.
Daniel C. Dennett. BRAINSTORMS. 1979.
Charles E. Marks. COMMISSUROTOMY, CONSCIOUSNESS AND UNITY OF MIND. 1980.
John Haugeland, Editor. MIND DESIGN. 1981.
Fred I. Dretske. KNOWLEDGE AND THE FLOW OF INFORMATION. 1981.
Jerry A. Fodor. REPRESENTATIONS. 1981.
Ned Block, Editor. IMAGERY. 1981.
Roger N. Shepard and Lynn A. Cooper. MENTAL IMAGES AND THEIR TRANS-FORMATIONS. 1982.
Hubert L. Dreyfus, Editor, in collaboration with Harrison Hall. HUSSERL, INTEN-TIONALITY AND COGNITIVE SCIENCE. 1982.
John Macnamara. NAMES FOR THINGS. 1982.
Natalie Abrams and Michael D. Buckner, Editors. MEDICAL ETHICS. 1982.
Morris Halle and G. N. Clements. PROBLEM BOOK IN PHONOLOGY. 1983.
Jerry A. Fodor. MODULARITY OF MIND. 1983.
George D. Romanos. QUINE AND ANALYTIC PHILOSOPHY. 1983.
Robert Cummins. THE NATURE OF PSYCHOLOGICAL EXPLANATION. 1983.
Irwin Rock. THE LOGIC OF PERCEPTION. 1983.
Stephen P. Stich. FROM FOLK PSYCHOLOGY TO COGNITIVE SCIENCE. 1983.
Jon Barwise and John Perry. SITUATIONS AND ATTITUDES. 1983.
Izchak Miller. HUSSERL'S THEORY OF PERCEPTION. 1984.
Elliot Sober, Editor. CONCEPTUAL ISSUES IN EVOLUTIONARY BIOLOGY. 1984.
Paul M. Churchland. MATTER AND CONSCIOUSNESS. 1984.
Ruth Garrett Millikan. LANGUAGE, THOUGHT AND OTHER BIOLOGICAL CONSIDERATIONS. 1984.
Myles Brand. INTENDING AND ACTING. 1984.
Zenon W. Pylyshyn. COMPUTATION AND COGNITION. 1984.
Herbert A. Simon and K. Anders Ericsson. PROTOCOL ANALYSIS. 1984.
Robert N. Brandon and Richard M. Burian. GENES, ORGANISMS, POPULATIONS. 1984.
Owen D. Flanagan. THE SCIENCE OF THE MIND. 1984.
Norbert Hornstein. LOGIC AS GRAMMAR. 1984.

Logic as Grammar

Norbert Hornstein

A Bradford Book
The MIT Press
Cambridge, Massachusetts
London, England

Second printing, 1986
Copyright © 1984 by
The Massachusetts Institute of Technology

This book was set in Palatino
by The MIT Press Computergraphics Department
and printed and bound by The Murray Printing Co.
in the United States of America

Library of Congress Cataloging in Publication Data

Hornstein, Norbert.
  Logic as grammar.

  "A Bradford book."
  Bibliography: p.
  Includes index.
  1. Semantics. 2. Grammar, Comparative and general.
3. Language and Logic. 4. Language acquisition.
I. Title.
P325.H62 1984   415   83–43036
ISBN 0–262–08137–7

For Isaac, Noam, and Sidney

Contents

Preface

For many years I have been convinced of two points on the problem of meaning in natural language. First, I believe that current model-theoretic semantical approaches to meaning do very little to explain the nature of a native speaker's interpretive abilities. Second, I believe that people interested in the problem of meaning in natural language are doing themselves a disservice by ignoring the approach to natural language (both the general methodological issues and the more specific technical devices) characteristic of work in generative grammar. This book is my attempt to redeem this pair of convictions. I adopt the central methodological assumptions of generative grammar in toto, and I try to show how they can be used to elaborate specific analyses. The analyses themselves eschew semantical notions almost entirely.

In many respects, I believe, the correct approach to issues in the theory of meaning hinges on an appreciation of how it is that the theory of meaning relates to a theory of understanding. Since its beginnings, work in generative grammar has focused attention on this crucial link by emphasizing the sorts of properties a linguistic theory would have to have if it were to enjoy psychological plausibility. What I call "the logical problem of language acquisition" attempts to state the minimal features a plausible theory of language understanding must have and how this should affect the process of theory construction in the domain of meaning. In the more technical chapters, I try to show how the very general considerations discussed in chapter 1 manifest themselves in particular analyses of quantifier-quantifier and quantifier-pronoun interactions.

If the importance of the generative perspective to issues in the theory of meaning is underestimated, the centrality of semantic notions for a theory of natural language interpretation is too often overestimated. It is simply assumed that semantical notions such as "truth," "reference," "object," "property," "model" will be central elements of an adequate theory of meaning. Little has been done to redeem this assumption, or at least this is what I will suggest in chapters 6 and 7. Chapter 6 argues that for a large part of what we consider pretheoretically the domain of a theory of meaning, the crucial concepts—in whose terms the explanatory principles are articulated—are syntactic rather than semantic. In chapter 7 I revive some skeptical doubts concerning the value of semantical notions for theoretical concerns.

Acknowledgments

In writing a book, no sentiment so dominates an author as a sense of heroism. If he is not exactly leaping tall problems with a single bound, the author does at least feel like a solitary yet determined Stanley hacking steadfastly through miles of difficulties. When he has finished, he finds that the phenomenological landscape changes with gestalt-like alacrity and totality. The heroic solitary investigator now resumes his place in the community of researchers. And if not exactly feeling like the right man in the right place, he feels like a man in a place. Other people occupy neighboring places, and it is their ideas and insights that he has just nudged along a bit. At this moment I clearly (and correctly) see that my efforts amount in large part to having organized the influences of others. At any rate, I would like to say here how grateful I am to all who have been kind enough to help. Special thanks go to Noam Chomsky, without whose work this book could never have been written, to the Columbia Philosophy Department and the Society of Fellows in the Humanities at Columbia for an extremely enjoyable and intellectually exhilarating four years, to Sidney Morgenbesser and Isaac Levi for never-ending, thought-provoking discussions, to Joseph Aoun, David Lightfoot, Dominique Sportiche, and Edwin Williams for invaluable help in untangling the issues discussed here, to Amy Weinberg, whose emotional support and tough intellectual standards made this book better than it would have been without her, to the junior faculty of Columbia for being great friends and colleagues, to Hilary Putnam, Burton Dreben, Warren Goldfarb, and Ed McCann for discussing the intricacies of Wittgenstein and meaning theory with me, and to The MIT Press and Bradford Books for the wonderful help and support they provided all through the writing of this book.

Logic as Grammar

Chapter 1
Semantic Competence

The purpose of this book is to consider how meaning in natural languages should be handled theoretically—in particular, how and to what extent phenomena usually construed as falling within the domain of a theory of meaning can be incorporated into a theory of the kind currently proposed by generative grammarians.[1] In this sense the book can be seen as a continuation of earlier efforts to extend the coverage of current grammatical theory from syntactic data to include phenomena characteristically described as semantic. What will make this effort somewhat different from many of these earlier (many still extant) approaches is that marrying semantic concerns with a generative approach to language demands wholesale changes in both the techniques and the basic concepts seen as relevant to a theory of meaning for natural language. In particular, once one tries to integrate issues of meaning within a generative framework, one must face a host of technical and, more important, methodological concerns that more standard treatments by and large ignore. Foremost among these is the logical problem of language acquisition, whose content and bearing on these issues I will investigate. Once such technical and methodological issues are taken to heart, I believe that it can be argued that semantic theories of meaning for natural languages—theories that exploit semantical notions such as "truth," "reference," "object," "property"—are not particularly attractive in explaining what speakers know when they know the meaning of a sentence in their native language. In short, a theory of meaning that is viewed as responsive to the same set of concerns characteristic of work in generative grammar to a large extent will not be a semantic theory, a theory cast in terms of a semantical theoretical vocabulary, but instead a syntactic one, a theory whose rules exploit a syntactic vocabulary and syntactic principles of well-formedness.

This thesis has both a weaker and a stronger interpretation. The weaker one simply says that we must redraw the boundary between syntax and semantics. Many of the phenomena earlier believed to be semantic (i.e., to be due to the generation of semantic rules and/or principles of the grammar) are better characterized in syntactic terms. The stronger interpretation is that the theory of language can dispense with the standard idealization of language, an idealization that crucially involves a semantic level of description. In other words, to explain what competent, mature, native speakers know about their language, it is unnecessary—and indeed quite misleading—to postulate a level of semantic representation halfway between the syntax of the sentence and the pragmatics of the utterance.

I believe the stronger interpretation is by and large correct, and I will advance reasons for this belief. However, it is important to see that even if this should prove incorrect, the weaker interpretation may nonetheless remain. Supporting the weaker claim can proceed straightforwardly. I will argue that properties of quantification such as relative quantifier scope and pronoun binding in natural language are best explained in purely syntactic terms. Not only are the explanations best construed syntactically but, more important, the distinctions and concepts needed to articulate them cut against the semantic distinctions one would naturally make.

Arguing in favor of the stronger interpretation will be a much touchier affair. This is because such an argument aims to dislodge a specific idealization rather than to discredit specific concrete proposals. Such arguments are never and cannot really hope to be conclusive. In a modified late Wittgensteinian vein, however, I will suggest that the reasons people have for assuming that such an approach must be correct are not very good, that alternatives are available, and that the burden of proof regarding the explanatory relevance of semantical notions is on those who insist on invoking them. In effect, then, I will argue that Fregean and Neo-Fregean idealizations of language, which regard semantical notions as essential to the correct characterization and explanation of the speaker's linguistic abilities, though perfectly coherent, have not borne fruit and that their "obvious" theoretical relevance to the study of language ought to be reconsidered.

To accomplish this, I must clarify some preliminary issues, which I propose to do in this introductory chapter. I will begin by stating what I take to be the central question that a theory of language ought to address, and by looking at how this question determines what types of theories of meaning will be considered adequate.

Next I will discuss what a semantic theory is a theory of, and I will propose some terminological conventions that will make it easier to consider the question of whether a theory of meaning must be a semantic theory. This is more important than might appear, since I believe that part of the problem surrounding theories of meaning revolves around certain preconceptions regarding what shape a theory of meaning must take. That these preconceptions are rather contentious is obscured by the terms used in talking about meaning. At any rate, a modest number of terminological revisions will help clarify the issues I would like to discuss. Last, I will outline the substantive issues that the succeeding, more technical chapters will elaborate.

The Methodological Setting

The framework of assumptions within which I will be working intimately links three questions:

1. What does a sentence S or construction C mean in a natural language like English?
2. What does a native speaker of English (tacitly) know about the meaning of S or C?
3. How is it that native speakers could have come to acquire this (tacit) knowledge about S or C?

These questions are obviously related and have been linked together by approaches that in all other respects are at right angles. Philosophers and linguists have exploited the fact that the sorts of answers that one can give to (3) will delimit the answers that one can give to (1) and (2). Linking questions (1) and (2) amounts to acknowledging that the properties that one attributes to a language must ultimately be grounded in some capacity the native speaker has in dealing with that language; languages and their properties have no existence apart from their potential speakers. In short, an account of the meaning of a sentence S or construction C must be tied to an account of how a native speaker understands and comes to understand the meaning. Thus, linking questions (1)–(3) indicates that I will consider a theory of meaning to be intimately tied to a theory of understanding.[2]

These assumptions are fairly standard. What language is, is at least in part a function of what speakers of the language (tacitly) have internalized. What one knows is a function of what it is possible for one to know. What is novel about the generative approach to these issues— the Extended Standard Theory (EST) approach, at least—is not that it links questions (1)–(3). Rather, it is the conditions that it places on an adequate answer to (3). Generative grammar highlights two salient facts about language acquisition and makes them central to its theoretical concerns: that a normal child can learn any language if raised in the appropriate speech community and that language acquisition proceeds despite extreme deficiencies in the data available to the child. In other words, the nub of this approach is to view explanations of linguistic abilities in the context of the problem of how a child growing up in any given linguistic community masters a rich and highly structured linguistic system on the basis of degenerate and deficient data. The deficiencies are these:

a. The speech that children hear consists not of uniformly complete, grammatical sentences but of utterances with pauses, slips of the tongue, incomplete thoughts, etc.

b. The data available to children are finite, yet as mature native speakers they come to be able to deal with an unbounded number of sentences, going far beyond the utterances actually encountered during the childhood acquisition period.

c. Speakers come to know things about the structure of their language for which no evidence is available in the primary linguistic data (i.e., the data to which they are exposed as children). Crucial evidence for such knowledge consists of judgments about complex and rare sentences, paraphrase and ambiguity relations, and ungrammatical "sentences," all of which are available to the theoretician but lie outside the primary linguistic data. Children are not systematically informed that some hypothetical sentences are in fact ungrammatical, that a given sentence is ambiguous, or that certain sets of sentences are paraphrases of each other, and many legitimate and acceptable sentence types may never occur in a child's linguistic experience. The distinction between the data available to the theoretician and the more limited data available to the child is of vital importance to the generative view of things.

The problem demanding explanation is compounded by other factors: despite variation in background and intelligence, speakers attain this complex but fairly uniform mature capacity in a remarkably short time, without much apparent effort, conscious thought, or difficulty; and it develops with only a narrow range of the logically possible "errors." Children do not test random hypotheses, rejecting those that are found to yield unacceptable sentences. We know this because in each language community the unacceptable sentences produced by very young children seem to be few in number and quite uniform from one child to another—a pattern of behavior that falls far short of random hypotheses. Normal children attain a fairly rich system of linguistic knowledge by the age of five or six and a mature system by puberty, an impressive feat when compared with the laborious efforts of squads of adult theoretical syntacticians, phonologists, and semanticists, who, with only moderate success, try to characterize explicitly what people know when they know a natural language.

These, then, are what I will take to be the salient facts about the acquisition of language: a rich system of knowledge emerges despite the poverty of the stimulus and deficiencies in the data available to the child. As the significance of the three kinds of data-deficiency has often been misconstrued, it is worthwhile to consider each kind in greater detail.

Suppose one tried to give an inductive account of language acquisition, where the mature ability was determined more or less entirely by the child's linguistic experience, by the "data" the child encounters. Deficiencies (a) and (b) offer difficulties because the inductive base (i.e., the evidence) is not straightforward; it is both *degenerate* and *finite*. Though an obstacle, such features are not necessarily fatal for inductive accounts. Neither (a) nor (b) denies that the relevant evidence exists in the database, but they point out that it is not as readily available as one might have supposed. In principle, one could overcome (b) by invoking a sophisticated inductive theory, one that induces a system of rules based on finite data—a second-order induction. To overcome (a) it would be necessary to incorporate some sampling techniques to sift out the good, relevant data from those that must be ignored at any given stage in the child's development; alternatively, one could claim that the child's linguistic experience is organized in such a way as to facilitate the learning of his native language (as an example, see Snow and Ferguson 1977 and references cited there). It is often claimed, for instance, that mothers speak to children in a simplified language and that one can identify a "motherese." It is alleged that this enables the child to circumvent the deficiency of data and provides sufficient structure for language acquisition to take place on an inductive basis, without the aid of a rich set of innate principles. Thus, it is claimed that the linguistic environment does not suffer as much from deficiency (a) as might be supposed.

It is certainly true that mothers and other people sometimes adopt a simple style of speech when addressing children, but it is scarcely plausible that this "motherese" provides a sufficient inductive base for language learning. First, although children no doubt ignore much of their linguistic environment, we have no way of knowing exactly what any particular child registers. It is certainly not the case that children register sentences only when they make eye contact with the interlocutor, as is sometimes claimed. By general observation, young children are great mimics and often imitate the speech of adults or older children who are paying no attention to them, or even imitate the radio (particularly by reproducing intonation patterns). Therefore, there is no factual basis to the claim that children "register" only what is filtered for them through "motherese"; see Newport, Gleitman, and Gleitman 1977, who show that what children do hear bears little resemblance to "motherese." Children have access to more than what is filtered through "motherese," including defective sentences. As Chomsky 1975 observes, exposure to only a small number of defective sentences would suffice to cause problems for a purely inductive theory. If only 5 percent of the sentences the child hears are ungrammatical, the problem will be significant because the sentences are not labeled as such. As an analogy, consider the difficulty one would have in deducing the legitimate moves of chess without the benefit of instruction or explicit correction, when exposed to fabricated games where one knew in advance that 5 percent of the moves were illegal but not which particular moves. Imagine the experience needed to figure out in those conditions the rules for castling.

Second, even if we were to abstract away from the immense difficulty of showing which sentences children actually register and suppose that the child notices only perfectly well formed sentences (i.e., even if we were to assume that deficiency (a) does not exist), we would have to claim much more to show that the child has a sufficient inductive base for language learning. In particular, the child would need to know in which order data should be registered, and the "mother" would need to know in which order data should be presented. Presumably, if the child were entirely dependent on his linguistic environment, whether he first registers regular or irregular verbs, finite or infinitival relative clauses, etc., would make a difference to the final state attained. Deficiencies (a) and (b), then, entail a great deal of elaboration in inductive theories, but they do not alone suffice to discredit such learning theories in general. Deficiency (c), however, does.[3]

The fact is that for a substantial part of mature linguistic knowledge the data provide no evidence that one can reasonably believe the child has access to. This deficiency shifts the nature of the problem dramatically. No inductive theory can possibly be adequate unless some data exist from which induction can proceed. If the child's experience affords no such data (contrast this, again, with the more extensive data available to the theoretician), no inductive learning theory can suffice, because there is no way that inductive learning can get started. In effect, then, it is (c) that offers the most challenging problem for any theory of acquisition. Even if the child had perfect evidence along dimensions (a) and (b), the logical problem of language acquisition would exist in essentially its present form. The problem is not that the data are inadequate but that for certain areas they do not exist at all.

There is substantial evidence that (c) is correct. Much of the recent linguistic literature has focused on areas of grammar where the best description is underdetermined by the data the child has access to. If these descriptive claims are correct, then it follows that inductive theories must be abandoned, because there is no inductive base. If the child's linguistic experience does not provide the basis for establishing some particular aspect of mature linguistic knowledge, that knowledge will have to have some other source. It will have to be a priori in the sense that it arises independently of linguistic experience. It may be present innately or arise from some nonlinguistic experience. Moreover, if such a priori knowledge must be attributed to the organism in order to circumvent deficiency (c), it will also provide a way to circumvent (a) and (b). Theorists need not concern themselves with the real extent of deficiencies (a) and (b); the degeneracy and finiteness of the data are not real problems for the child, because he is not totally dependent on his linguistic experience and he knows certain things a priori. In many areas, exposure to a very limited range of data will enable a child to attain the correct grammar, which in turn will enable him to utter and understand a complex range of sentence-types.[4]

In summary, the central problem is set by deficiency (c). Even if deficiencies (a) and (b) did not exist, the essential logic of the problem would remain the same. Therefore, recent work claiming that deficiency (a) is not pernicious has no significance for an account of language acquisition. It would be significant only if it were accompanied by a *plausible* claim that deficiencies (b) and, in particular, (c) also did not exist, and therefore that there is a sufficient inductive basis for language acquisition.

The Form of the Solution

What picture of language acquisition emerges, given these considerations, and what restraints do these considerations place on prospective explanations and theories concerning specific linguistic abilities? In other words, what should we expect of any particular explanation of a linguistic ability if it is to come to terms with the logical problem of language acquisition?

First, any adequate theory will approach deficiency (c) by postulating a rather rich set of innate mechanisms that language learners bring to the task of acquiring their native language. The reason for this is straightforward. There can be only two sources for the mature speaker's (tacit) knowledge of his language: it is a result either of the linguistic environment or of the intrinsic structure of the acquisition system. No one has ever proposed a third possibility. Since deficiency argument (c) rules out an inductivist account, which would exploit the structure of the linguistic environment, we are left with the only other choice: nativism. These innate mechanisms—the "universals" of "Universal Grammar"—are taken to describe the language faculty, a mental faculty causally responsible for whatever specifically linguistic knowledge one must have in order to acquire a human language in the way humans characteristically do. It is possible that there is no specific linguistic knowledge of this kind and that what is being studied can be explained on the basis of less specific cognitive principles. However, the view outlined here strongly suggests that this is wrong. More important, on such a view not everything reflected in language necessarily pertains to a theory of linguistics—only those features of linguistic knowledge for which this faculty is responsible. It is an empirical issue to determine how much this covers. After all, it is readily conceded that the operations of other cognitive faculties are reflected in what speakers say and comprehend. On the approach adopted here, then, the main task for a theory of language is to specify the nature of this mental faculty.

Considering deficiency argument (b) helps illuminate the nature of the innate mechanisms that characterize the language faculty. A native speaker can utter and comprehend an unlimited number of sentences; in other words, for all practical purposes the language system is infinite. Since we are finite beings, it must be the case that what we attain is a finitely specifiable rule system or grammar that operates to yield the theoretically infinite number of sentences. Moreover, given the obvious diversity of the world's natural languages and the fact that a child can learn any of them, the innate mechanisms cannot be language-specific; what is innately specified cannot be the set of rules for a particular language.

Taken together, these points suggest that the innate principles underlying language acquisition restrict the nature of the possible rule systems or *grammars* that can be acquired and that they are abstract enough to hold universally—for any possible human grammar—yet rich enough to show how any particular grammar might be acquired given the stated boundary conditions.

A natural approach combining these two points sees a theory of language as articulating a set of deductively related innate principles placing restrictions on possible grammars—called *Universal Grammar* (UG)—which have certain open parameters whose values are fixed by the primary linguistic data. Language acquisition consists largely of fixing these values on the basis of the data available to the child. Viewing things in this way will yield approximately the right results. The surface diversity of natural languages is accommodated, since assigning different values to open parameters of highly deductive systems (in this case grammars) can result in outputs (in this case sentences) whose surface properties are extremely diverse. Given the recursive/iterative nature of grammatical rules, a small change in the grammar of a language can have wide-ranging effects and lead to extensive differences at the surface level, that is, in the surface syntax of sentences.

Issues involving the poverty of the stimulus are accommodated by limiting the role of primary linguistic data to fixing the values of specific parameters of otherwise innate principles. Given this, explanations of specific abilities will take the following form: each will propose certain universal principles that, in conjunction with data one can reasonably suppose to be part of the child's linguistic experience, will yield the system of knowledge that by hypothesis underlies the mature native speaker's linguistic competence. In short, each account will consist of two parts: a set of universal principles one can presume to be innate, which bear on the ability in question, and a set of data one can presume to be part of the primary linguistic data relevant to fixing the requisite knowledge.

Constructing such an argument is by no means easy. In fact most work on the semantics of natural language has failed to show that there is any real *structure* to semantic systems at all. However, short of showing this, there is little reason to believe that any substantial part of the semantic ability is innate and hence bears on the structure of the language faculty as characterized by Universal Grammar. To be valid, a poverty-of-stimulus argument requires the existence of a rich ability—indicative of a rich system—in relation to which the stimulus is poor. By failing to show that such conditions exist in the domain of semantics, most work in this area has failed to provide the necessary ingredients for a successful poverty-of-stimulus argument. As it is this kind of argument that buttresses claims about Universal Grammar, it will be incumbent upon anyone wishing to address these questions to offer arguments of this sort. In what follows, as the aim of the discussion will be to define how the language faculty relates to issues of meaning, such explanations will be crucially important.

This view of language has other implications for linguistic explanations. First, the theoretical focus of such explanations will be *rules* and *grammars* rather than the sentences that are the outputs of rules and grammars. Recall that the innate principles in terms of which a solution to the logical problem of language acquisition proceeds are conditions on possible grammars. Grammars yield surface strings or sentences. However, our theoretical focus is not simply on surface strings, but on structured strings. Following traditional usage, let us distinguish between the *strong* and *weak generative capacity* of a grammar.[5] Two grammars are equivalent with respect to weak generative capacity (or are "weakly equivalent") if they both generate the same surface strings. They are strongly equivalent if they generate the same strings with the same labeled bracketings. Thus, for example, if grammar A generates the labeled string $[_\alpha \text{ a } [_\beta \text{ ab}]]$ and grammar B the string $[_\alpha \text{ aa } [_\beta \text{ b}]]$, they are weakly equivalent but not strongly equivalent.

Once one adopts the poverty-of-stimulus viewpoint, it is *strong* generative capacity that is of primary theoretical interest, and weak generative capacity is important only to the degree that it bears on the issue of strong generative capacity. Why? Because the innate principles in terms of which a solution to the logical problem of language acquisition proceeds are conditions on the *structure of grammars*—for example, conditions on what constitutes a possible grammatical rule— and it is strong generative capacity that bears most directly on the nature of rule systems. Thus, the primary concerns of a theory of language adopting the above perspective will be the notion of grammar rather than language and strong rather than weak generative capacity. It is the nature and properties of rules rather than simply their outputs that will be of primary interest in evaluating proposals for dealing with specific problems. Proposals will be highly valued if they invoke rules of the right kind. Coverage of the data (demonstrating the ability to weakly generate the acceptable sentences of a language) is not the ultimate aim of the theory being considered here. It is at best one desideratum among many and surely not the most important. Specifically, theoretical explanations are subject to evaluation along three dimensions:

    a.   Coverage of empirical data, showing that a class of facts follows from the principles we hypothesize.

    b.   Standards of simplicity and elegance, showing that the principles meet the usual general requirements of scientific theorizing.

    c.   A demonstration that the principles give insight into the central problem of acquisition.

Any specific proposal will be evaluated in terms of its explanatory ability according to these criteria. The criteria do not have equal weight, however, and (c) is clearly of paramount significance on the approach being adopted here.

The importance of (a) is sometimes overestimated because of a widespread belief that one can know which facts some theory is responsible for independently of any particular theory of those facts. Certainly it is necessary to show that some class of facts follows from the principles one postulates, but I do not accept that there can be valid pretheoretical notions about what facts must follow from any given principle. For example, suppose that it is a fact that children generally acquire the use of simple, one-clause structures before compound sentences; there is no reason to assume that this fact must follow from some particular principle of the theory of grammar, as opposed, let us say, to some property of perceptual maturation or of the developing short-term memory capacity. To take another example, some linguists assume that *himself likes John* is ungrammatical by virtue of a misapplied transformation; others that an interpretive semantic rule is involved. Since unacceptability judgments, like facts in general, do not come labeled as inherently syntactic or semantic, there is no a priori way of evaluating these alternative analyses. One will prefer whichever analysis of this string is compatible with the overall most explanatory theory of grammar. From this assumption it follows that a theory cannot be refuted simply by showing that some particular fact does not follow from some particular principle. A principle is responsible only for the *relevant* facts; since facts do not come labeled, one cannot know which facts are relevant until one has a theory. The relevance of some fact—i.e., the reason for treating the fact as a function of a particular principle—lies in the overall, global success of the theory. There is a certain circularity to this, whereby we justify a theory in terms of the relevant facts for which it accounts and determine the relevance of the facts by the success of the theory that entails them. This kind of circularity, however, is inescapable; it is not vicious and our theories are refutable and subject to rational debate, as will become clear. They are not, however, trivially refutable by the citation of a single recalcitrant or unexplained fact.

Part of the problem of a theory of meaning is to determine *which* facts ought to be explained. We should not assume ahead of time which facts a theory of meaning *must* explain and which notions it *must* invoke in order to be acceptable.[6] The main desideratum of a theory of meaning as conceived here will be to explain some "significant" part of the data *pretheoretically* construed as relating to meaning *and* as being able to provide an answer for the logical problem of language acquisition. The first point is intended to be quite weak; we do not know and should not strongly prejudge what does and does not pertain to a theory of meaning. This is crucially important for theorizing of the generative variety, since it is assumed that Universal Grammar characterizes a specific cognitive faculty—the language faculty—and this is only one faculty among many others. To treat a sentence as part of a theory of meaning on this account is to consider that its interpretive properties can be traced to the operation of the mechanisms of this faculty rather than some other. It is indisputable that much of what we naively take to pertain to the meaning of a sentence will not be assimilated to a theory of this kind, just as many aspects of meaning traditionally are not taken as belonging to a theory of sense. However, as will become apparent, I believe that the need for revision of our current views concerning the shape of theories of meaning is more extensive than might be supposed by those trying to wed Frege and Chomsky. All I wish to point out here is that such a conclusion should not be considered a priori absurd. The aim of a theory of meaning as construed here is to describe those aspects of a native speaker's "semantic" abilities that can be tied to the operation of the language faculty. Other aspects of meaning, though very important, are not part of such a theory any more than the Gricean theory of implicatures, say, is part of a theory of sense.

Criterion (c), that explanatory principles should illuminate the nature of the acquisition process, is fundamentally important because of the way the problem of linguistic explanation is conceived. In particular, a principle meeting conditions (a) and (b), but not (c), is a generalization of no explanatory force. One might postulate a simple, elegant principle entailing a significant range of facts, which makes no psychological sense in terms of language acquisition; one would accept it on the basis of conditions (a) and (b), but reject it on the basis of the paramount importance of (c). Thus, for example, one would reject any principle that could be shown to be attainable only on exposure to nonprimary data, such as the information that a certain multiclausal sentence is unacceptable.

The explanatory depth attained by different theories can also be compared as a function of criteria (a)–(c). It is not the case that theories either are or are not explanatorily adequate; rather, they are more or less so. Moreover, they may offer different kinds of explanation. Thus, given the primacy of criterion (c), a theory shedding greater light on the acquisition process and thereby attaining greater explanatory depth will be preferred; a theory will not be preferred simply because it allows greater coverage of data, meanwhile sacrificing either elegance or insight into the acquisition process. Two theories equivalent under criterion (c) will be evaluated under (a) and (b), but (c) has primacy.

This, then, is the methodological setting. In the chapters that follow, my goal will be to construct a theory able to explain the properties of certain quantifier-quantifier interactions and quantifier-pronoun interactions that is responsive to the concerns I have noted. It will turn out that the best account of the data using these criteria need invoke virtually *no* semantic notions. Thus, for these phenomena at least, many of the more traditional semantic approaches are on the wrong track. To see this more clearly, let us consider the aims and methods of certain more common and influential *semantic* theories of interpretation.

Semantic Theories of Meaning

How have philosophers (and linguists) working on meaning generally conceived of their project? It has been a rather standard assumption of philosophical (and philosophically inspired) work on meaning in natural language that the proper approach will be semantical.[7] Indeed, this view is so pervasive that the terms 'meaning' and 'semantics' have become virtually interchangeable; a theory of meaning *is* a semantic theory and it is constitutive of such a theory that it be cast in semantical terms. Note that a theory of meaning thus construed is not outlined in terms of the kinds of data or problems it deals with, but in terms of the theoretical apparatus it exploits. To be more precise, let us give the name *interpretation theory* to one that deals with those linguistic phenomena (relative quantifier scope, tenses, modality, etc.) that we would pretheoretically classify as pertaining to meaning. The classical philosophical view, stemming originally from the work of Frege and Russell, is that the bulk, or a very large and central explanatory part, of interpretation theory will be exhausted by semantics. The key theoretical notions of interpretation theory will be semantical ones such as "truth," "proposition," "object," "denotation," and "model." Understanding the meaning of a sentence will consist in understanding the proposition it denotes. Understanding a proposition will be explained in terms of understanding its truth conditions, which are in turn explained in terms of what kinds of objects specific terms denote— individuals, properties, relations, etc. From this point of view, the linguistic ability of a native speaker then includes knowledge of how language relates to a nonlinguistic reality and, in fact, it is *in virtue* of such knowledge that a speaker's interpretive abilities are explained.

This, then, is roughly the background of most current work in the theory of meaning. What is its articulated structure? A semantic theory of the Fregean variety as applied to natural language can be seen as advancing two major points. (A Russellian theory will be roughly similar.) First, the main explanatory burden of interpretation theory is carried by rules that relate syntactically specified linguistic items to corresponding nonsyntactically specified objects. The latter objects are described by semantic terms of the sort mentioned earlier, such as "truth," "object," "proposition," "reference," "model." These semantic objects play a central explanatory role in a theory of meaning; semantic rules relate syntactic objects to semantic ones, e.g., sentences to propositions. These semantic objects are then related to the specific meaning of utterances—sentences in use—via pragmatic rules. The first rules are often characterized as the object of a theory of sense, the second as the object of a theory of force. The underlying claim, then, is that a level of representation lying *between* the syntactic aspects of the sentence and the pragmatic aspects of the utterance must crucially be invoked to explain what a native speaker understands when he understands the full meaning of an utterance; moreover, that this level—the level of the proposition—is best characterized using a semantical vocabulary.

Such an approach, which I will call *Neo-Fregean*, involves subsidiary theoretical questions such as whether expressions denote the same objects in every linguistic environment (e.g., the problem of opacity), whether a particular expression (e.g., a fictional term) denotes at all, and so forth. However, the central theoretical intuition is that a level of semantic analysis lying between the syntactic and the pragmatic is crucial to any interpretation theory for natural languages.

The second important claim is that the rules underlying the semantic level are by and large not context sensitive.[8] Syntactic linguistic items have semantic roles that are largely determinable independently of pragmatic factors. This is a natural claim for such Neo-Fregean theories to make, given that one of their aims is to provide a level of interpretation that acts as imput to rules that then determine pragmatic import. If the notions "object," "truth," etc., or the rules relating syntactically specified items to semantic ones were themselves pragmatically determined or overly sensitive to context, intention, etc., it is hard to see how such a level of interpretation could exist. If the rules underlying the semantic level were context sensitive, it would seem that pragmatic factors would determine semantic ones; that is, a theory of force would be prior to a theory of sense. Thus, the rules of a neo-Fregean interpretation theory are of the form "x denotes y" or "x has sense y" where 'x' is a syntactically specified item and 'y' a semantic object. In more familiar terms, interpretation theory on this construal includes a context-insensitive set of rules of sense that give the sense of a sentence—what *proposition* it expresses. This sense is then input to context-sensitive rules of force that determine the other aspects of what we would call the full meaning of the *utterance*. To summarize, a Neo-Fregean theory of interpretation advocates the necessity of a set of context-insensitive rules that take syntactically specified things—sentences—into semantically specified ones—propositions—and specifies that the latter are themselves input to pragmatic rules of force that yield the full meaning of the utterance.

Both these aspects of a Neo-Fregean semantic approach to interpretation theory can be challenged. One might question the extent to which semantic notions are needed to explain the phenomena for which interpretation theory is pretheoretically held responsible. In other words, one might question the explanatory appropriateness of a semantic theory as the correct theory of interpretation. More radically, one might question whether the data we pretheoretically believe a theory of interpretation must explain can be explained by a single theory or indeed by any theory. To relate these points to earlier ones, one might ask whether native speakers interpret sentences as they do *in virtue* of understanding that certain syntactic items have certain semantic roles (e.g., pick out certain types of objects). If the Neo-Fregean approach is correct, the semantic account will be crucial for successful accounts of a wide range of phenomena pretheoretically seen as pertaining to meaning. Furthermore, if Frege's theories are to be wed to generative grammar, the sort of rules that Neo-Fregeans envisage will form part of Universal Grammar. In fact, a way of formulating the Neo-Fregean theory in generative terms is to claim that there is a set of rules of Universal Grammar of the kind semantic theories claim to exist. Included in the theory of Universal Grammar will be a theory that claims that understanding language involves understanding certain semantic concepts and their link to syntactic ones. This is a coherent thesis, but it is important to see that it may be false. Put this way, it is an open question whether a semantic theory indeed forms part of a theory of interpretation; whether such a level of analysis is important or central in explaining certain aspects of a speaker's linguistic abilities, or how he understands the meaning of an utterance.

Similarly, one might challenge the view that context-insensitive semantic rules really exist. Perhaps most interpretive rules are highly context sensitive, i.e., sensitive to pragmatic features of the discourse situation. Or, if context-insensitive rules do exist, perhaps they make no essential use of the fact that an item has a certain semantic role; for example, perhaps they are syntactic. Thus, one might agree with the Neo-Fregeans that there exist levels of analysis more abstract than surface syntax that must be invoked in explaining a native speaker's linguistic competence but deny that such levels must be, should be, or can be described in semantic terms.

I believe that both these objections to traditional semantic theories of natural language interpretation can be maintained. If this is so, it will be necessary to rethink certain basic presuppositions concerning a theory of interpretation. Earlier theorists have not seen this, I believe, because natural language has been investigated using the tools and concepts developed for the investigation of mathematical languages. Such languages are logically perfect (or can be treated as such) in the sense that syntactic structures and semantic rules mirror one another. Moreover, focusing on such languages essentially abstracts away from all pragmatic questions, given the special use to which such languages are put. Consequently, if such a view of language is transferred over to the study of natural language, it is not very urgent to decide, for example, whether a certain interpretive phenomenon is syntactically or semantically licensed, or how to relate the "meaning" of the items semantically construed to their uses or pragmatic import. Such a mathematical perspective essentially abstracts away from both syntax and use (pragmatics). Once natural language is treated on its own terms, such an "idealization" is no longer obviously relevant. Natural languages need not be logically perfect, nor are they used in only one way. These points, and related ones, will be elaborated considerably in later chapters.

However, before offering a more general abstract critique of the semantic endeavor, I will advance arguments on a more modest scale. In what follows, I will try to show that many phenomena surrounding quantifier scope and pronoun binding in natural languages like English are best described in syntactic terms. Moreover, I will argue that a natural semantic approach leads in the wrong direction. I will argue that one can give a full and interesting characterization of the speaker's competence in this domain in terms of Universal Grammar specifying the principles and open parameters in terms of which the logical problem of language acquisition could be solved. This project will occupy the next several chapters. Though these chapters are somewhat technical, I believe that the discussion that follows them depends on this technical sort of work. I do believe that the Neo-Fregean program is correct in one sense—namely, in the belief that accounting for human linguistic abilities requires a more abstract description of linguistic entities than surface syntax provides. My claim is that this can be done *without* reaching for semantic notions, which I don't believe advance the discussion very much. The following chapters are meant to show that this belief can be substantiated.

Chapter 2
Two Types of Quantifiers

I will argue that there are basically three types of quantificational NP expressions, which can be described roughly as follows:

I.   a set of NP expressions whose interpretive scope domain is always wide;

II. a set whose interpretive scope domain is restricted to the clause in which the quantified NP is situated;

III. a set whose scope domain is unbounded if originating in some syntactic positions but sententially bound when originating from others.

Each kind of quantified NP expressions has other properties as well. The aim of the next several chapters will be, first, to describe these distinct kinds of quantifiers more carefully and, second, to show how these properties follow from a version of the general principles—the *binding principles*—currently being developed within a version of the Extended Standard theory (EST) called the Government-Binding framework (GB).

Within this version of EST, the theory of quantifier structure is seen as one aspect of a more general theory of logical form. Within EST, the problem of defining the logical structure of quantified expressions in natural language (partially) translates into the question of how to derive the logical syntax of quantified expressions *step by step* from a level of representation known as S-structure. In other words, given a grammar organized as in (1), what sorts of rules are needed to yield a structure appropriate to the interpretation of quantified sentences?

(1)   D-structure
            ↓
         Transformations
            ↓
         S-structure
         ╱   ╲

Phonetic form (PF)   Logical form (LF)

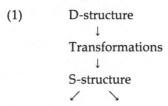

In this grammar, organized according to the views of GB theory, D-structure is analogous to the deep structure of earlier interpretive theories. It is a level of representation that is input to the syntactic transformational component but *not* to semantic interpretation. The representation of a sentence that is relevant to semantic interpretation is its S-structure, a string with syntactic labeled bracketings that is the output of the transformational component. This S-structure is input to the rules of LF. LF rules operate on S-structures to yield structures that represent certain aspects of the "meanings" of sentences, called their *logical form*.[1] To determine just *which* aspects of natural language that we would pretheoretically see as relating to meaning are to be represented at LF, and *how* they are to be represented, is the task of a theory of linguistic semantics. In particular, what are the properties of LF representations and what is the nature of the rules that transform S-structures into structures representing logical form?

This problem is by no means trivial. Many logically possible solutions are excluded because although the rules invoked are observationally adequate (i.e., they describe the data correctly), they do not comport with the general restrictions on rule types that linguistic theory must impose if it is to achieve its main research goal of providing a solution to the logical problem of language acquisition. I will argue that by embedding questions concerning the logical form of quantified expressions within a model of language of the sort advocated within EST, one can gain considerable insight into how such information is actually expressed within natural language.

This belief has a more general and a more specific expression. The general view is that seeing semantic competence as responsible to the same poverty-of-stimulus considerations that motivate much current work in syntax will allow us to bring comparatively refined empirical considerations to bear on competing proposals concerning the logical syntax of natural language. As characterized in chapter 1, current linguistic theory views the process of language acquisition essentially as the fixing, on the basis of the primary linguistic data, of certain open parameters of a deductively organized innate language schematism. This view leads one to look for linguistic interdependencies, clusterings of phenomena that result from a parameter's being set one way or another. When cast against the background of the acquisition problem, many of the traditional philosophical analyses of LF can be a fertile source of specific proposals concerning the nature of the innate schematism and its parameters. Furthermore, by reinterpreting various philosophical proposals concerning LF as a subpart of a general theory of linguistic competence, responsible to the same set of considerations as other aspects of grammatical theorizing, we are able to sharpen aspects of these proposals in several ways and so better appreciate their differences. In particular, "capturing" the phenomena in some logical notation yields to explaining why the phenomena pattern as they do. Hopefully these skeletal remarks will gain flesh as we consider specific issues regarding natural language quantification.

The more specific application of this viewpoint is that many of the theoretical devices that have been developed within EST can be used to probe the features of LF in natural languages. I will make crucial use of the idea that rules relating S-structure to LF are of the same kind that operate in the syntax (i.e., Move-α), and that the Empty Category Principle (ECP) is a condition on LF and thus can be used to probe the features of logical form in natural language. Different theories of quantifier structure interact with these independently motivated devices in different ways. Thus, at least in principle, it is possible to exploit these grammatical constraints in assessing the relative empirical merits of different proposals concerning the logical syntax of quantified expressions in natural language.

I thus hope to show that by embedding versions of familiar philosophical theories about logical form within the framework of current linguistic theorizing, one can turn many questions of a logical or philosophical flavor into empirical questions associated with quite definite debits and credits; a sort of cost accounting that can be used to assess the empirical value of competing approaches to logical form in natural language.

In this chapter, I will concentrate on the distinction (developed in Hornstein 1981) between type I and type II quantifiers. In the next, I will trace the implications of the results developed here for an analysis of definite descriptions and 'belief'-sentences with quantified expressions in the content clause—the embedded 'that'-sentence of a 'believe-that' construction. In chapter 4, I will turn to the properties of type II and type III quantifiers, arguing that the special clause-bounded features of each can be explained. In chapter 5, I will deal with certain puzzles that arise from treating quantified NPs in the way I have proposed. This will lead to developing certain grammatical mechanisms that can fruitfully be used to explain other interpretive phenomena. I will close this section of the book with a brief review of the results and a discussion of what they show about a theory of natural language interpretation.

Moved and Unmoved Quantifiers: Types I and II

The standard logical treatments of quantified sentences in natural language construe them as having a logical syntax of operator-variable form, i.e., $\ulcorner(Ox)(P(x))\urcorner$.[2] Currently, in EST, the logical form of quantified sentences is derived via a rule of quantifier raising (QR)[3] that Chomsky-adjoins the operators to the most proximate sentential node (S node), yielding a structure like (2b) from a structure like (2a)(in matrix clauses):

(2)   a. $[_s[_s \ldots Qx \ldots]]$

   b. $[_s[_s Qx[_s \ldots x \ldots]]]$

QR is a "movement" rule—it moves a constituent from one position in the phrase marker to another position. Moreover, it is conceived to be an instantiation, in the LF component, of the more general movement rule operative in the transformational component, the rule Move-α. Given that QR applies at LF, the effects of its application cannot be detected by inspecting the linear order of the string at surface structure. Some evidence for such abstract movement comes from considering the interpretation of certain multiply quantified sentences. The standard scope ambiguities apparent in such simple sentences can be represented in a standard disambiguated format via the repeated application of this rule. For example, consider a sentence like (3):

(3)   Everybody loves somebody

(3) is ambiguous with either the universal quantifier 'everybody' or the existential quantifier 'somebody' enjoying wide scope. The free, unordered application of QR will in fact yield two separate representations of (3):

(4)   a. $[_s[_s \text{ everybody}_x \ [_s \text{ somebody}_y \ [_s \ x \text{ loves } y]]]]$

   b. $[_s[_s \text{ somebody}_y \ [_s \text{ everybody}_x \ [_s x \text{ loves } y]]]]$

In (4a) QR applied to 'everybody' before applying to 'somebody', resulting in a structure in which 'everybody' dominates or c-commands 'somebody'; in (4b) it applied in the opposite order, with the result that 'somebody' dominates or c-commands 'everybody'.[4] On the assumptions that 'everybody' and 'somebody' are quantified expressions that are moved in LF by QR and that scope relations are determined in LF by c-command relations, Move-α can be used to generate the scope ambiguities of a sentence like (3).

These interpretive features of a simple example like (3) are not strong evidence in favor of a rule of QR. They are at most suggestive. However, we will see that construing the relative scope interactions of quantifiers as being dependent on the application of a rule like QR has very rich consequences. To take just one example, we will expect certain kinds of scope interactions to be impossible given the limited way in which QR applies, namely, by adjoining a quantified phrase (QP) to the most proximate S node. At any rate, we will expect QPs whose scope domains are determined by the application of QR to have rather intricate and interesting properties. In what follows, we will assume that quantified phrases subject to QR exist and that phrases such as 'everyone', 'someone',[5] 'every man', 'a woman' are noun phrase (NP) expressions of this kind—*type II quantifiers*.

In the literature on logic, quantified expressions have traditionally been contrasted with names. Names, unlike quantified phrases, do not form operator-variable structures. Their logical form can be represented as ⌜P(a)⌝ ('a' stands for a name, 'P' for a predicate). Translated into the terms of the above discussion, names and namelike expressions are not subject to QR. What, however, is a name or a namelike expression? NPs like 'John', 'Mary', 'Susan' are paradigmatic instances. However, I would like to suggest that many other phrases fall into this category as well; in particular, quantified expressions involving 'any' and 'a certain'. Phrases such as 'anyone', 'a certain woman', 'any gift', 'a certain toy', I would like to argue, have a logical syntax like that of names. Specifically, they are not subject to QR and do not form operator-variable structures in LF. Interestingly, these kinds of quantified expressions—the type I quantifiers—are the ones usually characterized as having wide scope interpretation in relation to other logical entities such as quantified NP negation and modals (see Evans 1977). For example, consider a sentence like (5):

(5)   Everyone loves a certain woman

Unlike (3), (5) is not ambiguous. Rather, it has only the interpretation associated with representation (4b); that is, the NP 'a certain woman' has wide scope over the universally quantified expression. However, if it is namelike, 'a certain woman' is not moved by QR and has the LF structure shown in (6):

(6)   [$_S$[$_S$ everyone$_x$ [x loves a certain woman]]]

In short, type I quantifiers do not form operator-variable structures and are generally interpreted as having wide scope.

In what follows, we will consider evidence concerning the behavior of type I and type II quantifiers and show that the distinction is empirically well motivated. Given even the brief description of these two kinds of quantifiers above, we should expect to find important differences in their linguistic behavior. Since the phrase marker representing the logical forms of the sentences that contain type I quantifiers is derived via the movement rule QR, we should expect these quantifiers to be sensitive to conditions or principles constraining movement rules. On the other hand, type II quantifiers, which do not move, should not be affected by such conditions or principles. Moreover, we can expect the two types to differ in their interpretive properties. In fact, we would expect type I quantifiers to act in many respects like ordinary names, particularly where the behavior of names and variables diverges in natural language. Variables are the entities that type II quantifiers leave behind and bind or coindex as a result of QR (see note 2). Last, and most important, we will expect these properties to cluster. That is, wherever a QP is insensitive to movement, we will expect its interpretation to be namelike in certain respects, and vice versa. In short, the distinction between type I and type II quantifiers predicts in a principled manner, in the context of current grammatical theory, rather specific kinds of behavior dependencies. From the point of view of a theory of interpretation, such dependencies are particularly interesting. If they cut a wide enough empirical swath, we can expect the analyses to support just the sorts of features that should be characteristic of a program for which poverty-of-stimulus considerations are central. I will return to this point after considering the empirical data.

The Data

Let us look at the behavior of the type II quantifiers 'every', 'a'/'someone' and the type I quantifiers 'any', 'a certain'.[6]

Pronouns as Bound Variables
Consider sentences (7a–g):

(7) a. *John likes every dog$_i$ and it$_i$ likes him

 b. *If John owes every man$_i$ money then Sam pays him$_i$

 c. *Every soldier kissed someone$_i$ if she$_i$ said hello

 d. *Every soldier loves a gun$_i$ because it$_i$ never jams

 e. *John likes every dog$_i$ and Sam feeds it$_i$

 f. *If a/some large man$_i$ loves every woman, then Sally loves him$_i$

 g. *That every wooden house$_i$ is highly inflammable makes it$_i$ expensive to insure

In these sentences, the indexed pronoun cannot be bound by the coindexed quantifier. That is, the interpretation of the pronoun is not determined by the coindexed NP. This is as expected if QR applies as indicated in (2), adjoining the operator to the most proximate S. In (7a), for example, the rule will adjoin the QP 'every dog' to the most proximate S, yielding a structure like (8):

(8) $[_s[_s$ every dog$_i$ $[_s$ John likes $x_i]]$ and $[_s$ it$_i$ likes him]]

For a pronoun to be interpreted as a bound variable of a type II QP, it must be c-commanded by that expression in LF.[7] Therefore, in a structure like (8) since 'it' is not c-commanded by and hence not in the scope of the quantified expression 'every dog', it cannot be construed as a bound variable. By claiming that 'every' is subject to the movement rule QR—that it is a type II quantifier—we can account both for its behavior in such cases and for the unacceptability of the sentence interpreted as in (7a). Similar considerations hold for the other examples in (7).

Contrast this with the sentences in (9):

(9) a. If John likes any man$_{i'}$ then Sam lends him$_i$ money

  b. Every knight loves a certain sword$_i$ because it$_i$ cannot break

  c. John likes a certain dog$_i$ but it$_i$ only likes Sam

  d. Take any number$_i$ and divide it$_i$ by two

  e. That any wooden house$_i$ might be highly inflammable makes it$_i$ expensive to insure

In these sentences, coindexing is possible. This could not be explained if the quantifiers were moved by QR and treated as in (7). What is happening here? If these quantifiers were type I quantified NPs, their logical form would parallel the logical form of names in simple sentences. Thus, it would not be surprising if they had the same coindexing properties as names. Consider sentences (10a–e):

(10) a. If John likes Fred$_{i'}$ then Sam lends him$_i$ money

  b. Every knight loves Excalibur$_i$ because it$_i$ cannot break

  c. John likes Fido$_i$ but he$_i$ only likes Sam

  d. Take four$_i$ and divide it$_i$ by two

  e. That Buckingham Palace$_i$ might be highly inflammable makes it$_i$ expensive to insure

The sentences in (10) are just those in (9) with names in place of the quantifiers. Clearly, these sentences allow coindexing. As is well known, the coindexing possibilities for names are not governed by the same c-command conditions that operate in the case of type II quantified NPs. In particular, coindexing can occur between a name and a pronoun, even if the name does not c-command the pronoun. Indeed, generally speaking, coindexing is impossible between a name and a pronoun if and only if the pronoun c-commands the name. Otherwise it is possible. (See chapter 4 for discussion.) In short, by treating 'any' and 'a certain' as type I quantifiers, we can explain the similar behavior of the sentences in (9) and (10) by citing a common logical form. In other words, we can explain the binding properties displayed by 'any' and 'a certain' by claiming that as far as coindexing is concerned, logical form is the relevant determinant and by treating the logical form of sentences with type I quantifiers in a manner parallel to those with names.

The parallel between names and quantifiers like 'any' and 'a certain' in fact extends beyond sentence grammar. Names can be coindexed with pronouns even across a discourse:

(11) a. Everyone likes $Fido_i$. John sees him_i on the way to work every day.

b. Take $four_i$ for example. If you multiply it_i by two, the product is even.

If 'any' and 'a certain' are type I quantifiers, we would expect them to act in a similar fashion:

(12) a. Everyone likes a certain dog_i. John sees it_i on the way to work every day.

b. Take any $number_i$. If you multiply it_i by two, the product is even.

The behavior of 'any' in examples like (12b) makes it very difficult to interpret it as a type II quantifier of any kind. I mention this because it has often been suggested that 'any' should be treated, in at least some cases, as a wide scope universal quantifier, that is, as a wide scope version of 'every' (see Quine 1960, Hintikka 1976a,b). There are problems with such an approach, however, one of which is relevant here. Briefly, the problem is that the notion of scope relevant to explaining the behavior of universal quantifiers like 'every' is different from the one needed to account for 'any'. The facts in (12) indicate that a non-sentence-bound notion of scope is needed to account for the behavior of 'any', since here its coindexing possibilities appear to extend beyond the sentence. In example (13), however, a narrower sentence-bound notion of scope is crucially utilized to explain the phenomena.

(13)   *$Everyone_i$ bought a beer. He_i drank it quickly.

Thus, even though 'every' can have *sententially* wide scope in (13), coindexing across a discourse with the indicated pronouns is not possible because of the sentence-bound nature of this scope. Taken together, these observations seem to indicate that treating 'any' as a wide scope version of 'every' will simply not suffice to predict the full range of its behavior. The relevant notion of scope in the two cases is just not the same.

The Leftness Condition

Chomsky 1976 and Higginbotham 1980 point out that a variable cannot be coindexed with 'a pronoun to its left. In other words, variables in natural language appear to obey a Leftness Condition with regard to their coindexing possibilities:

(14) a. *That he$_i$ might be sent to the front doesn't bother every good soldier$_i$

   b. *That he$_i$ might be sent to fight doesn't bother someone$_i$/ a good soldier$_i$[8]

   c. *His$_i$ being sent to the front doesn't bother every good soldier$_i$

   d. *His$_i$ being sent to the front doesn't bother a good soldier$_i$/ someone$_i$

   e. *Who$_i$ doesn't his$_i$ being sent to the front bother x_i

In LF these sentences have the structure shown in (15):

(15) [$_S$[$_S$ every good soldier$_i$ [$_S$ that [$_S$ he$_i$ might be sent to fight doesn't bother x_i]]]]

Note that in (15) the quantified NP 'every good soldier' c-commands the pronoun 'he$_i$'. Therefore, (14a) cannot be ruled unacceptable for the same reason as (7 a–g). In the case of (15), the quantifier has full sentential scope. Instead, (14a) is unacceptable because the coindexing violates the Leftness Condition. Similar considerations hold for the other sentences in (14).

The Leftness Condition does not apply to unstressed names,[9] which can be coindexed with pronouns to their left:

(16) a. That he$_i$ might be sent to the front doesn't bother Bill$_i$

   b. His$_i$ being sent to the front doesn't bother Bill$_i$

Thus, the behavior of proper names and variables diverges with regard to the Leftness Condition: the former can violate it, but not the latter. This being so, the Leftness Condition can be used as a diagnostic for whether some position is occupied by a variable or a namelike expression. The issue will turn on whether an expression can coindex a pronoun to its left.[10] Given the analysis of 'any' and 'a certain' as type I quantifiers, we would expect them to behave like names with regard to the Leftness Condition. This prediction is borne out:

(17) a. That he$_i$ might be sent to fight doesn't bother any good soldier$_i$

b. His$_i$ being sent to the front doesn't bother any good soldier$_i$

c. That he$_i$ might be sent to fight doesn't bother a certain good soldier$_i$

d. His$_i$ being sent to the front doesn't bother a certain good soldier$_i$

The Relative Scope of Quantifiers

So far I have discussed some aspects of quantifier "scope" in natural language by focusing on the pronoun binding behavior of various English quantifiers. In this section, I will consider another feature of the interpretation of quantifiers that has traditionally been discussed in terms of scope: the interpretation of multiply quantified sentences. In multiply quantified sentences the different semantic interpretations of the sentence have been analyzed in terms of differences in the relative scopes of the quantifiers in logical form.

In this discussion, I will make two major points. The first is an observation: certain kinds of quantifiers have a property that I will call *interpretive independence*. By this I mean that certain quantifiers are relatively insensitive to their logical environments as far as their interpretations are concerned.[11] This observation is by no means novel. It simply renames a feature of the interpretation of certain quantifiers that has often been discussed in terms of scope considerations. Thus, for example, it has often been claimed that 'any' is a universal quantifier that always takes wide sentential scope. As my remarks indicate, I think it is wrong to describe this feature in terms of a formal notion like scope. However, I will discuss the phenomenon itself, under the name of *interpretive independence*.

Second, I will suggest that this phenomenon of relative interpretive independence correlates with a more formal feature of quantifiers: whether the quantifier is moved by QR to form an operator-variable structure. In effect, lack of QR is a necessary condition for this sort of interpretation in natural language. Although I will discuss in passing how the interpretation of nonmoved quantifiers should be approached theoretically, this correlation between wide scope interpretation and lack of movement is the point I wish to emphasize.

Let us first consider the interpretation of 'a certain', with the aid of the following sentences:

(18) a. A man/Someone likes every woman

    b. Every man likes a woman/someone

    c. A certain man likes every woman

    c. Every woman likes a certain man

(18a,b) are ambiguous. Either the universal or the existential quantifier can be regarded as having wide scope. Thus, for example, (18b) can be represented as having the structure (19a) if QR applies to 'a woman'/ 'someone' after it applies to 'every man', or (19b) if the order of application is reversed.

(19) a. $[_S$ every man$_x$ $[_S$ a woman$_y$/someone$_y$ $[_S$ x likes $y]]]$

    b. $[_S$ a woman$_y$/someone$_y$ $[_S$ every man$_x$ $[x$ likes $y]]]$

(19b) corresponds to the interpretation where there is a single woman whom every man likes. (19a) says that for every man there is some woman that he likes; for example, it is true if Bill likes Sally, Fred Ann, and Max Golda.

For (18c,d), however, only the interpretation corresponding to (19b) is available. In other words, the reading of 'a certain man' is interpretively independent of the information provided by the universally quantified phrase 'every woman'.

The interpretation of 'a certain' also tends to be independent of the interpretation of other logical elements such as modals and negations:

(20) a. John didn't kiss a woman/someone at the party

    b. John didn't kiss a certain woman at the party

    c. John must kiss a woman/someone to get in

    d. John must kiss a certain woman to get in

The favored interpretation of (20a,c) corresponds to a structure where the existentially quantified phrase lies within the negation or the modal:

(21) a. not [a woman at the party$_x$ [John kissed x]]

    b. must [a woman$_x$ [John kiss x to get in]]

In (20b,d), however, there is a different interpretation. In these cases the existentially quantified phrase is interpreted as having "wide scope" over the negative and the modal. These sentences would have interpretations parallel to those represented in (22):

(22) a. a woman$_x$ [not [John kiss $_x$]]

    b. a woman$_x$ [must [John kiss x to get in]]

In other words, phenomenally speaking, the interpretation of a quantified noun phrase involving 'a certain' can proceed without regard for the interpretation of other logical elements such as negations, modals, or quantifiers in the phrase.

How should these facts about 'a certain' be incorporated within a theory of meaning for natural language? One way would be to treat them as scope facts, scope being a syntactic property of formal configurations. On such a view, 'a certain' is a quantifier that is mandatorily moved by QR to the widest possible scope position. This would in effect assimilate the behavior of quantified phrases with 'a certain' to standard quantifiers with 'a' or 'every' by appending an additional proviso to QR in the case of 'a certain', namely, that 'a certain' must be moved to widest possible scope position.

There are several problems with such an approach. First, I have already provided evidence that quantifiers like 'a certain' are not moved by QR at all. If this is correct, the property of interpretive independence that they appear to have should not be traced to syntactic features of the logical forms of the sentences in which they occur. However, a scope analysis involves just such a suggestion. On such an approach the ambiguity is related to the specifics of the logical syntax of such sentences yielded by the LF rule of QR.

A second problem is that it does not seem right to treat the interaction of negatives and quantifiers as scope facts, as such a QR analysis of 'a certain' suggests. A scope approach claims that the lack of ambiguity in sentences like (20b) arises from QR assigning mandatory wide scope to 'a certain', i.e., a scope wider than the scope of the negation. However, QR in general seems unable to do this. Thus, sentences like (23) are unambiguous, 'every' being *mandatorily* interpreted as lying within the scope of the negation 'not':

(23)   John didn't kiss every woman at the party

If the reason that 'a certain' is not interpreted as within the scope of 'not' in (20b) is that QR mandatorily assigns it wide scope, why can't 'every' *optionally* have wide scope over 'not' when QR optionally assigns it wide scope as in (19a)? Accepting that a scope mechanism of the sort QR embodies is responsible for the interpretation of 'a certain' will require complicating QR not only as it applies to 'a certain', but also as it applies to 'every' in examples like (23). Given that such complications exact a cost with respect to the acquisition of such rules, this type of approach is not highly favored.

Another set of facts also suggests dealing with the interpretive properties of 'a certain' independently of any mechanism of syntactic scope. QR encodes the observation that the scope of quantifiers like 'every' and 'a'/'someone' is generally limited to their minimal sentential domain. This accounts for the lack of quantifier ambiguities in sentences like (24a,b):

(24) a. Everyone believes that a pretty woman loves him

b. Someone believes that everyone ate well

Given QR as described in (2), the lack of ambiguity in (24) follows. (24b) will have only the logical form (25), where the universal quantifier 'everyone' is in the scope of the existential quantifier 'someone':

(25) [$_s$ someone$_i$ [x_i believes][that [everyone$_j$ [x_j ate well]]]]

Now consider (26):

(26) Everyone believes that a certain pretty woman is here

In (26) there is a single pretty woman of whom all have the same belief. If 'a certain' were subject to QR, it would have to be moved beyond the minimal S that contains it so that it would have wide scope over 'everyone'. This would be a further complication of QR for the case of 'a certain'. Even worse, as we shall see in the next section, structures of the sort that QR would yield in this case are, in general, ill formed. Thus, not only would QR have to be complicated, but the very acceptability of (26) would be difficult to account for given the illicit nature of the structure underlying it.

In light of these considerations it seems worthwhile to divorce the interpretive independence of 'a certain' from a syntactic scope mechanism embodied in a rule like QR. More positively, it is interesting to note that interpretive independence is shared by names. Consider sentences like (27a–d):

(27) a. John likes everyone

b. Everyone likes John

c. Sam doesn't like John

d. Everyone must kiss John

In (27) the behavior of 'John' is quite parallel to that of 'a certain'. Its interpretation is independent of its logical environment. Thus, for example, as Kripke and others have stressed, names are rigid with respect to modal interpretation. The same is true of the interaction of names with negations and quantifiers. The interpretation of names is by and large oblivious to the interpretation of other elements in the clause. In short, names and 'a certain' seem to have many interpretive similarities. We have seen that they also share a significant number of pronoun binding properties. Why not deal with the interpretive behavior of 'a certain' in much the same way that we dealt with its pronoun binding properties—by assimilating the interpretive properties of quantifiers like 'a certain' to those of names? More specifically, let us say that *all* noun phrases not forming operator-variable structures (i.e., all phrases, not only names, that are not moved by QR) are interpreted in a manner functionally independent of the interpretation of other logical operators in the clause.[12] This proposal amounts to saying that the rules of interpretation make a distinction between rules for the interpretation of unmoved elements and rules for the interpretation of moved ones. In particular, these two kinds of rules cannot monitor each other; hence, each is insensitive to the values that the other assigns. On such an account, names and quantifiers like 'a certain' are cases of unmoved elements, and this fact, together with the above suggestion concerning interpretation procedures, accounts for their interpretive independence.

This suggestion regarding interpretation is related to the claim that branching quantification of the sort that Hintikka has suggested occurs in natural languages. Given that on this proposal such phrases are not moved, they do not in fact form branching structures. Still, these phrases act as if they were represented in a branching structure, and we find interpretive effects analogous to those a branching account would imply. The suggestion here is that there are two fundamentally disjoint classes of interpretive rules that are clearly linked with certain syntactic features of operators, i.e., their movability. In earlier proposals such as Hintikka's, quantifiers were treated as a single class. In sum, the present proposal has the interpretive effects of these earlier ones but differs from them considerably in detail by divorcing certain aspects of interpretation from structural features like syntactic scope. I will have more to say on this topic when I discuss the interpretation of 'any'.

A similar, though more complex and interesting, version of the phenomenon of interpretive independence occurs in the case of 'any'. Consider the following sentences:

(28) a. John doesn't like any woman

b. John doesn't like every woman

c. John will be richer than any man here

d. John will be richer than every man here

In (28a,c) the 'any' phrase is interpreted independently of the interpretation of the negation or the modal, as can be seen by comparing these sentences with the corresponding 'every' sentences in (28b,d). This interpretive independence has often been explained by glossing 'any' as a wide scope universal quantifier. On such an approach sentences (28a,c) are given the structures in (29):

(29) a. for all men here$_x$ [not [John like x]]

  b. for all men here$_x$ [will [John more rich than x]]

Thus, under this analysis of 'any', what I have been calling interpretive independence is linked to a special feature pertaining to its scope possibilities in the syntactic sense of scope. As in the case of 'a certain', this approach seems to me beset with many difficulties.

First, I will show in the next section that a scope treatment of 'any' in terms of QR would yield structures that are generally unacceptable. Second, as with 'a certain', there is evidence that 'any' is not moved by QR and does not form operator-variable structures. Scope is a property of syntactic configurations, the scope of an operator being a feature of that operator in a given formal configuration. In a situation where QR does not take place, this syntactic concept cannot apply, and it is therefore not clear how it can be relevant. The problem is this: what sense is there to talking about the scope of an operator where there is no difference at the level of logical syntax between names and quantifiers like 'any'? What is clearly needed is not the notion of scope but its interpretive analogue; something like Kripke's notion of rigidity, for example, or some other notion specifying what interpretive independence amounts to. In any event, the previous two sections have provided evidence against adopting the standard scope treatment of 'any' as an account of how it functions within a natural language like English.

In light of these two considerations, I do not think it would be fruitful to explicate the various aspects of the interpretation of 'any' in terms of a scope mechanism like QR. Rather, it seems more promising to divorce this semantic property of interpretive independence, trying instead to extend the observation concerning names and 'a certain' to the case of 'any'; that is, interpretive independence is a feature of NP elements that are not moved by QR. As in the case of names and 'a certain', the rules for the interpretation of 'any' will be disjoint from other interpretive rules; hence their lack of interaction with the modal and negation in (28).

This said, interpretive independence in the case of 'any' is much more complex than in the case of 'a certain'. In what follows I will briefly consider some of these peculiar interpretive properties and touch on some of the proposals that have been advanced to deal with them.

Linguists and philosophers have adopted two approaches to the treatment of the interpretation of 'any'. One approach postulates two homophonic 'any's'. One of these lexical items receives a reading related to those of existential quantifiers and found when the 'any' resides in a negative polarity environment, for example, in the vicinity of 'not' or 'nobody'. The other 'any'—called *free choice 'any'* by Linebarger

1980—has an interpretation related to universal quantification and is found for example in modal environments. As a concrete example, consider how such a dual approach would interpret the sentences (28a,b). (28a) would have an interpretation analogous to that of (30a):

(30) a. not [∃x [John like x]]

b. ∀x [will [more [John rich than x]]]

(28c), on the other hand, would be treated as having an interpretation parallel to that of (30b).

The second approach gives 'any' a uniform interpretation. Both negative 'any' and free choice 'any' are treated like universal quantifiers. The existential import of negative sentences such as (28a) comes from treating 'any' like a wide scope quantifier and exploiting the logical equivalence between "for all x not . . . " and "it's not the case that there exists an x such that . . . " And since sentences like (28c) appear to have no existential import,[13] it is clear that a uniform approach to the interpretation of 'any' would have to select the universal reading.

In what follows I will consider how certain facts concerning the interpretation of 'any' and the proposal concerning the logical syntax of 'any' both bear on these two approaches.

Consider the following sentences:[14]

(31) a. Someone doesn't like anyone

b. Someone likes every woman

c. Someone doesn't like every woman

In (31a) the interpretation of the existential phrase 'someone' is not affected by the interpretation of the 'any'-phrase. In other words, whereas (31b,c) are ambiguous with either the universal or the existential enjoying wide scope, in (31a) 'someone' is construed as unambiguously taking wider scope; significantly, this means that 'any' appears *not* to be taking wide scope.

Consider what this means for the two approaches to 'any'. For the two 'any's' theory this is in some sense expected. Thus, for example, Linebarger's theory (1980) holds that 'any' must be interpreted as being in the immediate scope of the negation if there is one—a provision called the *Immediate Scope Condition*.[15] Thus, (31a) would have an interpretation corresponding to the logical form (32):

(32) someone$_x$ [not [someone$_y$ [x likes y]]]

Given that quantifiers in subject positions are generally not interpreted as being in the scope of a negation in VP position, and given the Immediate Scope Condition that Linebarger motivates, the correct interpretation of (31a) follows.

What about the single 'any' thesis? In and of itself (31a) poses no problem for treating 'any' as a universal quantifier. What it does show, however, is that the scope properties of 'any' are unusual; it takes interpretive precedence over a negative or a modal but not over other quantifiers in the clause. In other words, though 'any' is a wide scope quantifier, it is not a widest scope quantifier. What this means, I believe, is one of two things: either 'any' has the property that it takes wide scope over at most one logical operator—in (31a) the negation but not the existential quantifier—or it is an operator that takes wide scope but is interpreted in a branching manner. Let us consider these possibilties.

If we wished to treat 'any' in a unified manner as a special type of universal quantifier, we could account for (31a) by saying that 'any' takes wide scope over at most one operator, in this case the negation. This proposal would amount to reformulating the Immediate Scope Condition to read, in the case of 'any', that the negation must appear in the immediate scope of 'any'. The interpretation of (31a) would then parallel the interpretation of a sentence with the logical form (33):

(33)   someone$_x$ [everyone$_y$ [not [x likes y]]]

However, based on our discussion of 'a certain', a more attractive solution presents itself—the second alternative above—which allows us to maintain the claim that 'any' has wide scope in (31a) despite the interpretation of 'someone' noted. As discussed in the case of 'a certain', the interpretation of unmoved elements is functionally independent of the interpretations of the moved quantified NPs. If this idea were extended to the case of 'any', the interpretation of (31a) would be parallel to the *interpretation* (but would not have the *form*) of structures like (34):

(34)   someone$_x$
       >[not (x likes y)]
       everyone$_y$

If the interpretation of sentences with 'any' is parallel to those represented in (34), then the interpretation noted for (31a) follows. In structures like (34) the quantifiers in different arms of a branching structure are interpreted independently of one another. Thus, the interpretation of (34) will be equivalent to the interpretation of (35):

(35)   some$_x$ [every$_y$ [not [x likes y]]]

The structure represented in (35) correctly accounts for the interpretation that (31a) in fact has. Thus, by accepting this branching view of the interpretation of unmoved elements, of which 'any' is one, we can maintain an analysis of 'any' as a wide scope universal quantifier.[16]

Others (most notably Hintikka) have suggested that natural languages do in fact have interpretations involving branching quantification. My suggestion, though compatible with theirs, nonetheless differs from it. What I have considered above (and throughout this study, following the EST paradigm) is a question concerning the format of certain mental representations: should the interpretation of sentences having quantifiers like 'any' be represented as involving branching interpretation procedures? In Hintikka's discussion of branching quantifiers (1974, 1976b) the argument is that in certain rather complex sentences involving four quantifiers—two universal and two existential in $\forall \exists \forall \exists$ linear order—interpretations of the quantifiers arise that a nonbranching theory would forbid. Such interpretations hang on the informational independence of the two sets of $\forall \exists$ quantifiers. As Hintikka observes, one way of neatly representing this sort of informational independence is to claim that the interpretation of such sentences involves branching rules. However, by itself Hintikka's argument does not force the conclusion that the theory of *grammar* should allow branching quantification. An obvious alternative would trace the interpretation of such sentences to considerations of processing rather than grammar. We might claim that the rules of grammar yield linear interpretive formats but that because of the complexity of the sentences involved, processing limitations lead to interpreting the pairs of quantifiers independently of one another. In this way the effects of branching quantification in *complex* constructions could be obtained even if the actual representation of the sentences in the grammar involved only linearly ordered interpretation procedures for quantifiers.

In the cases discussed here, however, a branching format for the interpretation rules seems more clearly implicated. (31a) is not particularly complex, so that processing limitations do not seem very relevant. Moreover, the cases involving 'any' *only* allow a reading in which the quantifiers are interpreted independently, even though such sentences are no more complex than sentences involving 'every', where ambiguity is possible.

(36) a. Someone at the party likes anyone who was invited

b. Someone at the party likes everyone who was invited

(36a) has an interpretation parallel to (37a), whereas (36b) can also be interpreted as in (37b):

(37) a. some y [every x [[x likes y]]]

b. every x [some y [x likes y]]

The general conclusion is that in dealing with the grammar of natural language, one must distinguish acceptability from grammaticality. The latter is a theoretical notion relating to the actual rules characterizing the mental representation of linguistic entities. The former is a far less theoretically loaded concept. Significantly, sentences that are not grammatical may still be acceptable, though their acceptability will be due to *extragrammatical* factors such as processing.[17] My remarks on branching differ from Hintikka's in trying to keep these different possible sources of acceptability in focus and in suggesting that, in the case of 'any', a grammatical approach is the most reasonable one to pursue.

A second important difference is that under Hintikka's proposal sentences like (31a) form branching structures, whereas under mine they do not. To be more precise, if Hintikka's proposal were taken literally and embedded within the assumptions adopted here, it would suggest that type I quantifiers *do* move, though the positions to which they move branch with respect to the other linearly ordered elements. In other words, the interpretive independence of 'any'-phrases is due to their having structures like (34). On my account, 'any'-phrases do not move. They do not form syntactic structures like (34) in LF. Rather, I associate a certain kind of interpretive rule with unmoved NPs. Since Hintikka's own discussion of branching does not proceed within the assumptions adopted here, it would be fair to see my proposal as only a slight modification of his. Still, if we are to explain the phenomena of earlier sections, it is important to keep this modification of Hintikka's proposal in mind.

Of the two approaches to a uniform treatment of the interpretation of 'any', I prefer the branching analysis. Despite some difficulties, such an analysis seems worth pursuing, since it allows 'any' and 'a certain' to be treated alike. However, either uniform treatment of 'any' seems preferable to the dual interpretation homophonic theory. To support this belief, I offer the following indirect suggestive evidence: namely, that regardless of whether one gets the existential reading ((38b,d,f)) or the universal reading ((38a,c,e)), 'any' acts uniformly with regard to the Leftness Condition, pronoun coindexing, and cross-discourse reference.[18]

Leftness Condition
(38) a. That he$_i$ might get shot would bother anyone$_i$
   b. That he$_i$ might get shot didn't bother any soldier$_i$
   Pronoun Coindexing
   c. Sam will hit anyone$_i$ if he$_i$ wins
   d. If anyone$_i$ wins, Sam will hit him$_i$

Cross-Discourse Reference
e. Take any number$_i$. Divide it$_i$ by two.

f. John$_j$ didn't kiss any woman$_i$ at the party. Why? Because she$_i$ would have hit him$_j$ if he$_j$ had.

In other words, as far as these interpretive procedures go, the distinctions that a dual approach would make between existential and free choice 'any' disappear. One could retain the dual analysis despite these facts, concluding that 'any' is a single element in the syntax of LF and none-theless interpretively ambiguous. However, such an approach would be less favored than one that treated 'any' as interpretively singular in both LF and interpretation.

In this section I have briefly discussed some aspects of 'any' inter-pretation and have hesitantly opted for a treatment of 'any' and 'a certain' that involves branching interpretation procedures, though not a branching syntactic form at LF. More important, however, are the two basic facts (a) that both elements have relative interpretive inde-pendence and (b) that both act as if they are not moved by QR to form operator-variable structures. The main goal of the discussion was to suggest that these two facts should be seen as correlating as a matter of grammatical principle. It is a principle of Universal Grammar that unmoved elements are interpretively independent and moved elements interpretively dependent.

The Empty Category Principle
In this section I will focus on the fact that QR is a *movement* rule.

Kayne 1979, Aoun, Hornstein, and Sportiche 1980, and Chomsky 1981 have argued that all movement rules, including those in the LF component of the grammar, of which QR is one are subject to a condition called the *Empty Category Principle* (ECP).[19] This condition prohibits "long" movement of the quantifier phrase from the subject position of tensed clauses. As a result of ECP violations, the following sentences are marked unacceptable:

(39) a. *Jean n'exige que personne aime le gâteau
'John doesn't demand that anyone like the cake.'

b. *Who believes that who left the party

A sentence like (39a) would have the structure in (40):

(40)   [$_s$ personne$_x$ [$_s$ Jean n'exige [$_s$ que [$_s$ x aime le gâteau]]]]

In a structure like (40) the quantifier 'personne' controls the variable 'x' in a nonlocal manner from outside the clause within which the variable resides. It is binding of this sort between a moved element and its trace left in the subject position of a tensed sentence that the ECP prohibits.

Importantly, the ECP is a condition on the residue of *movement* rules (i.e., the empty categories such rules leave behind) and thus can be used to distinguish elements that move from those that do not. Given the analysis I have proposed, we should expect the latter—type I quantified NPs—never to lead to ECP violations despite a "wide scope" interpretation. We should also expect the former to be subject to the ECP and so possibly violate it. In English, the second hypothesis is harder to test, since type II quantifiers are generally assigned scope in their minimal sentential domains, thus, no "long" movement takes place and no ECP violations result. However, cases of this sort do occur in French, as (39a) indicates. The scope of 'personne' is determined by the position of 'ne'. It will have scope over the clause of which 'ne' is an element. In (39a) 'personne' is moved to the matrix clause—as shown in (40)—by QR. However, since the variable in the most embedded S is now not locally bound, an ECP violation occurs and the sentence is unacceptable. That the ECP holds in English is attested to by (39b).[20] The ECP forbids interpreting (39b) as a double question of the following form:

(41)   (For which x, which y) (x believes that y left the party)

Since the rule Move-α is involved in the formation of the structure that underlies sentences of this sort, the same "long" movement prohibitions are in force.

As we have seen, both 'any' and 'a certain' are generally construed as having widest possible scope:

(42)   a. Everyone believes that *a certain pretty woman* is here

   b. Sam doesn't believe that *anyone* came to the party

The fact that (42a,b) are fully acceptable corroborates the argument given in the previous section that such sentences are not derived from structures where QR has moved the indicated phrases. If QR were involved, we would expect the same unacceptability noted in (39), for here too the ECP would be violated.[21] However, by treating 'any' and 'a certain' as type I quantifiers not subject to a movement rule like QR, we have no more reason to expect unacceptability in (42) than in (43):

(43)   John believes that Harry is here

A Cluster of Effects

We have seen that there are two distinct *kinds* of quantifiers in English. On the one hand there are type II quantifiers, which are moved by

QR. As a result of being subject to a movement rule like this one, these expressions obey the Leftness Condition, have restricted scope and coindexing properties, are subject to the ECP, and have interpretive rules that are sensitive to the interpretation of other quantifiers.

On the other hand there are type I quantifiers, which in many respects act like names. These are not moved by QR. Thus, they are interpreted in a branching manner, have extensive coindexing properties, and are subject neither to the Leftness Condition nor to the ECP.

In a word, my proposal is that the two kinds of quantifiers are distinguished by whether or not they are subject to QR, that is, whether or not they form operator-variable structures. Moreover, by explaining the coincidence of properties noted above by reference to the *single* fact of whether the quantifiers do or do not undergo QR, we predict that the phenomena will appear together.[22] This prediction is borne out. Let us consider in more detail the French quantifier 'ne . . . personne':

(44)   *Jean n'exige que personne aime le gâteau

The scope of 'personne' is determined by the position of 'ne'. It is moved by QR, which adjoins it to the clause that 'ne' inhabits. The unacceptability of (44) is due to an ECP violation. The proposed analysis thus predicts that 'ne . . . personne' is a type II quantifier and that it will pattern accordingly. It does:

(45) a. *Qu'il$_i$ soit arrêté par la police n'a jamais empêché personne$_i$ de voler   (Leftness Condition)
'That he would be arrested never deterred anyone from stealing.'

   b. *Si personne$_i$ n'est arrêté par la police, il$_i$ continuera à voler   (limited coindexing)
'If anyone is not arrested by the police, he will continue to steal.'

   c. *Personne$_i$. n'aime quelqu'un. Il$_i$ aime seulement les gâteaux.   (no cross-discourse coindexing)
'Nobody likes anyone. He only likes cakes.'

Thus, 'ne . . . personne' not only falls under the ECP but also has limited scope and coindexing possibilities, obeys the Leftness Condition, and cannot coindex across a discourse. As predicted, the properties cluster together.

That this should be the case is particularly interesting evidence in favor of the analysis presented here. It predicts an interdependence of phenomena that is by no means obvious or logically necessary.[23]

These 'ne . . . personne' facts support the analysis in a more subtle way as well. In providing the relevant explanations, the above account focuses on the *formal* property of whether quantifiers are moved by QR to form operator-variable structures rather than on the interpretation of the quantifiers. The French facts corroborate this focus because, although the two expressions pattern very differently with respect to the relevant formal phenomena, 'ne . . . personne' and 'any' are virtually synonymous. For most purposes, the best English translation of a sentence with 'ne . . . personne' is almost always a sentence with 'any'. By locating the difference between quantifiers in a difference in their logical syntax, we allow for the possibility that their intepretive procedures will be similar. Comparing 'any' and 'ne . . . personne' vividly shows that these two features—interpretation and logical syntax—must be kept distinct. If the interpretation and the logical form of an expression co-varied, we would expect items with similar interpretive properties to behave similarly in all cases. But, as we have seen, this is not the case.

Acquiring Quantificational Competence

Before we continue, it is worthwhile pausing a moment to see how the logical problem of acquisition drives the arguments presented above.

I have argued that bifurcating the class of quantifiers and representing them as either type I or type II allows a *principled* explanation for a broad and interesting range of linguistic phenomena. I have *not* argued that it is impossible to treat 'any', 'every', 'a', 'someone', 'a certain' in a unitary fashion. It is indeed possible to capture or represent the relevant phenomena in a theory exclusively exploiting an operator-variable approach. Pronoun binding and relative quantifier scope could be accounted for simply by adjusting QR so that it moved 'any' and 'a certain' to their proper places in the course of applying. The facts pertaining to the Leftness Condition, cross-sentential coindexing, and the ECP could always be accommodated by special devices distinguishing QR as it applies to 'any'/'a certain' and 'every'/'a'/'someone'. Although these alternatives may be inelegant, they will suffice if the goal is simply to cover the data. However, if the goal is to explain how a child could acquire these rules, such approaches lead to insurmountable problems. What could lead a child to treat these quantifiers differently, especially given the often close similarity in meaning, for example, between 'any' and 'every' or even more strikingly between 'any' and 'ne . . . personne'? Why shouldn't the child bring these quantifiers together under one generalization? One might answer that the evidence cited above is surely what forces the child to treat these quantifiers differently. But how reasonable is this? Is it really reasonable to believe that sentences bearing on the Leftness Condition, such as (15)–(17), abound or even exist in the primary linguistic data? Would anyone ever use the unacceptable sentences in (14)? If not (as seems most likely, given their unacceptability), what evidence could force the distinctions noted? Even if relevant data are available, is it reasonable to think the child pays attention to them? How likely is it that the facts concerning the ECP can be winnowed from the primary linquistic data? In English, neither 'every' nor 'any' violates the ECP, so they appear to act alike. However, this similarity is mere coincidence arising from the local nature of QR, as the French facts and the double-'wh' facts cited in (39) show. Is it plausible that English speakers refer to French data in constructing their grammars and vice versa? Why does the child learning French not treat 'ne . . . personne' in the same way that the English child treats 'any'? The meanings are very similar. Moreover, why do the phenomena cluster as they do? Why does 'ne . . . personne' not act like 'every' with respect to pronoun coindexing and the ECP but like 'any' with respect to the Leftness Condition?

The answers seem obvious. There is no reason to believe that the different patterns of phenomena can be explained by citing features of the primary linguistic data. As this is what a uniform treatment implies when viewed in relation to the logical problem of acquisition, such an approach appears untenable. Though it can "cover" the data, the difficulties that confront a uniform approach when viewed as an explanation for the acquisition of quantifier competence demonstrate its empirical inadequacy.

An account that bifurcates the class of natural language quantifiers does not face these difficulties. The quantifiers behave differently because they are different kinds of quantifiers in Universal Grammar. The different patterns of behavior can be traced back to a single difference encoded in Universal Grammar: whether or not the quantifier forms operator-variable structures. That there are two types of quantifiers and that they have their associated properties and features of Universal Grammar and, as such, are innate. Thus, the fact that different quantifiers exemplify different paradigms of behavior can be accounted for without invoking the shaping effects of the primary linguistic data. Moreover, the child can accomplish the (simpler) task of *classification* quite easily on the basis of evidence from the linguistic environment. For example, from hearing sentences like (18a,b), the child gains evidence that 'every' and 'a'/'someone' are type II quantifiers. From hearing sentences like those in (9) and (28) and discourses like those in (11) and (12), the child learns that 'any' and 'a certain' are type I quantifiers. To classify the quantifiers, given that the classification scheme is itself innate, the child can rely exclusively on the positive data available in these kinds of simple sentences. Contrary to what happens in the other scenario, the child is not dependent on the kinds of data available only from complex sentences involving the ECP or even more exotic ones involving the Leftness Condition. Furthermore, the child needs no negative data, i.e., data to the effect that certain sentence types are unacceptable. From the perspective of the logical problem of acquisition, a theory of this kind makes far fewer demands on the language learner. The child need only decide whether a given quantifier is type I or type II, a manageable task since all the relevant information is contained in simple sentences of the kind noted above. Everything else follows from the child's innate grammatical endowment.

To be empirically adequate, any account will have to deal with the central fact that language acquisition proceeds despite an extremely poor data base. Embedding semantic questions like the nature of quantifier structure within the larger concerns of current linguistic theory forces one to hypotheses compatible with this most prominent of linguistic facts. In effect, it highlights a set of empirical costs and benefits that can be used to evaluate the relative merits of competing proposals about the logical structure of natural language. Judged by these costs and benefits, a bifurcated theory of quantifiers in natural language seems clearly superior to a unitary treatment.

Conclusion

The arguments of this chapter have shown that there exist two fundamentally different kinds of quantifiers. To put it more accurately, understanding the semantic aspects of natural language quantifiers requires distinguishing two axes that until now have generally been merged: an *interpretive* axis and a *logical syntax* axis. The interpretive axis is what philosophers have by and large concentrated on. 'Any', 'every', 'a'/'someone', 'a certain' do share important similarities when contrasted with names. Unlike names, none of them is a denoting expression. There is no anyman or anywoman. Rather, these expressions are interpreted relative to a given domain of entities.[24] Moreover, 'any' and 'every' both have general interpretations; 'a'/'someone' and 'a certain' do not.

The nature of the logical syntax axis should be clear; some phrases are of operator-variable form and some are not. Traditional logical analyses have treated all phrases that are quantifiers on the interpretive axis as also having operator-variable form. The above considerations show that this conflation is incorrect for natural language. More precisely, call elements having the interpretive properties noted above *quantifiers*, and those not having them *names*. Call NP elements moved by QR and so forming operator-variable structures *operators*, and those not so moved *terms*. The discussion above can be seen as claiming that not all quantifiers are operators and that some terms are quantifiers. An NP element has two axes relevant to predicting its semantic behavior; it can be [±:operator] ([−operator] = term) and [±quantifier] ([−quantifier] = name). Type I quantifiers such as 'any' and 'a certain' are [+quantifier, −operator]. Type II quantifiers such as 'every', and 'a' are [+quantifier, +operator]. Both features are relevant in explaining how what are pretheoretically called quantifiers behave semantically in natural language. In particular, distinguishing these two axes makes it possible to capture the namelike properties of certain kinds of quantifiers.

Furthermore, this typology of quantifiers is an aspect of Universal Grammar, an innate feature of the language faculty. There is simply not enough evidence to presuppose that the typology itself could be acquired on the basis of primary linguistic data. However, there is no a priori basis for expecting *in general* that a quantifier will fall into one or another class. Which element falls into which class is clearly a parameter set by the primary linguistic data. In short, the parameter [±operator] is innate. The specific value accorded a particular expression is a function of the linguistic environment.

Chapter 3

The Logical Syntax of Definite Descriptions and 'Belief'-Sentences

I have suggested that Universal Grammar makes available two types of quantifiers, distinguished by whether or not they form operator-variable structures of the form (1):

(1) $[_S Op_i [_S \ldots x_i \ldots]]$

These two kinds of quantifiers, type I quantifiers like 'any' and 'a certain' and type II quantifiers like 'every' and 'a'/'someone', behave differently in five important ways:

A. Type II quantifiers are more restricted than type I in their ability to treat pronouns as bound variables. Specifically, type II quantifiers seem capable of treating a pronoun as a bound variable only if it is in the same clause.

(2) a. *If Bill likes everyone$_i$, then Sam lends him$_i$ money

b. Bill gave every$_i$ man his$_i$ due

Type I quantifiers have far wider coindexing possibilities. They are not restricted to pronouns in the same clause, as sentences with 'any' illustrate:

(3) If Bill likes anyone$_i$, then Sam lends him$_i$ money

In fact, type II quantifiers, but not those of type I, can be characterized as having minimal sentential (S) scope. The operator must be construed as hanging from the minimal clause that contains it. Consider a sentence like (4):

(4) Someone believes that every man is a Republican

Here the only interpretation available is that there is just one person. 'Someone' cannot be interpreted as being within the scope of 'every'. (5) is not a possible representation of the logical form of (4).

(5) $[_S$ every man$_x$ $[_S$ someone$_y$ $[_S y$ believes$_S$ that x is a Republican]]]]

This reflects the minimal clause-bound nature of the interpretation of 'every' in particular and of type II quantifiers more generally.

B. Type I quantifiers, but not those of type II, can coindex pronouns across a sentence boundary, that is, they can bind across a discourse. Consider the following contrasted sentences with 'any' and 'every':

(6) a. Take any number$_i$. Divide it$_i$ by two.

b. Pick every peach$_i$. Give $\begin{Bmatrix} \text{them}_i \\ \text{*it}_i \end{Bmatrix}$ to Harry.[1]

c. Any citizen$_i$ can own a gun. In some countries he$_i$ must.

d. *Every citizen$_i$ can own a gun. In some countries he$_i$ must.

C. A type I quantifier, but not a quantifier of type II, can bind a pronoun to its left:

(7) a. That he$_i$ was drafted shouldn't bother $\begin{Bmatrix} \text{any} \\ \text{a certain} \end{Bmatrix}$ patriot$_i$

b. *That he$_i$ was drafted shouldn't bother $\begin{Bmatrix} \text{every patriot}_i \\ \text{someone}_i \end{Bmatrix}$

D. Type I quantifiers, unlike those of type II, are relatively insensitive to their "logical" environments with regard to their interpretation. They are *interpretively independent* of other logical elements in the clause. In other words, type I quantifiers are generally interpreted as if they had widest possible scope. Their interpretation neither depends on nor contributes to the interpretation of other logical elements in the clause. Consider the following sentences:

(8) a. Every man loves a woman/someome

b. Someone/A woman loves every man

c. Every man loves a certain woman

d. A certain woman loves every man

e. Sue doesn't love every man

f. Sue doesn't love any man

(8a,b) are ambiguous and can have either of the readings (9a,b):

(9) a. [every man$_x$ [a woman$_y$ [x loves y]]]

b. [a woman$_y$ [every man$_x$ [x loves y]]]

(8c,d), however can only be interpreted as (9b). The interpretation of an 'a certain' NP is not conditioned by the interpretation of other quantified expressions such as indefinite NPs or 'someone'. Thus, such an NP is *interpretively independent,* a term that singles out the phenomenon often explained in terms of scope.

Similar observations hold for 'any' and 'every'. As has often been noted, 'any' is relatively interpretively independent of its logical environment. This has often been described by saying that 'any' is a wide scope quantifier. Thus, phenomenally speaking, in (8f) 'any man' is not in the scope of the negation, whereas 'every man' in (8e) must be so interpreted.

E. Type II quantifiers, but not those of type I, are subject to locality restrictions on movement like the Empty Category Principle (ECP), a condition prohibiting the "long" movement of elements in the subject position of tensed clauses. Consider (10a–d):

(10) a. Who believes that John bought what

b. *Who believes that what was bought by John

c. Jean n'exige que Jean voit aucun des enfants

d. *Jean n'exige qu'aucun des enfants aille en vacances

(10a) is fully acceptable and can be interpreted as a double question of the form 'For which x and what y does x believe that John bought y'. An answer to (10a) might be 'Harry believes John bought a radio, Frank believes John bought a car . . . '. This interpretation as a double question does not exist for (10b). 'What' can only be interpreted as an echo element, as in 'John said *what*', where the questioner did not hear the last word (due to noise, for example); the phrase cannot be interpreted as a double question analogous to (10a). This is because the ECP prevents the "long" movement of the 'what' in the subject position of the tensed embedded clause, which is a necessary feature of sentences carrying such interpretations. To be interpreted as a double question, (10b) would have to have structure (11), but this structure is prohibited by the ECP.

(11) $[_S$ who$_x$, what$_y$ $[_S$ x believes $[_S$ y was bought by John]]]

Similar considerations hold for the French examples (10c,d). Movement from object position is permitted, but movement from subject position is not, resulting in the acceptability of the one example the unacceptability of the other.

The ECP does not apply to type I quantifiers, however:

(12) a. John doesn't believe anyone is home

b. Everyone believes a certain woman is in the yard

In (12a) 'anyone' is not interpreted as if it were in the scope of the matrix negation, and in (12b) 'a certain' has "wide scope" over the matrix 'everyone'. Moreover, the sentences are perfectly acceptable with these interpretations.

We have seen that these five differences can be accounted for by considering type II QPs to be subject to the movement rule QR, as a result of which they form operator-variable structures, and by grouping type I QPs together with names with respect to their logical syntax, i.e., considering them as not being moved by QR and not forming operator-variable structures. In other words, type II QPs are operators, and type I quantified expressions are terms (see chapter 2).

In what follows in this chapter the technical details concerning QR are not very important. The following correlations are crucial, however: (a) Noun phrase elements having a logical syntax of operator-variable form will act like type II quantifiers with respect to properties (A)–(E), and those having the logical form of names, i.e., non–operator-variable form, will act like type I quantifiers. (b) If an element has any of the properties (A)–(E), it will have them all. This follows from the account in chapter 2, according to which these properties are all linked to a *single* parameter: whether or not an element forms operator-variable structures.

This analysis claims that certain features of the logical syntax of a natural language quantifier are crucial for predicting certain of its interpretive properties. Furthermore, logical syntax must be distinguished from interpretation. Though 'any' and 'a certain' have the interpretations of quantifiers, they have the logical syntax of names. Whether a quantifier is treated as forming operator-variable structures is a parameter whose value must be fixed by primary linguistic data. Just how this is done will be discussed below.

The goal of this chapter will be to apply the theoretical apparatus motivated in chapter 2 to the case of definite descriptions and propositional attitude sentences. The discussion will proceed as follows. First, I will show that definite descriptions can be best described as type I QPs. I will then argue that this fact about definite descriptions follows from an interpretive property peculiar to definite descriptions when considered in the context of the logical problem of acquistion. In effect, given the focus of the theory of language assumed here, it is predicted that definite descriptions must be type I quantifiers. Next, I will investigate what this account of definite descriptions implies for the explanation of certain "scope" properties that Russell's analysis associated with the logical syntax of definite descriptions. Finally, I will extend the discussion to 'belief'-type sentences and consider their logical form.

Definite Descriptions

Given the distinction between type I and type II quantifiers, consider how definite descriptions ought to be treated in natural language. As is well known, two different approaches have been proposed to the logical syntax of definite descriptions.[2] One approach, associated with Frege, treats descriptions as singular terms with a logical syntax parallel to that of names. The other approach, associated with Russell, considers definite descriptions to be like quantifiers, on a par with 'every' and 'some'. It is important to note that this difference between Frege's and Russell's analyses involves not only the interpretation of definite descriptions but also a disagreement about the logical form of sentences of the structure ⌜[[the A] B s]⌝. In any event, our central concern will be the logical form of such expressions. Exploiting the resources of the analysis in chapter 2, we can investigate the question of the logical form of definite descriptions with respect to natural language. Does a phrase of the form 'the A' behave like a type I or a type II quantifier with respect to properties (A–E)? Depending on whether it behaves like a type I or a type II quantifier, it will constitute evidence in favor of either Frege's approach or Russell's, respectively. We will see that the facts favor the Fregean approach.

(13) a. If John likes the man in the corner$_i$, then Fred will lend him$_i$ money

b. John likes the man in the corner$_i$. Fred lent him$_i$ money.

c. That he$_i$ was insulted didn't bother the man in the corner$_i$

d. $\begin{Bmatrix} \text{Every} \\ \text{A} \end{Bmatrix}$ man likes the man in the corner

e. That the man in the corner$_i$ was insulted bothered his$_i$ mother

(13a) indicates that pronoun binding for definite descriptions is like pronoun binding for 'any'. (13b) shows that, like 'any', pronoun coindexing involving a definite description can occur across a discourse. (13c) shows that a definite description can bind a pronoun to its left, just like 'any' and unlike 'every'. In (13d) there is no apparent interpretive interaction between 'every', 'a'/'someone', and the definite description, a fact often explained by the uniqueness conditions on the interpretation of definite descriptions and usually encoded by permitting the permutations of definite descriptions with all other quantifiers. (13e) indicates once again that definite descriptions act like 'any' and unlike 'every'. If it were a type II quantifier like 'every', the definite description would have to be moved by QR[3] and appended to the matrix S node to be assigned the scope of the matrix clause and so be able to coindex the indicated pronoun:

(14) [$_S$ the man in the corner$_x$ [$_S$ that [$_S$ x was insulted]] disturbed his$_x$ mother]

But a structure like (14) would violate the ECP. Thus, we must conclude that, like type I quantifiers such as 'any', definite descriptions are not subject to the ECP.

Taken together, these facts indicate that definite descriptions behave like type I rather than type II quantifiers. Given the assumptions we have been making, it appears that a Fregean treatment of the logical syntax of definite descriptions is more adequate. Contra Russell, definite descriptions do not parallel type I quantifiers like 'every' in their logical form; instead, they have logical structures reminiscent of sentences containing names. In any event, this analysis will fully account for the behavior of definite descriptions with respect to properties (A)–(E). Though certain individual features of the behavior of definite descriptions can be accommodated piecemeal by citing other considerations— recall the standard explanation of (13d) concentrating on the uniqueness feature of the interpretation of definite descriptions—why it is that definite descriptions have *all* the properties cited and why their behavior parallels that of names and type I quantifiers is not so easily explained. Alternative approaches become even less appealing when we note that the facts of language acquisition discussed in chapter 1 and the proposal concerning quantifier types made in chapter 2 *predict* that definite descriptions will behave precisely as they in fact do with respect to properties (A)–(E).

Deriving the Properties of Definite Descriptions

As we have seen a theory of language that acknowledges the poverty of the stimulus will aim at adumbrating innate principles with certain parameters whose values are fixed by the primary linguistic data. In this light, how can we recast the above discussion? The innate principle involved is that natural language quantifiers differ in whether or not they are subject to QR, that is, whether or not they form operator-variable structures. Considering the data given in this chapter and in chapter 2, it seems initially reasonable to isolate the data concerning the interpretive independence of quantifiers (D), cross-sentential coindexing (B), and possibly pronoun binding (A) as relevant to setting the value of this parameter. The facts concerning the ECP (E) and leftward binding of pronouns (C) seem too exotic to be reasonably considered part of the primary linguistic data. Of the facts cited under (A), (B), (D), the evidence for the limited scope of type II quantifiers like 'every' comes from considering certain unacceptable sentences involving them.

In other words, until we focus on unacceptable sentences, there is no stark difference between type I quantifiers like 'any' and type II quantifiers like 'every'. How likely is it that such negative evidence is available to the child (as opposed to the linguist)? Since sentences like (2a) and (7b) are unacceptable and therefore unlikely to be used, there is little reason to believe the child will ever hear them. Moreover, even if they were used, what evidence would they provide, given their unacceptability? It seems reasonable to suppose that the evidence they provide will not be part of the primary linguistic data and is therefore not available to the child learning its first language. To circumvent some of these problems, we might assume that Universal Grammar predisposes the child to assume that elements interpreted as quantifiers, syntactically form operator-variable structures unless evidence arises to the contrary, i.e., that being subject to QR is the unmarked case.[4] If this is accepted, only the positive data displayed in acceptable sentences like (3) and (7a) will be relevant in fixing the value of the parameter.

The data displayed in (D) are reasonably straightforward. All the sentences are acceptable. The evidence for classifying a quantifier one way or another will be whether it is interpretively independent or not, that is, whether or not it can interact interpretively with other quantifiers. Moreover, the types of sentences discussed under (D) will suffice to show that type I quantifiers, but not those of type II, are terms in the sense of chapter 2.

In sum, the three likely sources of evidence in the primary linguistic data for assigning specific quantifiers to one innately given class or the other are the positive data found in acceptable sentences like those of (A), (B), (D). Since Universal Grammar makes operator-variable structures the unmarked case for quantified NPs, only positive data are needed to determine type I quantifiers. Consider the implication of this for definite descriptions.

As noted, in standard logical treatments, it is a logical feature of the uniqueness aspect of the interpretation of definite descriptions—the *unique a* such that A(a) and B(a)—that allows the definite description to permute freely with any other quantified element without affecting the interpretation of other logical elements in the clause. Thus, in sentences like (13d) the definite description appears to be interpretively independent of the other quantified elements in the clause. Under the proposed analysis, this property of definite descriptions will suffice to have them classified as terms and therefore as elements not forming operator-variable structures. In the case of definite descriptions, then, an inherent interpretive feature will suffice to determine their logical syntax. Specifically, the uniqueness feature characteristic of the interpretation of definite descriptions suffices to have them treated on a par with names and type I quantifiers like 'any' with respect to their logical form.

To put this another way, we have distinguished two axes relevant to the behavior of quantified expressions: their interpretation and their logical syntax. By and large, knowing a quantifier's value along one axis will not suffice to determine its value along the other. The independence of the values of the axes, however, will fail just in case the specific interpretive aspect of a quantifier has a feature that results in its being interpretively independent of other quantified and logical elements in the clause. The language faculty will take this as an indication of *termhood*, and will thus construe the quantifier as not forming operator-variable structures. The uniqueness aspect of the interpretation of definite descriptions has just this result. Hence the prediction that definite descriptions have the logical syntax of names and therefore pattern like type I quantifiers.

In sum, the general approach to language outlined in chapter 1, coupled with the specific proposal concerning quantifier types in chapter 2, predicts the full behavioral range of definite descriptions. By considering what types of data can reasonably be expected to be accessible to the child, we find that one type will suffice to induce the language faculty as characterized above to treat definite descriptions as terms. The fact that definite descriptions have a uniqueness clause as part of their interpretation (in the acceptable, correctly used cases) and hence are interpretively independent leads the language learner to treat them as not forming operator-variable structures. As the full range of properties (A)–(E) hangs precisely on this single syntactic feature of quantified NPs, the paradigm noted in (13) with respect to definite descriptions follows straightforwardly.[5]

Further Considerations

We have concluded that definite descriptions should be treated in a Fregean rather than a Russellian manner. One implication of this conclusion is worth emphasizing: namely, that certain ambiguities concerning the interpretation of definite descriptions in negative and modal sentences, first noted by Russell, should *not* be treated as resulting from different scope possibilities.

"Scope" is a syntactic notion describing formal relations among elements in a string. In current versions of EST scope assignment is a feature of the rule QR. A quantifier has the scope of the S to which it is appended. Thus, definite descriptions cannot really be said to have scope, for they are not affected by this rule. How does this apply to

Russell's ambiguities? At first blush, it might be tempting to employ a scope mechanism to represent them:

(15) John didn't see the present king of France

Russell noted that (15) could be true under at least two different situations: if there was no present king of France or if it was true of that individual who was the present king of France that John did not see him. A Russellian approach to definite descriptions could explain the possibility of the two interpretations by claiming that in the two cases the relative scopes of the negative and the definite description differed. More specifically, the ambiguity could be accounted for by assuming that sententially negated sentences like (15) have structures like (16) and that definite descriptions are moved by QR to form operator-variable structures. Depending on whether QR moved the definite description inside or outside the scope of the negation, one or the other reading would result. Thus, with (16) as a representation of negated sentences, QR could derive (17) and (18).

(16) [$_S$ not [$_S$ John saw the present king of France]]

(17) [$_S$ not [$_S$ the present king of France$_x$ [$_S$ John saw x]]]

(18) [$_S$ the present king of France$_x$ [$_S$ not [$_S$ John saw x]]]

The interpretations noted under (15) would correspond to (17) and (18), respectively; (18) but not (17) carrying ontological import. On such an approach the key mechanism employed to explain the ambiguity is that of differential scope embodied in QR, the rule grammatically responsible for scope assignment.

There are several problems with such an approach. First and foremost, as we have seen, there is good reason to think that treating definite descriptions as subject to QR and forming operator-variable structures is simply incorrect.

Beyond this, however, such an approach encounters several technical problems. First, it seems incorrect to propose (16) as the logical form of sentential negatives. If it were the correct analysis, we would expect 'any', which is generally acceptable only if it appears in the scope of a negative or a modal, to appear in the subject position of such sentences:

(19) *Anyone didn't see John

Furthermore, we would incorrectly expect sentences like (20a) to have interpretations like (20b):

(20) a. Everyone didn't like the play

       b. Not everyone liked the play

Finally, claiming that QR is involved in yielding the two readings creates problems quite independently of what one takes the proper analysis of sentence negation to be. The reason is that we would expect parallel ambiguities with quantifiers like 'every'. (21) should have the two readings represented in (22):

(21) John didn't like everyone at the party

(22) a. [$_S$ everyone at the party$_x$ [$_S$ not [$_S$ John like x]]]

     b. [$_S$ not [$_S$ everyone at the party$_x$ [John like x]]]

(22a,b) are simply the analogues of (17) and (18). Why, then, can (22a) not be a representation of (21)? If the ambiguity of (15) is derived by allowing QR to optionally place operators inside or outside the negative, then reading (22a) should be available. We might doctor the rule of QR to yield the right readings, but this would be very artificial and would stipulate rather than explain the facts.

In sum, there are independent reasons to believe that a scope approach to Russell's ambiguities is ill advised for natural language. Add to this that one loses any account for why definite descriptions pattern like names and type I quantifiers with respect to properties (A)–(E), and the approach loses virtually all its appeal. As far as natural language is concerned, the ambiguity observed by Russell is not the result of scope ambiguities in the logical syntax.

How, then, can this ambiguity be explained? My own view is that it is not one that a theory about the logical form of sentences in natural language ought to account for; in other words, that it is not an ambiguity that can strictly be traced to the operations of the language faculty. The ambiguity turns on whether the referent of the definite description *exists*. However, whether a singular term refers to an existent entity seems to have no noticeable effect on how the term functions in a grammar. Thus, for example, both fictional and real names act in exactly the same way with respect to operations like pronoun binding, cross-discourse coindexing, and the Leftness Condition. This can be seen by considering (13a–e) with 'Thor' and 'Abraham Lincoln' in place of the quantified expressions. From the point of view of the language faculty, whether a term refers to an actual entity seems to be an entirely inert property, at least as far as these aspects of interpretation are concerned.

One way to accommodate this fact is to follow Chomsky 1975. Here the semantic component is divided into two parts, *SI-1* and *SI-2*. SI-1 is the level of semantic interpretation connected with the operation of the language faculty. SI-2 includes principles of interpretation due to the operation of other cognitive faculties that might perhaps be governed by relationships of the cognitive apparatus with facts about the world.

Aspects of interpretation that turn on whether or not a singular term refers to an actual object or to one that is believed to exist would be considered part of SI-2.

Barwise and Perry 1980 travel an independent route to a similar conclusion. Following the approach pioneered by David Kaplan,[6] they develop a three-level theory of semantic interpretation that generalizes certain distinctions first observed by Donellan. According to this theory of "interpretation evaluation strategies" for natural language (Barwise and Perry 1980:28), level 1 is the level of linguistic meaning, level 2 interpretation, and level 3 evaluation. *Linguistic meaning* is what language provides—the rules for the interpretation of a linguistic element, possibly in a context. Thus, for example, the rule for 'I', the first person singular pronoun, is something like: refers to the utterer of the sentence.

A sentence in use is a statement that has an *interpretation*. At the level of interpretation we find objects as the interpretation of names, variables, and other noncomplex terms, properties and relations as the interpretation of predicates, and propositions as the interpretation of statements (Barwise and Perry 1980:19).

The interpretation of a sentence can involve yet a third level—evaluation—and in particular what Barwise and Perry call *value loading*. As a result of step 2 each basic part of a sentence receives an interpretation. However, given a particular context of use, "secondary interpretations" can be generated by "feeding into the proposition not the interpretation itself but some other entity closely associated with it in the world" (p. 22)—in other words, its value, the thing the speaker is referring to in the context of use or something like this. In terms of value loading, Barwise and Perry analyze Donellan's referential/attributive distinction with regard to definite descriptions. A value-loaded definite description corresponds to Donellan's referential use, a non-value-loaded interpretation to his attributive use.

The particular interest of Barwise and Perry's remarks given the previous discussion of definite descriptions is that (as they note) their interpretation-evaluation procedure can account for Russell's noted ambiguity without invoking a scope mechanism. It does so by distinguishing value-loaded from value-neutral readings of the sentence in use. Leaving the interpretation of a definite description value neutral results in a reading parallel to (17). Value loading yields an interpretation parallel to (18).

As Barwise and Perry correctly note (1980: 27–28), value loading is quite highly context sensitive depending on the syntactic structure of a sentence, the relative accessibility of possible interpretations, stress, pointing gestures, and a host of far more obscure and subtle pragmatic factors. This context sensitivity of value-loaded interpretations coincides with the view suggested above that the language faculty alone should not be expected to account for the ambiguity of sentences like (15) and that extralinguistic abilities tied to the operation of cognitive faculties other than the language faculty must be involved in any account. In effect, Barwise and Perry isolate interpretive strategies capable of yielding Russell's ambiguities without invoking either syntactic or, indeed, context-insensitive semantic distinctions characteristic of a traditional (e.g., Fregean or Russellian) theory of sense. Combining their account with the logical syntactic considerations of previous sections, we develop a rather comprehensive analysis of the interpretation of definite descriptions in natural language.

Some caveats must be added, however. Value loading should not be interpreted as carrying with it any ontological commitments. A value-loaded interpretation of a definite description will result in a proposition that is about a specific object or entity. It need not be the case, however, that this object exists. Value loading and value neutrality are two strategies of interpretation. The specific ontological implications are context dependent. The fact that the range of interpretations value loading and value neutrality yield can occur in fictional contexts, for example, indicates that value loading need not feed existing entities into the proposition. Whatever value loading is (and for my purposes its properties are not crucial), it can go on insulated from features of the actual world.

Moreover, I think that the referential/attributive dichotomy that Barwise and Perry's theory incorporates and generalizes should be treated less as an absolute distinction and more in terms of the endpoints of a graded continuum of possible interpretations. Scheffler 1955 argues for just such a conclusion. In discussing various difficulties with Carnap's notion of intensional isomorphism, he points out that in many cases of indirect discourse we wish to have both a wider and a narrower conception than Carnap's (or indeed any plausible) semantic theory can provide. What is really desired, Scheffler argues (p. 41), is a *pragmatic* requirement on meaning. He points out that the interpretation of a sentence is highly dependent on what our purposes are in a given context and, as such, should be conceived as "graded" and "contextually variable with purpose" (p. 43, note 11).[7]

If seen as a version of the sort of approach advocated by Scheffler, a treatment like Barwise and Perry's, in conjunction with the above considerations, will account rather well for the interpretation of definite descriptions in natural language. Various aspects of "meaning" are parceled out between features of the logical syntax in which such expressions appear and pragmatically determined, graded, and continuous interpretation procedures.

'Belief'-Sentences

The points made above regarding definite descriptions can be extended to apply to 'belief'-sentences as well:

(23)   John believes that $\begin{Bmatrix} \text{a handsome Swede} \\ \text{someone} \end{Bmatrix}$ loves Ingrid

The two interpretations of (23), like the ambiguity of (15), have been related to scope mechanisms. The readings associated with (23), it is claimed, result from whether the quantified noun phrase 'a handsome Swede'/'someone' is inside or outside the scope of the opaque verb 'believe'.

(24) a. $[_S$ a handsome Swede$_x$ $[_S$ John believes $[_S$ that x loves Ingrid$]]]$

   b. $[_S$ John believes $[_S$ that $[_S$ a handsome Swede$_x$ $[_S$ x loves Ingrid$]]]]$

Structure (24a) allows the implication that there are such things as Swedes; (24b) could be true even if Swedes were mere figments of John's imagination.

The problem with this scope-based account of the ambiguity is that a structure like (24a) is quite generally ill formed. It violates the ECP, for example. Furthermore, QR, which would apply to yield the operator-variable structures in (24), generally attaches quantifiers to the most proximate S node. Consequently, (24a) could not be derived.

The general point, however, is that scope considerations cannot really be involved in the ambiguities of (23). If they were, we would expect sentences like (25) to display ambiguities like those represented in (26):

(25)   Someone believes that every Swede loves Ingrid

(26) a. $[_S$ every Swede$_x$ $[_S$ someone$_y$ $[_S$ y believes $[_S$ that x loves Ingrid$]]]]$

   b. $[_S$ someone$_x$ $[_S$ x believes $[_{\bar{S}}$ that $[_S$ every Swede$_y$ $[y$ loves Ingrid$]]]]]$

However, the reading of (25) corresponding to (26a) does not exist. This indicates that the mechanism involved in explaining the *relative scope* of quantifiers cannot be the same one involved in accounting for the opacity ambiguities in (23) i.e., that scope differences are not responsible for the ambiguities of 'belief'-contexts.[8]

This case supports the conclusions drawn in the previous section. Once again the ambiguity in question is not a matter for SI-1; once again it concerns whether an expression denotes actual existing objects.

Interpretations that depend on such ontological concerns fall outside the theory of linguistic competence properly speaking.

As in the case of definite descriptions, we could extend Barwise and Perry's account of value loading to cover these readings. The value-loaded interpretation of the existential phrase 'a handsome Swede' will yield the reading parallel to (24a); the value-neutral interpretation will correspond to (24b). However, in the case of 'belief'-sentences it is much clearer that a graded notion will be needed: something like *degree* of value loading (a notion pointing to a Schefflerian interpretation of Barwise and Perry's account) to accommodate the effect of scope in multiply embedded constructions. There is a degree of substitutivity allowed in the content clauses of propositional attitude constructions that falls short of the full substitutivity characteristic of pure *de re* readings but is less frozen than the pure *de dicto* interpretations. To accommodate this, I will follow Scheffler and view *de re* and *de dicto*, value loading and value neutrality as the ends of a graded continuum of context-sensitive interpretations rather than as the only two interpretive options available.

Such an approach to propositional attitudes seems to be what authors like Burge and Kaplan have been suggesting (Burge 1977, Kaplan 1970). As these authors point out, even in opaque readings pure *de dicto* and pure *de re* interpretations are very special cases. Often a term in such a context, though not freely substitutable, has a range of terms that can replace it without affecting the propositional content of the propositional attitude ascription. For example, if John says "Queen Elizabeth is pretty" and we know that John believes that Queen Elizabeth is the Queen of England, then it seems legitimate not only to ascribe to him the belief that Queen Elizabeth is pretty but also to say that for John this is the same belief as the belief that the Queen of England is pretty. In certain contexts, much harder to fully specify than to recognize, given what we know about John and how we interpret his sentences and beliefs, we can legitimately substitute in the content sentences of 'belief'-statements concerning him. What the actual range of substituends is will depend on a range of contextually determined pragmatic factors that determine when and by how much one can "export" the quantifier.

In sum, as in the case of definite descriptions, the behavior of 'belief'-sentences should be seen as following from a combination of logical syntactic properties and context-sensitive pragmatic features of interpretation. Incidentally, in these cases, context-insensitive semantic theories that focus on the objects words denote or the propositions sentences express yield either to more formal syntactic notions like whether the NP element is of type I or type II or to more context-sensitive, graded, and continuous pragmatic notions of interpretation. Semantics, traditionally conceived as a level of interpretation focusing on the relationship between words and the objects they denote context independently plays a very small role, if any. I will return to this issue in chapters 6 and 7.

Additional Semantical Caveats

Whatever the merits of the positive proposals suggested to handle the ambiguities of definite descriptions and 'belief'-sentences, the main conclusion of the previous sections is a negative one. Certain types of readings—those turning on the existence of the entities referred to—should not be associated with the mechanisms of scope and quantification. They should not be considered as bearing on the mechanisms underlying a speaker's linguistic competence properly speaking. The discussion centered on relative complex constructions involving definite descriptions and 'belief'-sentences but, as noted in passing, it need not have been so sophisticated. For example, in natural language the behavior of fictional names is virtually indistinguishable from that of names that refer to actual objects. Linguistically, whether a denoted entity exists seems entirely irrelevant. Similarly, how quantification works seems disjoint from the ontological issues that Quine and more recently the Davidsonians have seen as intrinsically related to explaining quantification. The objectual interpretation of quantification, interpreted as ontologically pregnant, is in no way intrinsic to the operation of quantifiers in natural language. Quantification theory in natural language is not *about* anything; nor is it about the very general features of everything. Quantification theory simply marks out linguistic dependencies and divides up domains of discourse. What the division "means" is a function of the kinds of entities involved. If the entities in the domain are real, then quantification will be objectually interpreted and the utterances of speakers so interpreted will reveal ontological commitments. If the entities in the domain are fictitious, then no ontological commitments will be revealed. What remains constant from domain to domain are the grammatical or syntactic aspects of quantification, plus some rules stating how specific quantifiers divide up or relate to arbitrary domains of entities. More detailed features of quantifier interpretation cannot be *specified* without considering the *use* to which the whole apparatus is being put. In short, the ontological aspects of quantification and reference are best seen as functions of use rather than as being intrinsically related to the apparatus itself.

In fact, a more radical thesis can be maintained. It might be suggested that even if the notion "object" or "actual existent object" is not very important as far as the interpretation of natural language is concerned, surely the notion "possible object" is, or perhaps even a looser one. One might say, for example, that 'Pegasus' denotes at least a possible object. However, not even this weak claim is obviously correct for much of what would be studied as part of the problem of meaning in natural language. How definite descriptions behave with respect to many aspects of meaning seems tied exclusively to the logical syntax of these expressions. Neither domains of objects nor possible objects need be invoked; the form of the inscription (at an abstract level of representation) suffices.

Consider, for example, sentences like (27a,b):

(27) a. That his$_i$ income is falling bothers $\left\{ \begin{array}{c} \text{the} \\ \text{*every} \end{array} \right\}$ average man$_i$

b. Its$_i$ definition as both round and square fully characterizes $\left\{ \begin{array}{c} \text{the} \\ \text{*every} \end{array} \right\}$ round square$_i$

No one wishes to claim that there are objects that are average men in any meaningful sense. Even less so for round squares. Nonetheless, mature speakers of English understand that the definite descriptions in sentences (27a,b) allow the indicated linking relations even though the phrases cannot be taken to denote anything at all—not even possible objects. The 'every'-phrases in (27a,b) are more unacceptable than the definite descriptions, and are perceived as such, because they violate grammatical constraints on coindexing. This is clear even though (27b) is already interpretively very strange because of the strange sorts of things it appears to be talking about. Despite this anomaly, the difference in relative acceptability is clear. These considerations indicate that for such issues concerning meaning semantic notions such as "object" or "possible object" are beside the point.

If this is the case, it would appear that several currently influential approaches to the semantics of natural language are misconceived. For example, programs of the Davidsonian variety that try to give truth theories of meaning for natural language will inevitably construe quantification in natural language objectually, and reference as a relation between a term and an actual object. In McDowell's pithy phrase, "truth is what a theory of sense is a theory of" (McDowell 1976). If so, then a theory of sense (in McDowell's terms) is not what people interested in meaning in natural language should be trying to construct. This approach conflates what is context-independently intrinsic to quantifiers, variables, and names with properties that these notions have in one special use of this apparatus. Moreover, this conflation raises problems that, naively considered, hardly seem problematic.

Nonreferring singular terms in natural language becomes semantically suspect or secondary, as do the myriad of uses unconnected with the conveying of information, namely, those uses at right angles with issues of truth and falsity. This truth-theoretic perspective leads us away from considering the possibility—and, if the above discussion is correct, the actuality—that names, variables, quantifiers, etc., have many properties that can be specified independently of the specific uses to which they are put, but that nonetheless determine how language functions in a wide range of what we would pretheoretically call semantic phenomena. As far as natural language is concerned, quantifiers that range over unicorns and Norse gods function no differently from those ranging over quarks, tables, or nineteenth-century presidents of the United States. Similar considerations hold for theories of meaning invoking notions like "truth in a model" or "entity in a model." If such theories are to be construed as saying anything at all, it will be that notions like "possible object" play a central role in explaining how meaning operates in natural language. If the above observations are correct, then for many cases, how meaning is determined has nothing at all to do with notions like "object," "truth," or "model." The key notions are not semantic, but syntactic or pragmatic. The semantic notions turn out to have no role in the generalizations that explain how meaning functions in natural language. If they do have a role to play, it will be elsewhere.

Conclusion

I have argued that the ambiguities in definite description constructions described by Russell, as well as opacity distinctions characteristic of propositional attitude constructions, are not properly treated as scope phenomena. How they are to be treated is another issue. I described some pragmatic approaches to the interpretation of such constructions advanced by Scheffler 1955 and Barwise and Perry 1980. Such approaches, I believe, are best interpreted as falling outside the theory of grammar (and hence linguistic semantics) properly speaking. If Scheffler, Barwise, and Perry are correct, the only reasonable approach to these phenomena will involve pragmatic considerations exploiting cognitive abilities far richer than those the language faculty alone provides and will fall outside the framework of assumptions noted in chapter 1. If they can be incorporated into any theory at all, they will form part of a theory akin to Chomsky's SI-2. I will return to these important issues in chapters 6 and 7.

Chapter 4

A Grammatical Basis for the Theory of Quantifier Types

In this chapter I will take a closer look at type II quantifiers. My goal will be to derive the most salient property of these quantifiers—the fact that their scope is generally limited to the S domain that most immediately dominates them—from more general principles concerned with the binding of null elements.[1,2]

In showing how this property of type II quantifiers can be derived from (and so explained by) independently motivated principles, I will consider yet another type of quantified expression—type III QPs—which are moved by QR to form operator-variable structures but whose scope is not clause bound. It will turn out that by adopting the binding principles suggested below, we can derive not only the basic properties of type II QPs, but also those of types I and III. Finally, I will relate the technical discussion developed to derive these three types of quantified expression to the logical problem of language acquisition.

The Problem

In standard logical treatments of quantification there is no limit to the possible scope interactions of quantified expressions within a clause. Quantified expressions arbitrarily far apart act no differently with respect to their possible scope dependencies than those residing in the same clausal neighborhood. For example, just as (1a) can be represented as having the quantifier dependencies illustrated in either (1b) or (1c), so too can sentences (2a–d):

(1) a. $\begin{Bmatrix} \text{Someone} \\ \text{A man} \end{Bmatrix}$ loves every woman

   b. $[_S \begin{Bmatrix} \text{someone} \\ \text{a man} \end{Bmatrix}_x [_S \text{ every woman}_y [_S x \text{ loves } y]]]$

   c. $[_S \text{ every woman}_y [_S \begin{Bmatrix} \text{someone} \\ \text{a man} \end{Bmatrix}_x [_S x \text{ loves } y]]]$

(2) a. Someone believes that everyone likes bananas

   b. Everyone believes that someone won the lottery

   c. Someone believes that Frank likes everyone

   d. Everyone believes that Frank likes someone

However, (2a–d) do not have the ambiguities illustrated in (1b) and (1c). In these sentences, the matrix quantified NP enjoys wide scope over the embedded quantified expression. Thus, in (2a) and (2c) 'someone' is interpreted as having wide scope over 'everyone' and in (2b) and (2d) 'everyone' is construed as having wider scope than 'someone'. These judgments would be explained if (2a–d) could be analyzed as having the logical form representations illustrated in (3) and were prohibited from having those illustrated in (4):

(3) a. [$_S$ someone$_x$ [$_S$ x believes [$_S$ that [$_S$ everyone$_y$ [$_S$ y likes bananas]]]]]

   b. [$_S$ everyone$_x$ [$_S$ x believes [$_S$ that [$_S$ someone$_y$ [$_S$ y won the lottery]]]]]

   c. [$_S$ someone$_x$ [x believes [$_S$ that [$_S$ everyone$_y$ [$_S$ Frank likes y]]]]]

   d. [$_S$ everyone$_x$ [$_S$ x believes [$_S$ that [$_S$ someone$_y$ [$_S$ Frank likes y]]]]]

(4) a. *[$_S$ everyone$_y$ [$_S$ someone$_x$ [$_S$ x believes [$_S$ that [$_S$ y likes bananas]]]]]

   b. *[$_S$ someone$_y$ [$_S$ everyone$_x$ [$_S$ x believes [$_S$ that [$_S$ y won the lottery]]]]]

   c. *[$_S$ everyone$_y$ [$_S$ someone$_x$ [$_S$ x believes [$_S$ that [$_S$ Frank likes y]]]]]

   d. *[$_S$ someone$_y$ [$_S$ everyone$_x$ [$_S$ x believes [$_S$ that [$_S$ Frank likes y]]]]][3]

The free application of QR will yield both types of structures in LF. However, only the interpretations associated with the structures in (3) seem acceptable. Why are the structures in (4) prohibited? If we can find a principled answer to this question and hence a principled means of ruling out such structures, we will have explained why quantified sentences in natural language do not have the full range of logically possible readings.

Possible Approaches

Subjacency
One solution immediately suggests itself. As May 1977 suggests, we might simply assume that, like other movement rules in the syntax, the LF rule of QR—the rule responsible for forming structures of operator-variable form, as in (3) and (4)—is constrained by the Subjacency Principle. Under this assumption, the Subjacency Principle would form part of the definition of movement rules in general, i.e., part of the definition of Move-α. As QR is simply a particular instance in LF of this kind of rule, we would expect it to be subject to Subjacency and thus have the limited scope options illustrated above.

Consider the details. QR is subject to Subjacency, which restricts the movement in the following way. In a structure like (5), where α, β are *bounding nodes*, a rule of the type Move-α can move an element A to a position like B, but not to one like C.

(5) $[_\gamma \ldots C \ldots [_\beta \ldots B \ldots [_\alpha \ldots A \ldots] \ldots B \ldots] \ldots C \ldots]$

The Subjacency Principle thus prohibits a moved element from crossing more than a single bounding node.

In English, bounding nodes will include S and $\bar{S}$. Therefore, the movement of the embedded quantified phrases by QR in (4) will violate the general subjacency restriction on movement rules and the structures will be disallowed.

There are, however, several empirical difficulties with such an account. First, it makes crucial use of the assumption that both S and $\bar{S}$ are bounding nodes. However, it has been shown that there are languages in which $\bar{S}$, but not S, is a bounding node (see Rizzi 1980 on Italian and Sportiche 1979 on French). Assuming that Subjacency accounted for the noted restrictions on quantifier scope, we would expect that in such languages representations like those in (4) would be generally well formed and that therefore (2a–d) would have scope ambiguities parallel to those of (1a). This, however, does not seem to be the case.

In French, for example, where $\bar{S}$ but not S counts as a bounding node, (6) is not ambiguous:

(6) Quelqu'un croit que Pierre aime chaque enfant
     'Someone believes that Pierre likes every child.'

The embedded quantified expression is interpreted within the scope of the matrix quantifier 'quelqu'un'. That is, the interpretation represented in (7) is not available:

(7) $[_S$ chaque enfant$_x$ $[_S$ quelqu'un$_y$ $[_S$ y croit $[_S$ que $[_S$ Pierre aime $x]]]]]$

A second problem facing the Subjacency account is illustrated by the behavior of 'wh'-elements that do not undergo syntactic 'wh'-movement, the so-called 'wh'-in-situ constructions. Consider (8a,b):

(8) a. Who saw a review of a book about who

     b. Who said that John bought what

These sentences are well-formed multiple questions. An answer to (8a) might be "Fred said that John bought a car and Frank said that Sheila bought a rug." These sorts of multiple questions are formed by the application of an LF movement rule, 'Wh'-Raising, which preposes a 'wh'-in-situ into a complementizer position already filled by a 'wh'-element.[4] For instance, the LF representation of (8b) is illustrated in (9).

(9) $[_S$ who$_x$ what$_y$ $[_S$ x said $[_S$ that $[_S$ John bought $y]]$

Note that (9) violates Subjacency. At least two bounding nodes intervene between 'what$_y$' and the variable 'y' that it binds. Nevertheless, the sentence with the indicated interpretation is fully acceptable. Under a Subjacency account of the clause-boundedness of QR we would therefore be forced to claim that Subjacency constrains one instance of Move-α (QR) but not another ('Wh'-Raising).

This is clearly an undesirable conclusion. It is well known that Subjacency constrains all syntactic instances of Move-α; that is, it applies to all instances of the rule that apply in the syntactic component of the grammar. Why, then, should the same not be true of instances of Move-α in LF, especially if Subjacency is part of the general definition of movement rules? Moreover, how could a child learn that Subjacency does not apply to 'Wh'-Raising? Effects of the Subjacency Principle are evident only in complex sentences involving *at least* three levels of embedding. For the reasons indicated in chapter 1, it is unreasonable to suppose that such sentences form part of the primary linguistic data. Thus, it is hard to see how a child would ever be able to distinguish the rules of 'Wh'-Raising and QR.

Given these considerations, it seems wrong to think that obeying Subjacency is part of the *general* definition of Move-α. Rather, Subjacency constrains syntactic instances of Move-α but not LF instances. One way of accounting for this is to assume that Subjacency is a condition on the well-formedness of representations at S-structure rather than being part of the definition of movement rules as such and constraining their application.[5]

In sum, it seems undesirable to invoke Subjacency to account for the phenomenon of limited quantifier scope.

The Empty Category Principle

Another possible approach is to begin with the observation that quantified expressions moved by QR are subject to the Empty Category Principle (ECP), which requires that such categories (the residue of movement rules, such as NP traces left by NP Movement and variables left by 'Wh'-Movement or QR) be properly governed by a lexical category. Roughly speaking, the ECP requires empty elements to appear only in the complement positions of verbs, nouns, or prepositions (see Chomsky 1981 for details).

As an illustration, consider the following sentences:

(10) a. Someone expects (that) every Republican will be elected

   b. Someone expects every Republican to be elected

The possible scope dependencies of the quantified NPs in (10b), but not in (10a), are ambiguous. (10b) can be interpreted with either the existential or the universal quantifier having wide scope. (Similar facts are noted by Postal 1974:222.) On the other hand, the only possible interpretation of (10b) is that the existential phrase 'someone' enjoys scope over the universally quantified phrase 'every Republican'.

Such facts can be straightforwardly explained in terms of the ECP. The structures underlying the readings of (10) on which the universally quantified phrase has wide scope are illustrated in (11).

(11) a. $[_s[\text{every Republican}]_x \ [_s[\text{someone}]_y \ [_s \ y \text{ expects } [_s \text{ (that)}[_s \ x$
    will be elected]]]]]

   b. $[_s[\text{every Republican}]_x \ [_s[\text{someone}]_y \ [_s \ y \text{ expects } [_s \ x \text{ to be}$
    elected]]]]

If we assume that *only* the empty category 'x' in (10b) is properly governed, the structure in (10a) will be ruled illicit by the ECP. (Definitions of government and proper government are given in note 19 of chapter 2.) This assumption is a natural one if, following Chomsky 1981, we observe that in (10a), but not (10b), the embedded subject is in an inflected clause. If we assume that Inflection (Infl) governs the subject, then in (10a), but not (10b), a governor intervenes between the matrix verb and the empty category. Thus, the empty category is not properly governed as the ECP requires. In short, the ECP will explain why 'every Republican' can have scope over 'someone' in (10b) but not (10a), by generally restricting the distribution of empty categories in the subject positions of inflected clauses.

Though the ECP partially explains the phenomenon of limited quantifier scope, it alone does not suffice to account for the data. Thus, consider (2c) once again.

(2) c. Someone believes that Frank likes everyone

Under an ECP account, we would expect the embedded universal quantifier to be extractable and have scope over the matrix existential QP, because the empty category left by QR would be properly governed by the embedded verb 'likes'. This interpretation is not available, however, and we therefore need something besides the ECP to rule it out.

Anaphors
As we have seen, the ECP can be invoked to explain the limited scope opportunities of QPs in subject position of inflected clauses. However, it still remains to be explained why the scope of nonsubject quantified NPs is also restricted—in particular, why the scope domains of type II quantifiers like 'every' in general do not extend beyond the clauses in which they originate. In other words, why does QR seem to append a type II quantifier only to a position within the most proximate clause containing it?

(12) a. *$[_S O_x [_S \ldots [_S NP \ V \ x] \ldots]]$

    b. $[_S \ldots [_S O_x [_S NP \ V \ x] \ldots]$

(12) displays the kinds of structures we must consider. Those like (12b) must be allowed, those like (12a) ruled out. Two possibilities suggest themselves: the limited scope of type II QPs is due (a) to the nature of the rule that moves the element to presentential position, namely, QR, or (b) to some condition that the variable 'x' must satisfy. The first option informs a Subjacency approach, which we have already found to be inadequate. Here I will suggest that the second option enables us to make the required distinction.

First, let us reconsider the data to see how the *variables* of type II quantifiers distribute. As (2a–d) indicate, a reasonable generalization is that QR is clause bound. In other words, the variable left behind by QR must be bound to an operator in the same clause. Strictly speaking, however, this generalization is incorrect. Sentences like (10b), repeated here as (13a), indicate that if the variable is in the subject position of an infinitive, it can be bound by an operator in the next clause.

(13) a. Someone expects every Republican to be elected

    b. $[_S$ every Republican$_x$ $[_S$ someone$_y$ $[_S$ y expects $[_S$ x to be elected$]]]]$

Furthermore, in such sorts of sentences, the operator must be in the next closest clause.

(14)   Someone wants John to expect every Republican to be elected

In (14) 'every Republican' cannot be interpreted as having scope over 'someone'.

This pattern of distribution is quite familiar within natural languages. In fact, it is the one displayed by anaphoric elements, such as 'himself' or 'each other'.

(15) a. $John_i$ likes $himself_i$

b.   *$John_i$ expects Mary to kiss $himself_i$

c. $John_i$ expects $himself_i$ to pass the exam

d.   *$John_i$ expects that $himself_i$ will pass the exam

e.   *$John_i$ wants Mary to expect $himself_i$ to pass the exam

As these sentences indicate, anaphoric expressions like 'himself' pattern just like the variables of type II quantifiers. They are fully acceptable if bound by (i.e., coindexed with) an antecedent in the same clause, as in (15a), or, if they are in the subject position of an infinitival expression, by an antecedent in the next immediate clause, as in (15c). Otherwise, they are unacceptable.

If we assume that the variables left behind by type II quantifiers are anaphoric, then those variables must be locally bound, and we thus have an explanation for the limited application of QR to such quantifiers.[6] The formal details of this solution will be given below. Note, however, that if we can generalize the notion of anaphor and antecedent so that the relation between a type II quantifier and its variable is analogous to the relation between an antecedent and its bound anaphor, then the limited scope of type II quantified NPs follows.

A Typology of Quantifiers

First, let us consider one more set of facts. Not all quantified NPs subject to QR have the limited scope options displayed by type II quantifiers such as 'every'. For example, Move-α in the form of QR can move 'personne' in 'ne . . . personne' constructions in an unbounded manner, and Move-α in the form of 'Wh'-Raising can move the 'wh'-in-situ to a complementizer position arbitrarily far away. However, elements can only be moved from object positions or the subject positions of non-tensed clauses. In other words, the movement, though not restricted to the immediate clause from which it originates, as in the case of type II quantifiers, is nonetheless subject to ECP restrictions, contrary to the case of type I quantifiers.

(16) a. Who expects that John bought what

b. *Who expects that what was bought by John

c. Who expects who to be convicted

d. Je n'ai exigé qu'ils arrêtent personne

e. *Je n'ai exigé que personne vienne

The existence of such quantifiers, which I will call *type III quantifiers*, is very interesting: they fill a logically possible gap in a theory of quantifier types in which the full typology of quantifiers is generated on the basis of the principles of the binding theory. In particular, we will see that the relevant parts of the binding theory—principles (A) and (C), which are conditions on anaphors and "variables," respectively—suggest that three and only three kinds of quantifiers exist: those subject to principle (A), those subject to principle (C), and those subject to both (A) and (C). We will see that these are exactly the properties of the quantifiers we have been discussing:

(17) a. Type I quantifiers like 'any' and 'a certain'

b. Type II quantifiers like 'every', 'a', 'someone'

c. Type III quantifiers like 'personne' and 'wh'-in-situ

Type II and III quantifiers are subject to the ECP. Type II quantifiers have severe restrictions on possible scope. Type I quantifiers pattern in many respects like names; type II quantifiers pattern very much like anaphors. Type II and type III QPs are subject to QR; those of type I are not. It remains to show exactly how type II quantifiers can be distinguished from type III. In the next section I will outline a version of the binding theory that accomplishes this and from which the typology of quantifier follows.

The Binding Theory

The version of the binding theory proposed in Chomsky 1981 is composed of three principles:

(18) *Binding Theory*

A. An anaphor is bound in its governing category.

B. A pronominal is free in its governing category.

C. An R-expression is free.[7]

"Governing category" and "bound"/"free" are defined as follows:

(19) a. α is a *governing category* for β iff α is the minimal maximal projection containing β, a governor of β, and a subject accessible to β. Subject = AGR or [NP,S].[8]

b. An element α is *bound* by an element β iff it is coindexed with β and β c-commands α. If α is not bound, it is *free*.

Finally, the following definition of "accessibility" is assumed:

(20) α is *accessible to* β iff β is in the c-command domain of α and coindexing of (α,β) would not violate principle (C) of the binding theory.[9]

On the revised version of the binding theory adopted here, (18) emerges as (21) (see Aoun 1981 for further details).

(21)   *Generalized Binding Theory*

A.   An anaphor must be X-bound in its governing category (X = A or $\bar{\text{A}}$).[10]

B.   A pronominal must be X-free in its governing category (X = A or $\bar{\text{A}}$).

C.   An R-expression must be A-free.

This version of the binding theory differs from the one in (18) by extending the notions "bound" and "free" to include both $\bar{\text{A}}$-binding and A-binding. In (18) the binding principles were restricted to A-binding. The extension of the notion "binding" to "X-binding" is necessary if we are to treat the relation between an operator and the variable it coindexes as analogous to the relation of an antecedent and the anaphor it coindexes. Within clause (A) of the generalized binding theory, $\bar{\text{A}}$-binding, which is relevant to operator-variable relations, and A-binding, which is a well-formedness condition on antecedent-anaphor relations, are both construed as instances of "X-binding." Given this more general notion of binding, we can account for the parallelism in the distribution of anaphors and type II variables by noting that they both are subject to principle (A) of (21).

Let us see how this version of the binding theory and the definitions in (19) and (20) interact to account for the properties of type II QPs. Consider first examples like (22a,b):

(22) a.   *John$_i$ said that Mary likes himself$_i$

b.   Someone said that Mary likes everyone

(22a) is unacceptable, as is (22b) with the interpretation where 'everyone' has scope over 'someone'. This can be explained as follows. Sentences (22a,b) have the structures (23a,b) under the relevant interpretation.

(23) a. [$_{S_2}$ John$_i$ said [$_S$ that [$_{S_1}$ Mary likes himself$_i$]]]]

b. [$_S$ everyone$_x$ [$_{S_2}$ someone$_y$ [$_S$ y said [$_S$ that [$_{S_1}$ Mary likes x]]]]]

If both 'himself' and 'x' in (23a,b) respectively, fall under (A) of (21), each must be X-bound in its governing category. But given definitions (19) and (20), in both cases the governing category is S_1: 'Mary' is the accessible subject (it is the first [NP,S] that c-commands 'himself' and with which it can have coindexing satisfying (20)), and 'likes' governs 'himself' and 'x'. However, both elements are X-free in this governing category, that is not coindexed with an element in the governing category (S_1). 'Himself' is coindexed, but only with an element in S_2, and 'x' is only coindexed with 'everyone', also an element outside S_1. Therefore, both structures violate (A) of (21), and the sentences with the indicated interpretations are ruled unacceptable.

Consider now the interpretation of (22b) where 'everyone' is within the scope of 'someone'. On this interpretation (22b) has the structure (24).

(24)   [$_{S_2}$ someone$_y$ [$_{S_2}$ y said [$_{\bar{S}_1}$ that [$_{S_1}$ everyone$_x$ [$_{S_1}$ Mary likes x]]]]]

In (24) S_1 is the governing category for 'x'. Thus since 'x' falls under (A) of (21), it must be X-bound. But it is X-bound in S_1; in particular, it is Ā-bound by 'everyone'.[11] (22b) with the interpretation indicated in (24) is therefore fully acceptable.

Finally, consider the following pairs of sentences:

(25) a. *John$_i$ expects (that) himself$_i$ will pass the exam

b. *Someone expects (that) every Republican will be elected ('every Republican' has wide scope)

(26) a. John$_i$ expects himself$_i$ to be elected

b. Someone expects every Republican to be elected ('every Republican' has wide scope)

(27) a. *John expects Mary to want himself to be elected

b. *Someone expects Mary to want every Republican to be elected ('every Republican' has wide scope)

The relevant structures for (25a,b) are (28a,b):

(28) a. [$_{S_2}$ John$_i$ expects [$_{\bar{S}_1}$ (that) [$_{S_1}$ himself$_i$ AGR pass the exam]]]

b. [$_{S_2}$ every Republican$_x$ [$_{S_2}$ someone$_y$ [$_{S_2}$ y expects [$_{S_1}$ (that)
[$_{S_1}$ x AGR be elected]]]]]

The governing category for both 'himself' and 'x' is S_1. Since the sentences are finite and have tense, AGR governs the subject position in each. Moreover, by definitions (19a) and (20), this is also an accessible subject. Therefore, by principle (A) of (21) both elements must be X-bound in S_1. Neither is. Therefore, the structures are ill formed and the sentences in (25) are unacceptable.

(26a,b) have the representations (29a,b):

(29) a. [$_{S_2}$ John$_i$ expects [$_{S_1}$ himself$_i$ to be
elected t$_i$]]

b. [$_{S_2}$ every Republican$_x$ [$_{S_2}$ someone$_y$ [$_{S_2}$ y expects [$_{S_1}$ x_i to be
elected t$_i$]]]]

In both structures, S_2 is the governing category for 'himself' and 'x', since 'expects' is the governor for each. Therefore, both must be X-bound in S_2. This is the case in both (29a) and (29b); thus, these structures are well formed and (26a,b) are acceptable with the indicated interpretations.

Finally, consider (27a,b), which have the structures (30a,b):

(30) a. [$_{S_3}$ John$_i$ expects [$_{S_2}$ Mary to want [$_{S_1}$ himself$_i$ to be elected]]]

b. [$_{S_3}$ every Republican$_x$ [$_{S_3}$ someone$_y$ [$_{S_3}$ y expects [$_{S_2}$ Mary to
want [$_{S_1}$ x to be elected]]]]]

The governing category for 'x' and 'himself' is S_2; 'want' is the governor and 'Mary' is the accessible subject. Therefore, both elements must be X-bound in S_2. Since both are X-free in S_2, the structures are ill formed and (27a,b) are ruled unacceptable with the indicated interpretations.

In sum, a version of the binding theory like the one in (21) (in particular, clause (A)), definitions (19) and (20), and the assumption that type II variables are anaphors combine to explain fully the scope possibilities of type II quantifiers.

Now consider type I quantifiers. As their behavior has been thoroughly examined elsewhere (Chomsky 1981), I will not repeat the details here. Briefly, though, all the properties of type I quantifiers discussed in chapter 2 follow in the customary manner, if we assume that they have the logical syntax of names and are R-expressions subject to principle (C) of the binding theory. Type I QPs will not be subject to the ECP because they never form operator-variable structures and, therefore, leave no empty category (variable) behind that would fall under this condition.

Moreover, type I QPs can be coindexed with pronouns in other clauses. As (31a,b) show, if a QP forms operator-variable structures, it can coindex a pronoun only if the operator c-commands that pronoun in LF (see Chomsky 1981, Higginbotham 1980 for details).

(31) a. $[O_x \ldots [\ldots \text{pronoun } x \ldots] \ldots]$

b. $*[\ldots [O_x \ldots] \ldots \text{pronoun } x \ldots]$

Type I quantifiers, however, like names, are not subject to this condition, because they do not form operator-variable structures.

Finally, binding principle (C) of (21) is relevant to the following cases,[12] ruling sentences like (32a) unacceptable:

(32) a. *He$_i$ doesn't believe that anyone$_i$ is home

b. His$_i$ heavy caseload doesn't bother any lawyer$_i$ in the firm

The structure of (32a) is indicated in (33):

(33) $[_{S_2}$ he$_i$ doesn't believe $[_{S_1}$ anyone$_i$ is home]]

By principle (C) 'anyone', a namelike expression, must be free in every governing category. However, it is coindexed by a c-commanding element 'He' in S_2 and is therefore bound in S_2, thus ensuring the unacceptability of the sentence.

Note that principle (C) does *not* apply to (32b). Here, since 'his' does not c-command the 'any'-phrase, the coindexing is permitted.

(34) $[_S[_{NP}$ his$_i$ heavy caseload] doesn't bother $[_{NP}$ any lawyer$_i$ in the firm]]

In short, the binding theory does not appear to pertain to the facts clustered around the Leftness Condition. Indeed, leftness violations occur only with QPs that form operator-variable structures, not with QPs in general (consider (32b) with 'every' in place of 'any' and the resulting unacceptability). This would seem to indicate that the phenomena described by the Leftness Condition should be traced to the fact that some QPs have syntactic scope whereas others do not. In other words, leftness phenomena are a result of certain illicit operator-pronoun-variable relations. This has in fact been proposed by Koopman and Sportiche 1981. They explain leftness violations in terms of the *Bijection Principle*, which allows an operator to bind *at most* one of two elements—i.e., pronoun-variable pairs— if these elements are not in a c-command relation. So, for example, a structure like (35) is ill formed by the Bijection Principle:

(35) $[_S O_x [_S \ldots [_\alpha \ldots \text{pronoun}_x \ldots] \ldots [_\beta x] \ldots]]$

Such a treatment of leftness phenomena comports quite nicely with the analysis presented here, which distinguishes QPs that are subject to QR (hence forming operator-variable structures) from those that are not. In particular, it traces leftness violations not to some general feature of the binding theory or QPs as such, but to a particular feature QPs might (but need not) have if they form operator-variable structures.

On the assumption that binding principle (A) of (21) pertains to type II quantifiers and principle (C) pertains to type I, we can derive their observed properties. What then of type III quantifiers? This is the truly interesting case. Since we have found that some QPs are subject to (A) and others are subject to (C), we would expect, for logical completeness, that some QPs are subject to both. And in fact type III quantifiers fill this gap in the expected pattern.

Since being subject to the ECP is the distinguishing property of type III QPs, we must show that from (A) and (C) together we can derive ECP effects. Moreover, we will have to show how these two principles interact to prohibit movement from subject position of a finite clause but permit it from nonsubject positions.

Consider first the ECP effects.

(36) a. *Who thinks (that) what was bought by John

     b. Who thinks (that) John bought what

The structure of (36a) is (37).

(37) $[_{S_2}$ who$_x$ what$_y$ $[_{S_2}$ x thinks $[_{\bar{S}_1}$ (that) $[_{S_1}$ y AGR be bought by John]]]]

A type III variable such as 'y' in (37) (a variable left by 'Wh'-Raising, an LF instance of Move-α) is subject to binding principle (A). Therefore, (37) should be parallel to (25b). AGR is both a governor of, and an accessible subject for, 'y'. Therefore, it must be X-bound in S_1, its governing category. However, it is X-free in S_1, with the result that (36a) is unacceptable.

Now consider (36b), whose structure is (38).

(38) $[_{S_2}$ who$_x$ what$_y$ $[_{S_2}$ x^i [AGR^i-Present] think $[_{\bar{S}_1}$ (that) $[_{S_1}$ John^i [AGR^i-Past] buy y]]]]

The subject 'x' in S_2 and 'John' in S_1 are coindexed with the AGR marker.[13] This cosuperscripting is a convention to indicate agreement between the subject of a clause and the agreement elements in a finite (in English, "tensed") clause, i.e., AGR (see Aoun 1981 for details). Consider now which sentence is the governing category for 'y'. 'y' has a governor in S_1, i.e., 'buy'. However, 'John' cannot be an accessible subject. Why not? By definition (20), 'John' is an accessible subject for

'y' iff coindexing between 'John' and 'y' is permitted. But coindexing them would lead to a binding violation. Recall that 'y', being a type III variable, is subject to binding principle (C) and therefore must be free in every governing category. But if coindexing between 'John' and 'y' took place in (38) 'John' would bind 'y', since 'John' c-commands 'y' and would be coindexed with it. In short, the sentence would violate binding principle (C).

What about considering the AGR element of S_1 to be an accessible subject, an option permitted by definition (19a)? Recall that AGR and the subject of (38), 'John', are coindexed. But AGR is in turn coindexed with 'y'; in other words, 'John' and 'y' are coindexed. But this is just the same case prohibited by binding principle (C) under the first option of choosing 'John' as the accessible subject. Similar reasoning will prevent 'x' or the AGR element in S_2 from being an accessible subject for 'y'. In fact, on the assumption that 'y' is subject to principle (C), 'y' can have no accessible subject in (38) and hence no governing category.

One more step is required to explain the well-formedness of (38). Chomsky 1981 has suggested, on independent grounds, the need for a principle such as (39).

> (39)   A root sentence is a governing category for a governed element that lacks an accessible SUBJECT.[14]

By (39), the whole clause counts as a governing category for 'y' in (36). In this governing category 'y' is X-bound by 'what$_y$' and principle (A) of (21) is satisfied.

In short, if we assume that 'y' is subject to both principles (A) and (C) of the binding theory (21), and adopt the independently motivated principle (39), the extractability of type III quantifiers in sentences like (36b) follows. That is, we derive the salient characteristics of the scope of type III QPs: that such QPs are clause bound in scope when originating from the subject positions of finite clauses and only in such positions. In sum, we derive the salient characteristics of the scope of type III QPs. 'Wh'-Raising has been examined in detail here but similar considerations will hold for other instances of Move-α in LF such as QR in the case of 'ne . . . personne' in French noted earlier. (For a full discussion of 'ne . . . personne' under these assumptions, see Aoun and Hornstein (forthcoming)).

In conclusion, we have seen how the relevant clauses of the binding theory can be used to predict the behavior of the three types of QPs described in the previous section. More interesting still, we see that the full range of logical possibilities exists: QPs that are namelike (type I, subject to binding principle (C)), those that are anaphoric (type II, subject to (A)), and those that are both (type III, subject to both (A) and (C)). In the next section I will discuss the issues such an analysis raises for the logical problem of language acquisition.[15]

Learning Quantification

I have argued that the proper setting for work on meaning in natural language is the logical problem of language acquisition, and I have shown how the distinction between type I quantifiers and types II and III might proceed. In this section, therefore, I would like to focus on the remaining issue: how the child could distinguish type II quantifiers from type III. If the child comes to language learning equipped with an innate schematism, setting the grammatical limits to possible theories of quantification, and if language learning is the fixing of the open parameters of this schematism on the basis of the simple sentences of primary linguistic data, then what sorts of information are relevant to classifying a particular QP as type II or type III?

I suggested in chapter 2 that type II quantifiers are the unmarked option with respect to Universal Grammar. In other words, the language faculty will consider a QP to be type II unless evidence arises to the contrary. We have already seen what sort of evidence the primary linguistic data could provide to indicate to a child that a QP is of type I. What would show it that a QP is of type III?

The two cases of type III QPs we have considered suggest an obvious answer. Multiple-'wh' constructions and 'ne . . . personne' sentences both contain an overt element to which a movement rule is sensitive in assigning scope to the moved element. In the former case, it is the 'wh'-element in COMP position, already moved by the syntactic movement rule 'Wh'-Movement (an instance of Move-α in the syntactic part of the grammar). In the latter case, it is 'ne'. I would like to suggest that the existence of these overt grammatical scope indicators is to be expected, given the nature of the acquisition problem as defined in chapter 1.[16] If type II quantifiers are the unmarked option in Universal Grammar, then evidence of this sort—overt evidence bearing on and indicating the scope of type III quantifiers—is called for. That it seems to exist, at least in the cases discussed, is further support for the general approach adopted.

In conclusion, if these considerations are correct, they give quite a complete account of how quantifiers work in natural language. Quantifiers are of three types, with three distinct sets of properties. Principles of Universal Grammar, in particular clauses (A) and (C) of the binding theory (21), plus more general considerations regarding language acquisition, can account for this trichotomy of quantifier types in natural language.

Chapter 5

Application of the Theory to More Problems and Puzzles

According to the theory developed so far, natural language quantifiers differ along two dimensions: (a) whether they move, and (b) what kinds of variables they leave behind if they move. (a) distinguishes type I quantifiers like 'any' and 'a certain' from both type II quantifiers like 'every', 'a', 'someone' and type III quantifiers like 'ne . . . personne' in French and the 'wh'-in-situ in multiple questions in English. (b) distinguishes type II QPs from type III and is the basis for explaining the different possible scopes that can be assigned to these quantifier types. In particular, viewing type II variables as subject to principle (A) of the Extended Binding Theory explains the fact that, generally speaking, their scope is limited to their smallest sentential domain, and viewing type III variables as subject to both principles (A) and (C) explains the ECP subject-object asymmetry characteristic of their movement.

In this chapter, we will be occupied primarily with two kinds of sentences whose behavior appears to differ sharply from what the theory would permit:

(1) $[_{S_2}$ $[_{NP}$ everyone $[_{S_1}$ who owns *a donkey$_i$*$]]$ beats it$_i]$

(2) $[_{S_2}$ $[_{NP}$ the woman $[_{S_1}$ that *every Englishman$_i$* loves$]]$ is his$_i$ mother$]$

In both (1) and (2) it appears that the type II quantified phrases—'a donkey' and 'every Englishman'—bind pronouns in clauses outside of their possible scope domains. That is, in both (1) and (2) the relevant quantified phrases appear to have scope beyond S_1, the minimal S that contains them, and in fact appear to be attached to S_2 so as to be able to coindex the indicated pronoun. Given the theory outlined above, the structures underlying (1) and (2) are ill formed and as such should result in the sentences themselves being judged unacceptable. However, (1) and (2), with the indicated interpretations, seem perfectly acceptable.

In what follows I will try to show why these examples constitute merely *apparent* counterexamples to the theory I have outlined. To accomplish this, I will argue (i) that the distinction between moved and unmoved QPs suffices to account for the properties of the so-called 'donkey'-sentences, and (ii) that the mechanisms needed to explain the 'Englishman'-sentences such as (2) are really quite general and form the basis of a theory of PRO interpretation.

Sentences (1) and (2) have been long-standing puzzles in discussions of natural language quantifier scope (see Geach 1962). Of particular interest here is that they have been used as strong *motivation* for semantical approaches to meaning in natural language. In showing how the theory of quantifier types developed above, in conjunction with some natural independently motivated extensions of current Government-Binding theory, suffices to explain these phenomena in a principled manner, I have a higher-order goal: to weaken the motivation for semantical theories of interpretation and to show that a principled alternative is available that exploits purely syntactic mechanisms.

'Donkey'-Sentences: The Problem

What, exactly, makes 'donkey'-sentences so puzzling? Consider once again a sentence like (1):

(1)   Everyone who owns a donkey beats it

In (1) it appears that 'a donkey' is within the scope of the universal quantifier 'everyone'. In other words, there is an interpretation of (1) in which more than one donkey is being discussed—in fact, one donkey per owner. The favored reading of (1) contrasts with (3), in which only one donkey is being discussed.

(3)   Everyone who owns a certain donkey beats it

In (3), but not (1), the 'donkey'-phrase has scope over the universally quantified phrase 'everyone'.[1]

This fact alone is not particularly irksome. Indeed, given the theory of type II quantifiers outlined above, we expect this to be the case. The (relevant) logical form of (1) is (4); thus, we expect the scope relations between 'everyone' and 'a donkey' that in fact hold, since 'everyone' c-commands 'a donkey'.

(4) $[_{S_2}$ everyone$_x$ [who $[_{S_1}$ a donkey$_y$ $[_{S_1}$ x owns y]] beats it]]

The problem is that the pronoun 'it' appears to be bound by the 'donkey'-phrase. Recall that for type II quantifiers, binding is possible only if the quantifier c-commands the pronoun that it coindexes at LF. In (4), however, this is not the case. 'A donkey' has scope only over elements in S_1 and not over those in S_2. Unfortunately, 'it' resides in S_2, not in S_1.

This, then, is the problem: given the assumptions we have been working with, it seems that we cannot simultaneously account for the quantifier-quantifier interaction and the quantifier-pronoun interactions in 'donkey'-sentences like (1). We do have a principled way of explaining the relative quantifier scopes of 'everyone' and 'a donkey'—the fact that 'everyone' has wide scope over 'a donkey'—but this appears to prohibit an explanation of the fact that 'it' is bound by 'a donkey'.

There are several possible approaches to solving this problem. We might deny that the logical form of relative clauses is the one displayed in (4). In particular, we might claim that, in relative clauses quite generally, quantified phrases that reside in the relative clause can have scope over that portion of the clause that the *whole* relative clause c-commands. For example, in (1) the whole relative clause 'everyone who owns a donkey' does c-command the pronoun 'it'; therefore, 'a donkey' is a possible binder of the pronoun. In short, such a solution would claim that for the purpose of pronoun binding in relative clauses the scope of a type II quantifier is determined not by its own c-command domain (the elements it c-commands in LF) but by the c-command domain of the whole relative clause of which it is a part.[2]

Though a perfectly coherent possibility, such an approach runs into immediate problems.

(5)   *A man who owns every donkey$_i$ beats it$_i$[3]

In (5) there is exactly the same logical form as in (1), the only difference being that the positions of the existential and universal QPs are reversed. If the above approach were correct, the two should behave alike. However, in (5), as we would expect, the existential phrase 'a man' has scope over 'every donkey' and 'every donkey' cannot bind the pronoun 'it'.

Sentences like (5) seem to indicate that it is far too strong to claim that the scope domain of a relative clause determines the scope domain of a clause-internal quantified expression. We might try to save the proposal by weakening it, claiming that for existentially quantified phrases contained in relative clauses (but not universally quantified ones), scope is determined by the whole relative clause. This would in fact distinguish (1) from (5). However, it does not *explain* the properties of 'donkey'-sentences, namely, why (1) does not behave like (5). The principle as refined merely stipulates that 'donkey'-sentences have the properties they do; but a stipulation is not an explanation. The proposed "solution" is not so much a solution as a restatement of the problem.

However, the restatement is helpful. It indicates that the properties of 'donkey'-sentences cannot be traced solely or primarily to structural factors. Sentences (1) and (5) have the same structures but diverge in their behavior. More important, consideration of both (1) and (5) suggests that the special properties of 'donkey'-sentences are tied to the *particular* quantifiers involved, i.e., an existential NP in the relative clause, a universally quantified NP heading the relative. Before pursuing this observation and developing another kind of solution, however, let us consider the properties of 'donkey'-sentences more fully.

'Donkey'-Sentences: Further Details

How are 'donkey'-sentences interpreted? A rough paraphrase of (1) is a sentence like (6).

(1)   Everyone who owns a donkey beats it

(6)   Every donkey owner beats the donkey he owns

As the paraphrase (6) indicates, the interpretation of (1) is quasi-generic; it says something about donkey owners. This becomes even clearer when we consider what would make (1) false. Consider Sheila, Edna, and Sally. Each of these individuals owns five donkeys. Each adores four of them and detests one. Each beats the detested beast, but only this one. The other four are never so much as yelled at. In short, each donkey owner beats one of the five and only one of the five donkeys that she owns. Under these conditions, on the assumption that Edna, Sheila, and Sally exhaust the class of donkey owners, (1) would be false. Though it is true that everyone owns a donkey—in fact, five— and everyone beats a donkey, still, it is not the case that everyone who owns a donkey beats it. For this to be true, the three owners would have to beat *all* the donkeys they own, not just one. In short, as (6) makes clear, (1) is true if and only if every donkey owner beats all the donkeys she owns. Thus, we see that the relationship between the universal NP 'everyone' and the existential NP 'a donkey' is more complex than that in a simple universal QP–existential QP sentence.

The quasi-generic feature of such sentences can be further highlighted by considering other 'donkey'-sentences and their paraphrases.

(7)   Everyone who sees a red-billed heron remarks on its coloring

(8)   Everyone who sees the red-billed heron remarks on its coloring

(8) is a reasonably good paraphrase of (7). In (8), however, the existential phrase 'a red-billed heron' is replaced by a definite description with generic import. (8), as well as (7), says something about all those who are red-billed-heron seers. The fact that an overt generic phrase can substitute for the existential NP to produce a reasonable paraphrase

further confirms the above observations about the interpretation of 'donkey'-sentences.

Consider one last set of observations. As is well known, a noun phrase of the form 'a N(oun)' does not always have a generic interpretation. Generic phrases appear only in certain contexts. For example, whether a generic interpretation is available for a noun phrase often depends on its grammatical context. Such an interpretation is often found in sentences of the present tense, for example, or in "general" sentences involving universal quantifiers in subject position:

(9)   A camel travels well in the desert

(10)   Everyone hunted the dodo mercilessly

(11)   Everyone likes $\left\{ \begin{array}{c} \text{the} \\ \text{a} \end{array} \right\}$ basset hound

When the local *grammatical* environment is altered, the generic interpretation vanishes:

(12)   Two men saw $\left\{ \begin{array}{c} \textit{the donkey} \\ \textit{a donkey} \end{array} \right\}$

(13)   *A donkey* has eaten the petunias

In (12) and (13) the italicized phrases do not have a generic interpretation. Now, if 'donkey'-sentences are indeed quasi-generic, we should find that their interpretations can be upset by altering the local grammatical environment. This in fact appears to be the case:

(14)   *Two men who own a racehorse$_i$ race it$_i$

(15)   *Everyone who has once owned a donkey$_i$ will beat it$_i$

(16)   *Everyone who owned a donkey$_i$ had beaten it$_i$

All that we have done in (14)–(16) is to change the tense of the sentences or replace a universal QP with 'two', and yet these sentences seem far less acceptable than the commonly cited 'donkey'-sentences. For example, if (14) is acceptable at all, it does not have the interpretation of a 'donkey'-sentence. It has only a reading where a single racehorse is being discussed; its only paraphrase is (17):

(17)   Two men who own a certain racehorse$_i$ race it$_i$

In short, 'donkey'-sentences are very sensitive linguistic objects. They seem best when they carry a present tense and have a general structure, i.e., a universally quantified subject. This would be expected if their interpretations are quasi-generic. More important, these observations concerning the interpretation of 'donkey'-sentences suggest that perhaps the quasi-generic character of these clauses is in fact partially responsible for their idiosyncratic properties. If this is correct, we would not expect sentences like (5) and (14)–(16) to behave like 'donkey'-sentences, since in (5) the phrase 'every donkey' is not generic and in (14)–(16) the indefinite phrase does not have a generic interpretation because of the local grammatical environment.

In what follows I will present a solution to the problems concerning 'donkey'-sentences that exploits these observations. To do so, it will be necessary first to consider generics in more detail and then to incorporate these observations into an overall account.

Generics

Consider once again the basic properties of 'donkey'-sentences.

(1)   Everyone who owns a donkey$_i$ beats it$_i$

Like a standard type II QP, the 'donkey'-phrase is interpreted as falling within the scope of the phrase 'everyone'. Note, however, that with respect to its pronoun-binding abilities 'a donkey' acts very much like a type I quantifier, or a name.

(18) a.   Everyone who owns a certain donkey$_i$ beats it$_i$

b.   ?Everyone who owns any donkey$_i$ beats it$_i$

c.   Everyone who sees Tom$_i$ hits him$_i$

As we have seen, 'donkey'-sentences have a quasi-generic interpretation. This leads to the question, what kind of QPs are generics? More specifically, are generics of the form 'a Noun' type I QPs?

The answer seems to be yes. For example, these generics appear to be capable of coindexing pronouns to their left:

(19) a.   Its$_i$ family is important to a raccoon$_i$

b.   That it$_i$ might go for days without water doesn't disturb a camel$_i$

They can coindex pronouns that they do not c-command at LF:

(20) a.   If a bear$_i$ is angry, it$_i$ will fight

b.   A man's$_i$ home reflects his$_i$ personality

They can coindex pronouns across a discourse:

(21) a.   A beaver$_i$ has a flat tail. It$_i$ can also swim under water.

b.   A nightingale$_i$ has a sweet voice. It$_i$ sings at night.

They are interpretively independent:

(22) a. Everybody loves a lover

b. A beaver builds every dam itself

Finally, they do not appear to be subject to the ECP:

(23) John doesn't believe that a beaver has a flat tail

Since these five properties are characteristic of type I quantifiers, it seems that generic phrases are type I QPs, just like 'any' and 'a certain'.

Seen from this point of view, the fact that the 'donkey'-phrase in 'donkey'-sentences like (1) can coindex a pronoun it does not c-command is not surprising: all type I quantifiers can do this. The remaining problem is to explain how 'a donkey' can be both a type I and a type II QP. If we can do this, we will have explained the basic properties of such phrases in a non–ad hoc manner. The explanation, in effect, turns on viewing 'a donkey' as an ambiguous phrase. In its guise as a type II QP it interacts with 'everyone' and has the relative scope dependency discussed earlier. In its guise as a type I QP, a generic, it coindexes the pronoun 'it' and yields the quasi-generic coloring characteristic of the interpretation of 'donkey'-sentences.[4] In short, the properties of such a phrase result from its having two related yet different structures, each of which explains half of the observed properties. What allows the pronoun binding is the fact that the phrase 'a donkey', as a generic, is a type I QP. Note, incidentally, that there is additional evidence for treating 'a donkey' as a type I QP. For example, 'donkey'-sentences violate the Leftness Condition.

(24) a. Until its$_i$ warranty expires, everyone who owns a Dodge$_i$ drives recklessly

b. Because it$_i$ can maim a person with one kick, everyone who owns a donkey$_i$ is careful

Furthermore, they allow coindexing across a discourse:

(25) Every farmer who owns a donkey$_i$ also owns several acres. They use it$_i$ to plow them.

This follows if the 'donkey'-phrase is a type I QP, but it would be totally inexplicable if the 'donkey'-phrase were construed as being moved by QR to mandatorily form operator-variable structures.[5] In short, any analysis that explained the properties of 'donkey'-sentences *exclusively* in terms of a revised version of QR, no matter how complex, would have trouble explaining why sentences like (24) and (25) act as though they contain type I QPs. Though it is no doubt part of the answer, invoking a movement analysis to explain *all* the properties of 'donkey'-sentences is a solution beset with great difficulties.

'Donkey'-Sentences Once Again

I have suggested analyzing 'donkey'-sentences as involving dual structural descriptions, namely, the logical forms in (26) and (27):

(26) $[_{S_2} [_{NP_2}$ everyone$_x$ $[_{\bar{S}}$ who$_x$ $[_{S_1}$ a donkey$_y$ $[_{S_1}$ x owns $y]]]]$ $[_{S_2}$ z beats it]]

(27) $[_{S_2} [_{NP_2}$ everyone$_x$ $[_{\bar{S}}$ who$_x$ $[_{S_1}$ x owns a donkey$_i]]]$ $[_{S_2}$ z beats it$_i]]$

The interpretive effects of relative quantifier dependency in these sentences are the result of their having LF structure (26); pronoun binding is possible because they have LF structure (27). The *full* range of properties characteristic of 'donkey'-sentences is the result of their having both (26) and (27) as possible structural descriptions. This, in turn, is just a way of theoretically representing the fact that phrases of the form 'a Noun' are ambiguous between regular indefinite descriptions–existentially quantified phrases that are type II QPs, on the one hand, and generic phrases that are type I QPs, on the other.

The technical device required for 'donkey'-sentences to have both of these structural descriptions is Kupin and Lasnik's formulation of the Extended Standard Theory (Kupin and Lasnik 1977). According to this formulation, which I adopt here, a sentence is identified with its set of structural descriptions. Most sentences will have a set of such structural descriptions, which together yield a unique phrase marker at any particular level of grammatical description. In some cases, however, such as Reanalysis (Hornstein and Weinberg 1981), 'easy-to-please'-constructions (Chomsky 1981), or restructuring (Rizzi 1978), more than one structural description is available. In such cases a single tree format is incapable of representing the grammatical processes, and sets of phrase markers must be invoked. I suggest that 'donkey'-sentences are another such case. The set of structural descriptions for 'donkey'-sentences includes *both* (26) and (27). (26) is relevant to determining relative quantifier scope; (27) to determining the possibility of coindexing 'it'. Exactly as in Chomsky's analysis of 'easy-to-please'-sentences, two mutually incompatible structures underlie 'donkey'-sentences and only in tandem do they determine all of their properties.

In sum, by (a) assuming the distinction between type I and type II quantifiers, (b) observing that phrases of the form 'a Noun' are ambiguous between generic phrases and existential phrases, (c) considering existential phrases as type II QPs and generics as type I, and (d) adopting

Kupin and Lasnik's approach to a sentence's structural descriptions, we are able to explain the salient properties of 'donkey'-sentences and the idiosyncratic interpretive and acceptability judgments in the examples given. Each of these four assumptions seems quite uncontroversial. The distinction between type I and type II quantifiers has been extensively motivated above. Kupin and Lasnik's formulation of current grammatical theory is generally accepted, and the resources it makes available that have been employed in this account have been used to explain other related phenomena. Points (b) and (c) amount to little more than commonplace observation. Thus, once the proposed distinction of quantifier types is granted, a straightforward syntactic apparatus is available within the current assumptions of Government-Binding theory, and we are able to account for 'donkey'-sentences at no extra theoretical cost.

Further Interpretation Remarks

Whatever the virtues of the above analysis of 'donkey'-sentences, it is somewhat odd to insist that a sentence has two different representations at LF but is not ambiguous.[6] In this section I would like to suggest that, far from being a problem, the dual analysis indeed helps to explain the source of the indicated interpretation of these sentences.[7] Recall how 'donkey'-sentences are interpreted:

(28)   Everyone who owns a donkey beats it

(29)   Every donkey owner beats the donkey that he owns

The 'donkey'-sentence (28) is paraphrased by (29). Why? In particular, why does (28) have the reading that *all* the donkeys are beaten? Let us sharpen this question a bit by considering some other sentences:

(30)   Everyone who bought a gift received a meal voucher

(31)   Everyone who owns a gun obtains a registration

Sentence (30) is ambiguous. It can have one of the two readings in (32):

(32) a. Everyone who bought a gift received a meal voucher when it was wrapped

     b. Everyone who bought a gift received a meal voucher when they were wrapped

Interpretation (32a) implies one meal voucher per gift; for example, if Harry bought three gifts, he received three meal vouchers. Interpretation (32b), on the other hand, implies one meal voucher per customer or gift buyer, regardless of how many gifts that individual bought. Similar remarks hold for (31). This sentence is also ambiguous. On one reading there is one registration per gun; on the other there is one registration per gun owner.

More specifically, (30) can be viewed as follows (see Kamp 1982 or Heim 1982). Consider the ordered pair of shoppers and gifts $(a.b)$. The ambiguity of (32a) can be represented as in (33a,b):

(33) a. Every shopper (a) gift (b) pair $(a.b)$ receives a meal voucher

b. Every shopper (a) receives a meal voucher if there is an ordered pair $(a.b)$, (b) a gift

On both readings only gift buyers receive a voucher. The issue is whether the premium is one voucher per gift or one voucher per shopper. What does this have to do with 'donkey'-sentences? 'Donkey'-sentences are relative clauses that permit only the reading parallel to the reading of one voucher per gift. In other words, a 'donkey'-sentence is interpreted as follows:

(34) For every owner-donkey pair $(a.b)$, if a owns b, then a beats b

'Donkey'-sentences do not receive a reading parallel to the other one available for relative clauses in general (i.e., parallel to (33b)), according to which every donkey owner beats at least one of the donkeys that he owns. Since, as (33) shows, there is nothing inherent in relative clause interpretation itself to account for the absence of this reading, we must seek some other interpretation. Another possibility is that, in such phrases, the operator 'every' is defined over the ordered pair for some reason. But this cannot be true. Consider a sentence like (35).

(35) Many farmers who buy a donkey beat the donkeys (all) they buy

(35) is interpreted as in (36):

(36) For many farmers a and every donkey b, if a buys b, a beats b

In other words, the range of b, the donkeys, is not determined by the operator of the head of the relative clause, nor is it interpreted as a regular existential quantifier.

As the background for a third possibility, let us consider one more type of sentence whose quantifiers are in universal-existential order.

(37) Everyone gave a book$_i$ to its$_i$ author

Under one reading, (37) is true if everyone gave at least one book to the author of that book (on the assumption that the set of books is not empty). In particular, (37) is true even if there were some books not given to the authors of those books. Now consider (38):

(38)   Everyone gave every book$_i$ to its$_i$ author

(38) will be true only if every book written by an author is given to that author by everyone (again assuming that the set of books is not empty). In particular, it will be false if some book written by author x is not given by everyone to x. It appears that these interpretations parallel those of the relative clause sentences discussed in (33). (37) parallels the reading of one voucher per shopper; (38) parallels the reading of one voucher per gift. In other words, the reading associated with 'donkey'-sentences is the one normally associated with a universal quantifier embedded within the scope of another universal quantifier, rather than the one associated with an existential NP embedded within the scope of a universal NP. Moreover, (38) implies (37). The two readings are compatible; (38) is simply a stronger statement.

Consider (39):

(39)   Anyone who owns any donkey beats it

Since 'anyone' is interpretively a universal quantifier, the quantifier order is the same here as in (38), namely, universal-universal. If generics are likewise "universal" in interpretation,[8] and if the 'donkey'-phrase in a 'donkey'-sentence can be interpreted as generic, we should expect 'donkey'-sentences to parallel (39) in interpretation. This is in fact the case. (39), like 'donkey'-sentences, is true if and only if every owner-donkey pair is also a beater-donkey pair.

In sum, relative clauses whose quantifiers are in universal-existential order are ambiguous unless the "existential" phrase is quasi-generic (hence, quasi-universal, type I), as is the case with 'donkey'-sentences. The fact that the 'donkey'-phrase binds the pronoun indicates that it has an analysis as a generic; if it were not a generic, it could not coindex the pronoun, since it does not c-command it. As a generic, its interpretation should parallel that of (38) or (39) with two universal quantifiers. Since the interpretation of the relative clause in 'donkey'-sentences is like (38), and since (38) inplies (37), the interpretations of the LFs of such sentences are not incompatible; in fact, the two LFs "blend" into a single reading, the generic 'donkey'-phrase acting like a universal quantifier.

The fact that 'donkey'-sentences are interpreted in this way and not as we might expect universal-existential phrases to be interpreted ('Everyone owns a donkey and beats it') results from the dual quality

of the 'donkey'-phrase as both a type I and a type II QP. Having the
LF of a type II QP helps to explain why owner-donkey pairs are considered in the interpretation and in particular that more than one donkey
is being discussed. It also helps to explain why the 'donkey'-phrase is
not a pure generic but a quasi-generic. The generic LF (type I structure)
is necessary to explain why leftness violations and cross-sentential
coindexing can occur with 'donkey'-sentences. 'A man who owns every
donkey$_i$ beats it$_i$' is unacceptable because 'every donkey' is, crucially,
not ambiguous. The ambiguous nature of the quantifier in a 'donkey'-
sentence accounts for the nonambiguity of the sentence as a whole
(the fact that it does not have a reading parallel to (33b)): the interpretations of the two LFs blend to yield the reading on which every
owner-donkey pair is a beater-donkey pair.[9]

Englishmen and Their Mothers

As we have seen, 'donkey'-sentences are not the only apparent counterexamples to the analysis presented in earlier chapters. 'Englishman'-
sentences like (2) pose a second set of problems:

(2)   The woman that every Englishman$_i$ loves is his$_i$ mother

(2) appears to have an interpretation in which 'every Englishman' binds
the pronoun 'his'. However, this should not be possible. Given the
theory developed so far, the LF representation of (2) would be (40):

(40) $[_S[_{NP}$ the woman $[_S$ that who$_y$ $[_S$ every Englishman$_x$ $[_S$ x loves
       $y]]]]$ is $[_{NP}$ his mother$]]$

In (40), 'every Englishman' does not c-command the pronoun 'his';
consequently, coindexing should not be permitted and the above-noted
interpretation of (2) should not be available. Moreover, the kind of
solution advanced to handle the 'donkey'-sentences will not work here,
despite the initial similarity of the two cases. The account of 'donkey'-
sentences turns on distinguishing 'every' from 'a' by noting that the
latter, but not the former, is an ambiguous element. Whereas 'a' can
be either a type I or a type II quantifier depending on whether it receives
a generic or an existential interpretation, 'every' is unambiguous in this
way and is always a type II quantifier. This assumption is crucial in
explaining the unacceptability of sentences like (5). Consequently, we
cannot now insist that 'every' need not c-command the pronoun it
binds in order to coindex it. 'Every' is a type II quantifier and as such
it must c-command any pronoun that it binds.

How then are we to treat this case? In what follows I will propose
a solution in terms of a theory of Reconstruction. Intuitively, Recon-

struction is a process that interprets a phrase by first placing it in the position with which it is coindexed. In other words, a phrase may be interpreted as if it were situated in a grammatical position different from the one it actually occupies at S-structure. Part of a theory of Reconstruction is to specify from which positions a phrase can be interpreted. I will suggest that the pronoun binding in sentences like (2) can be explained in terms of a theory of Reconstruction, in conjunction with some standard assumptions of trace theory. I will further propose that Reconstruction is a ubiquitous grammatical process and that it is also involved in the interpretation of PRO. As such, it is a process with substantial independent motivation; it is not being invoked merely to explain the difficulties sentences such as (2) apparently create for the proposed analysis of quantifier types.

Reconstruction

Reconstruction is the grammatical process underlying the acceptability judgments in the following sentences:

(41) a. *Which picture of John$_i$ does he$_i$ like

    b. Which picture of himself$_i$ does John$_i$ like

    c. *Which picture of John's$_i$ mother does he$_i$ like

    d. Which picture of his$_i$ mother does everyone$_i$ like

(42) a. *A picture of John$_i$ is easy for him$_i$ to paint

    b. A picture of himself$_i$ is easy for John$_i$ to paint

Take (41a) for example. Why is it that 'John' cannot be coindexed with 'he'? Generally, coindexing between a namelike expression and a pronoun is permissible unless the pronoun c-commands the name.

(43) $[_S[_{COMP}$ which picture of John$]_i$ $[_S$ he like $t_i]]$

(43) is the LF representation of (41a). Here, 'he' does not c-command 'John'. 't_i' is the trace of the phrase 'which picture of John'. A trace is an element that a moved phrase leaves behind and coindexes; in this case, 'wh'-Movement applies and the complex noun phrase leaves 't_i' behind. In turn, (43) is derived from a structure like (44):

(44) $[_S[_S$ he likes $[_{NP}$ which picture of John$]]]$

In (44) 'he' does c-command 'John'. One way of thinking about Reconstruction is that it replaces the moved phrase in the position marked by 't_i'; it undoes the effects of movement. Coindexing between two elements is well formed just in case it is permitted in the reconstructed configuration. In this case, Reconstruction turns (43) back into (44).

Since 'he' and 'John' cannot be coindexed in (44), such coindexing is also prohibited in (43).[10] Another way of thinking of Reconstruction, which I find preferable, is as a well-formedness condition of coindexing in LF. NP elements are coindexed with traces as a result of various syntactic movement processes such as 'Wh'-Movement and free indexing of NPs at S-structure. On this view, Reconstruction is a principle that conditions the coindexing of two elements. In particular, it can be thought of as follows:

(45)   In a structure like

$$[[_{NP_i} \ldots X \ldots] \ldots Y \ldots t_i \ldots]$$

coindexing is permitted between X and Y just in case such coindexing is permitted with the phrase NP_i interpreted from the position marked by 't_i'.[11]

As this is not permissible in the case of (43), sentence (41a) is unacceptable.

Now consider (41b), in which 'himself' and 'John' are coindexed. Such coindexing is generally prohibited unless 'John' c-commands 'himself'. In the LF structure (46) that underlies (41b), this is not the case:

(46) $[_S[_{NP_i}$ which picture of himself$]_i$ $[_S$ John likes $t_i]]$

However, given (45), coindexing is permitted just in case it is well formed with NP_i interpreted from the position marked by 't_i'. In such a reconstructed configuration—(47)—'John' does c-command 'himself'; therefore, coindexing is permitted in (46).

(47) $[_S$ John $[_{VP}$ likes $[_{NP}$ which picture of himself$]]]$

Thus, thanks to Reconstruction, the interpretation indicated in (41b) is available.

Similar considerations hold for (41c) and (42d). In (41c) Reconstruction of the 'wh'-phrase 'which picture of John's mother' yields a structure in which 'John' and 'his' cannot be coindexed without violating the binding principles. (41d) parallels (41b). Reconstruction allows coindexing between 'his' and 'everyone', which would otherwise involve a leftness violation. In sum, Reconstruction is an important condition of interpretation in that it rules out sentences that would otherwise be acceptable and permits interpretations that would otherwise be impermissible.

Reconstruction also accounts for (42). Following Chomsky 1981, the subject of an 'easy-to-please'-construction is coindexed with a trace in the object position of the embedded verb—in this case, 'paint'. The relevant logical forms of these sentences are (48a,b):

(48) a. $[_S[_{NP_i}$ a picture of John] is easy $[_S$ for him to paint $t_i]]$

   b. $[_S[_{NP_i}$ a picture of himself] is easy $[_S$ for John to paint $t_i]]$

By the Reconstruction rule (45), coindexing between 'John' and 'him' is permitted in (48a) just in case it is permitted with the phrase 'a picture of John' interpreted from the position marked by 't_i', i.e., just in case (49) permits coindexing between 'John' and 'him'.

(49) $[_S$ (it) is easy $[_S$ for him to paint a picture of John]]

However, coindexing between 'him' and 'John' in (49) would violate principle (C) of the binding theory; therefore, by (45) it is not permitted in (48a) either. Hence the unacceptability of (42a) with the indicated interpretation.

Similar considerations hold for (48b). In this case, however, if NP_i is interpreted from the position marked by 't_i', then coindexing is permitted between 'himself' and 'John'. Consequently, by (45) it is also permitted in (48b), and therefore (42b) is acceptable with the indicated interpretation.

These examples illustrate how Reconstruction operates and what sort of data motivate it. Sentences such as (41) and (42) bear no close resemblance in structure to sentences like (2). However, I will suggest that the properties of these sentences can also be accounted for by assuming this independently motivated condition.

Consider the relevant sentence once again.

(2)   The woman that every Englishman$_i$ loves is his$_i$ mother

If (45) is involved in the interpretation of this sentence, then it must be the case that via Reconstruction 'every Englishman' c-commands 'his' in LF. Consider the LF form of (2):

(50) $[_{S_2} [_{NP_1}$ the woman $[_S$ that who$_i$ $[_{S_1}$ every Englishman$_x$ $[_S$ x loves $t_i]]]]$ is $[_{NP_2}$ his mother]]

Let us assume, uncontroversially I believe, that the head of a relative clause—in this case 'the woman'—is coindexed with the 'wh'-phrase involved in forming the relative clause. In other words, 'the woman' and 'who$_i$' are coindexed. Let us further assume, again uncontroversially, that the whole relative clause carries the index of its head. These two assumptions lead to the conclusion that NP_1 and 't_i' are coindexed, i.e., the structure underlying (2) is (51):

(51) $[_{S_2}[_{NP_i}$ the woman$_i$ $[_S$ that who$_i$ $[_{S_1}$ every Englishman$_x$ $[_{S_1}$ x loves $t_i]]]]$ is $[_{NP_2}$ his mother]]

If we make one more assumption, then Reconstruction (45) can come into play. Assume that the satellites of a copula ('is' in (51)) are coindexed. In (50), then, NP_1 is coindexed with NP_2:

(52) $[_{S_2}[_{NP_i}$ the woman$_i$ $[_S$ that who$_i$ $[_{S_1}$ every Englishman$_x$
$[_{S_1}$ x loves $t_i]]]]$ is $[_{NP_i}$ his mother]]

In a structure like (52) 'his mother' is coindexed with 't_i', so that (45) comes into play. Coindexing between 'every Englishman' and 'his' is permitted in (52) just in case it would be permitted with 'his mother' in the position marked by 't_i'. However, 'every Englishman' c-commands this position (i.e., 't_i') in LF. Consequently, coindexing is permitted in (52) and (2), with the indicated interpretation, is acceptable.

If the assumptions made above are tenable, we have a principled account for the acceptability of (2) based on the independently motivated principle (45). How reasonable, therefore, are these assumptions? As noted, there is nothing very daring in the first two. Coindexing the head of a relative clause with the 'wh'-phrase in complementizer position is simply a way of representing the information that the "head" of the relative is also acting as object of the verb in the embedded clause, i.e., that 'the woman' is object of 'loves' in S_1 (see Vergnaud 1974). It is also a standard view that the index of a major category percolates up from the head, i.e., that the whole relative clause carries the index of the head. Thus, the only new suggestion made in explaining the properties of (2) is that the elements that orbit a copula should be coindexed. In the paragraphs that follow, I will present four reasons for thinking that such coindexing indeed takes place.

Copular Coindexing

The first argument for copular coindexing is relatively weak. In chapter 4, it was assumed that agreement relations are signaled by coindexing between the elements that must agree. For example, it was crucially assumed that the subject of a tensed clause in English is coindexed with the AGR element. In copular constructions agreement takes place as well. This is especially evident in Romance languages, like French, where the subject of a copular phrase must agree in gender with a postcopular adjective:

(53) a.   La fille est belle

b.   *La fille est beau

If we assume that agreement phenomena are generally signaled by coindexing, then sentences like (53) show that coindexing takes place between elements that flank a copula. The simplest assumption is that this is true not only in French but in English as well, and not only for predicate adjectives but for all phrases. At any rate, assuming this best of all possible eventualities, we have a reason to believe that the NPs in a sentence like (2) are coindexed.

The second argument involves a well-formedness condition on indexing called the *i-within-i* (henceforth *i/i*) *Condition*.[12] This condition prohibits an element from bearing the same index as a phrase that contains it, as in (54a,b):

(54) a. *$[_{NP_i}$ the owner of his$_i$ boat]

b. *$[_{NP_i}$ a fan of his$_i$ team]

Now consider a sentence like (55):

(55) *John$_i$ is his$_i$ cook

In (55) the indicated interpretation is disallowed. On what grammatical grounds can it be ruled out? A straightforward account is available exploiting the *i/i* Condition, if we assume that the NPs around the copula are coindexed. On this assumption the structure underlying (55) is (56):

(56) $[_S[_{NP_i}$ John] is $[_{NP_i}$ his$_i$ cook]]

'John' is coindexed with both the whole phrase 'his cook' and the pronoun 'his' under the interpretation indicated in (56). If so, however, 'his' carries the same index as the whole noun phrase 'his cook'— exactly the configuration prohibited by the *i/i* Condition. Hence the unacceptability of (55).

Now consider sentences like (57) (first brought to my attention by Robert Fiengo):

(57) John's$_i$ father is his$_i$ cook

This sentence has the structure (58):

(58) $[_S[_{NP_i}$ John's$_j$ father] is $[_{NP_i}$ his$_j$ cook]]

This structure does not violate the *i/i* Condition, and (57) is therefore fully acceptable. There is a minimal difference between (55) and (57). The fact that the acceptability of one and the unacceptability of the other can be explained by assuming copular coindexing is rather subtle evidence in favor of this assumption.[13,14]

The third argument is based on sentences such as (59), from Chomsky 1981:41–42.

(59) a. John$_i$ believes that it is a picture of himself$_i$

b. The men$_i$ believe that it is a picture of each other$_i$

The structure underlying (59a) is (60):

(60) $[_{S_2}$ John$_i$ believes $[_{S_i}$ that $[_{S_1}$ it is $[_{NP_1}$ a picture of himself$_i]]]]$

In (60) 'John' is coindexed with the anaphoric expression 'himself'. Such structures are generally ill formed, since the anaphor 'himself' is free in its governing category, S_1. The sentence, however, is fully acceptable. The problem, then, is that 'himself' is governed in S_1 and if 'it' is an accessible subject, then 'himself' is X-free in S_1 and (60) should be ill formed. However, if we assume that copular coindexing obtains and that the i/i Condition holds as a well-formedness constraint, then 'it' cannot be an accessible subject for 'himself'. If 'it' is coindexed with 'a picture of himself' as a result of copular coindexing, then the structure underlying (59a) is (61):

(61) $[_{S_2}$ John$_i$ believes $[_{S_i}$ that $[_{S_1}$ it$_j$ is $[_{NP}$ a picture of himself]]]]$[15]

Recall that for 'it$_j$' to be an accessible subject for 'himself', it must be possible to coindex it with 'himself'. However, such coindexing would violate the i/i Condition; 'himself' would bear the index 'j' and, because of copular coindexing, 'a picture of himself' also carries the index 'j'. Therefore, 'it$_j$' is not an accessible subject for 'himself' and S_1 is not its governing category. The governing category is S_2 and 'John' is its accessible subject. As a result, there is no binding violation in (61). It is well formed and (59a) is acceptable.

A similar account holds for (59b). On the assumption that 'it' and 'a picture of each other' are coindexed, 'the men' is the accessible subject for 'each other' and the matrix clause is the governing category for 'each other'. In sum, given the assumption that the NPs around a copula are coindexed, we can account for the acceptability of the sentences in (59).

The fourth argument in favor of copular coindexing involves sentences such as (62):

(62) *This picture of John$_i$ is the present he$_i$ liked

The structure underlying (62) is (63) (see Chomsky 1981):

(63) $[_S[_{NP_i}$ this picture of John] is $[_{NP_i}$ the present$_i$ $[_S$ which$_i$ [he liked t$_i]]]]$

Since the two NPs around the copula are coindexed and the head of the relative ('the present') is coindexed with the trace 't$_i$', the phrase 'this picture of John' is coindexed with 't$_i$'. Thus, principle (45) becomes relevant. 'John' and 'he' can be coindexed only if coindexing is possible with 'this picture of John' interpreted from the position 't$_i$'. But under these conditions 'he' c-commands 'John' and coindexing is forbidden by principle (C) of the binding theory. Therefore, (62) is unacceptable. Similar considerations hold for a sentence like (64):

(64)   *It was the picture of John$_i$ that he$_i$ liked

Following a suggestion by Sportiche and Stowell, Chomsky 1981 argues that an extraposed clause is coindexed with the 'it' in subject position; in this case, that 'it' and 'that he liked' are coindexed. By copular coindexing, 'it' is coindexed with 'the picture of John'. It has also been proposed that COMP is head of $\bar{S}$ and that COMP is coindexed with 'that' under certain conditions. (On the latter claim, see Aoun, Hornstein, and Sportiche 1980.) The structure of (64) is (65):

(65) $[_{S_2}[_{S_1}$ it$_i$ was $[_{NP_i}$ the picture of John]] $[_{\bar{S}_i}[_{COMP_i}$ that] $[_S$ he liked t$_i$]]]

In short, 'the picture of John' is coindexed with 't$_i$', so that (45) comes into play. In particular, 'John' cannot be coindexed with 'he'.

These last two cases are particularly interesting for, although they are rather complex, all the assumptions except copular coindexing have been extensively motivated on independent grounds. By assuming this last principle, also motivated independently in the second and third arguments above, we can explain the judgments in (62) and (64) in a straightforward way.

Thus, the principle of copular coindexing, for which we have seen considerable independent evidence, readily explains the properties of 'Englishman'-sentences like (2). Moreover, it does so without requiring any changes whatsoever in the analysis of type II quantifiers. This in fact is quite fortunate.

(66)   *$[_{NP_1}$ the woman that every Englishman$_i$ likes t$_j$] kissed $[_{NP_2}$ his$_i$ mother]

(66) is clearly unacceptable. The only difference between (66) and (2) is that 'kissed' replaces 'is' in (66). Since coindexing is limited to satellites of the copula, 'kissed' does not induce coindexing of NP$_1$ and NP$_2$ in (66), and (45) does not apply. Consequently, 'every Englishman' never c-commands 'his' and the two cannot be coindexed. NP$_1$ is not coindexed with 't$_j$', and (45) again does not apply. By assuming copular coindexing, principle (45), and the analysis of quantifier types outlined in the chapters above, we can explain both the acceptability of the 'Englishman'-sentences and the unacceptability of (66).

Rather than raising problems for the proposed theory of quantifier types, sentences such as (2) and (66) provide interesting confirmation for it. The fact that the proposal fits in so easily with current grammatical assumptions is further confirmation. To explain the pronoun binding properties of sentences like (2), only one assumption was needed—namely, copular coindexing, which enjoys substantial independent motivation.

PRO Interpretation and Reconstruction

In the rest of this chapter I will consider Reconstruction in more detail, arguing that a principle of Reconstruction like (45) can illuminate PRO interpretation. In particular, (45) will allow us to analyze properties of PRO without invoking any semantic or quasi-semantic notions such as those suggested in Chomsky 1981 to account for problems that arise from treating antecedent-PRO relations as an instance of variable binding.

PRO is the null element found in the subject position of infinitival clauses:

(67) a. John persuaded Harry [$_s$ PRO to leave]
     b. John promised Harry [$_s$ PRO to leave]

In (67a) the understood subject of the embedded clause is 'Harry'; in (67b) it is 'John'. The relation of 'Harry' and 'John' to 'PRO' in such sentences has been conventionally analyzed as parallel to the relation between an antecedent and the pronoun it coindexes. Indeed, within current versions of the Government-Binding theory, PRO is analyzed as a pronominal anaphor, subject to both principles (A) and (B) of the binding theory. This assumption allows a principled derivation of the distribution of PRO. However, though I do not wish to challenge the claim that PRO is subject to both principles (A) and (B) of the binding theory, it is clear on the basis of well-known data that the relation between an antecedent and the PRO it is related to is quite unlike the relation between an antecedent and the pronoun it binds or between an antecedent and the anaphor it binds. Such analogies regarding antecedent-PRO relations do not really account for the permissible coindexing and interpretation phenomena. The facts are as follows:

First, we see from (68) that a type II quantifier can coindex a PRO to its left, even though leftward coindexing generally violates the Leftness Condition (as in the case of pronouns and anaphors). In fact, as (68c,d) indicate, sentences that would normally result in leftness violations are fully acceptable if there is a PRO acting as intermediary in the coindexing relation.

(68) a. [PRO$_i$ planning to leave] annoys everyone$_i$
     b. *[his$_i$ planning to leave] annoys everyone$_i$
     c. PRO$_i$ to clear his$_i$ friend of charges is important to everyone$_i$

    d. PRO_i to keep himself$_i$ clean is important to every Marine$_i$

    e. *For himself$_i$ to win would annoy John$_i$

    f. PRO_i to win would annoy John$_i$

    g. *For each other$_i$ to win would bother John and Harry$_i$

    h. PRO_i to win would bother [John and Harry]$_i$

Similar observations hold for the acceptability contrasts in the rest of (68).

    Second, an antecedent of a PRO need not c-command it to coindex it, though this is generally necessary in the case of pronoun binding and bound anaphora.

    (69) a. *A picture of the men$_i$ bothered each other$_i$

        b. *That he$_i$ clear himself$_i$ of charges is important to everyone$_i$

        c. PRO_i to clear himself$_i$ of charges is important to everyone$_i$

        d. *John gave a book to everyone$_i$ [for him$_i$ to read]

        e. John gave a book to everyone$_i$ [PRO_i to read]

Consider, for example, (69e). Here 'everyone' is the object of the preposition 'to' and does not c-command the subject of the embedded clause. (69e) with PRO is fully acceptable, but (69d) is not. (69a), like (68g), indicates that an anaphor must, in general, be c-commanded by its antecedent. In (69c) 'everyone' interacts with PRO despite both being to its right and not c-commanding it.

    Third, as Fodor 1975 has observed, antecedent-PRO relations are not interpreted in the same way as relations between antecedents and the pronouns they bind.

    (70) a. Only Churchill$_i$ remembers PRO_i giving the blood, sweat, and tears speech

        b. Only Churchill$_i$ remembers that he$_i$ gave the blood, sweat, and tears speech

(70a) might well be true even if (70b) is false. This is a problem for any theory that views PRO as merely a pronoun without phonetic features.

    Fourth, PRO can be controlled by pleonastic elements that have no θ-role.

    (71)   It$_i$ rains after PRO_i snowing

In general, a variable, such as 'PRO_i' in (71) or a null element left by 'Wh'-Movement, must have a θ-role:

    (72)   *[what$_i$ [t$_i$ rains]]

If coindexed PRO is treated like a variabilized pronoun, the difference in acceptability between (71) and (72) must be explained. The 'PRO' in (71) functions like the weather-'it' of 'it rains', 'it snows'. (72) indicates that such elements have no θ-roles. Why then is (71) acceptable?

Fifth, consider the interpretation of the following sentences:

(73) a. Someone married everyone
   b. Someone wants to PRO marry everyone
   c. Someone tried PRO to take every course
   d. Someone expects that he will take every course
   e. Someone wants himself to marry everyone
   f. Someone wants Harry to take every course
   g. Someone expects John to win every prize

(73a) is ambiguous with either the existential or the universal QP enjoying wide scope. Oddly enough, (73b) and (73c) are also ambiguous. This is odd, because normally the embedded quantifier cannot have scope outside the minimal sentence containing it, as is the case with (73d–g), which are unambiguous. In all four, 'someone' is interpreted as having scope over the 'every'-phrase. What the data in (73) seem to indicate is that an embedded quantifier (e.g., 'everyone') can be interpreted as taking scope over a matrix quantifier (e.g., 'someone'), just in case the matrix quantifier controls a PRO in the embedded clause. That is, usually scope interaction is permitted between type II quantifiers only if they are in the same clause; but apparently it is also permitted if they are in different clauses but one controls a PRO in the same clause as the other.

In sum, the data indicate that the coindexing relations between an antecedent and a PRO are quite different from those between antecedents and pronouns or antecedents and variables. The antecedent-PRO relation is insensitive to quite general leftness conditions, c-command requirements, θ-Criterion restrictions, and scope limitations. The facts suggest that PRO should not be construed as a pronoun with null phonetic features, at least for many interpretive procedures.

In what follows, I will suggest that these phenomena can be explained if PRO interpretation is seen as an instance of Reconstruction.

Reconstructing PRO

Reconstruction (45) has some very nice properties in relation to the facts of the previous section. First, it is insensitive to left-right asymmetries. So, for example, it explains the acceptability of both (74a) and (74b):

(74) a. The woman that every Englishman$_i$ admires is his$_i$ mother

   b. His$_i$ mother is the woman that every Englishman$_i$ admires

As (74) further indicates, Reconstruction can take place even if the element that is reconstructed does not c-command the trace position in which it is reconstructed. Nor, for that matter, need the trace position c-command the reconstructed element. In short, (45) applies regardless of the c-command relations between the reconstructed element and the position in which it is reconstructed.

Given these facts about Reconstruction, if we assume that PRO interpretation is an instance of Reconstruction, we can explain why antecedent-PRO relations are free of any special c-command or leftness restrictions, as the examples in (68) and (69) seem to indicate. If the antecedent-PRO relation is really an instance of Reconstruction, then it is not surprising that it does not act in a manner parallel to antecedent-pronoun or antecedent-anaphor relations.

Consider again Fodor's examples (70a,b), repeated here. If we construe PRO interpretation as an instance of Reconstruction, then these sentences have different structures:

(70) a. Only Churchill$_i$ remembers [PRO$_i$ giving the blood, sweat, and tears speech]

   b. Only Churchill$_i$ remembers [that he$_i$ gave the blood, sweat, and tears speech][16]

Only in (70b) does the subject of the embedded clause contain a variable. In short, this analysis results in a structural difference on which we can hang the interpretive differences observed by Fodor. On the other hand, by treating PRO interpretation as an instance of pronoun binding,[17] the analysis of Chomsky 1981 cannot account for this interpretive difference between the two sentences.

As we noted previously, it seems that certain quantifier-quantifier interactions obtain in the case of PRO sentences that are normally prohibited.

(75) a. Someone wants PRO to marry everyone

   b. Someone wants Harry to marry everyone

   c. Someone tried PRO to register for every course

   d. Someone expected Harry to register for every course

   e. Someone expects himself to win every prize

In (75a,c) it is possible to interpret the existential quantifier 'someone' as within the scope of the universally quantified 'every'-phrase. This interpretation does not appear to be available in (75b,d,e), where, because of the limited scope domains of 'everyone', the only possible interpretation gives 'someone' wide scope. However, the ambiguities in (75a,c) can be explained if PRO interpretation is viewed as an instance of Reconstruction.

The structures of (75a,c) would be (76a,b):

(76) a. [$_S$ someone$_i$ wants [$_S$ PRO$_i$ to marry everyone]]

b. [$_S$ someone$_i$ tried [$_S$ PRO$_i$ to register for every course]]

If Reconstruction applies between 'someone' and the position marked by PRO, it should be the case that 'someone' can be interpreted as within the scope of the 'every'-phrase just in case it could be so interpreted if it were in the position marked by 'PRO$_i$'. If it were in this position, however, 'someone' and the 'every'-phrase would be clausemates, and their possible scope dependencies should be exactly like those of the quantifiers in (77):

(77) a. Someone married everyone

b. Someone registered for every course

(77a,b) are ambiguous, with either the existential or the universal quantifier enjoying wider scope. Therefore, if PRO interpretation is an instance of Reconstruction, the possible scope interactions between the quantifiers in (76) are predicted.[18] Note, incidentally, that such quantifier scope ambiguities arise in regular Reconstruction cases as well.

(78) a. John brought a book for everyone to read

b. John bought a sandwich for everyone to eat

c. *John made a film about everyone$_i$ for him$_i$ to see

d. *John brought Bill$_i$ for him$_i$ to see

The proposed Reconstruction account explains the unacceptability of (78c,d). The structure of (78d) is (79) (see Chomsky 1981 for relevant discussion):

(79) [$_S$ John [$_{VP}$ brought Bill$_i$] [$_{\bar{S}}$ for wh$_i$ [$_S$ him$_i$ to see t$_i$]]]

In (79) 'Bill$_i$' and 't$_i$' are coindexed. Consequently, (45) comes into effect: the indicated coindexing is permissible just in case it would be allowed with 'Bill' interpreted in the position marked by 't$_i$'. This, however, is impossible, since 'him$_i$' would then bind 'Bill$_i$', which is forbidden by principle (C) of the binding theory. A similar account will explain the unacceptability of (78c).

What is particularly interesting for present purposes is that sentences (78a,b), parallel to (78c,d) exhibit the same scope ambiguities as (75a,c). As (78c,d) indicate, Reconstruction applies in these cases. Thus, for example, the structure of (78a) is (80):

(80) [$_S$ John [$_{VP}$ brought a book$_i$] [$_S$ for wh$_i$ [$_S$ everyone to read t$_i$]]]

'A book$_i$' is coindexed with 't$_i$'. Therefore, it should be possible to construe 'a book$_i$' as within the scope of 'everyone' just in case it can be so construed in position 't$_i$'; and in fact it can be. The interpretation in which John brought many books (i.e., one for each person) is therefore available. Similar considerations hold for (78b). In short, Reconstruction cases exhibit virtually the same ambiguities as PRO interpretation cases, which is just what we would expect if they were really instances of the same phenomenon.

To bring these quantifier cases within the scope of principle (45), the definition of Reconstruction presented there must be generalized to accommodate them. The principle in (45) is stated in terms of "coindexing." However, although it is possible to represent quantifier-quantifier interactions, in terms of coindexing, it is not necessary to do so. The generalized Reconstruction principle is (81):

(81) *Reconstruction Principle*

In a structure like

[... [$_{\alpha_i}$ ... X ...] ... Y ... t$_i$ ...]^{19}

X and Y can be related just in case such a relation is permitted with the phrase α_i interpreted from the position marked by 't$_i$'.

In (81) we need not specify that the relation is an *interpretive* relation, because this follows from the fact that Reconstruction is a condition on LF operations. The only difference between (45) and (81) is that the former is stated in terms of coindexing, whereas (81) includes other interpretive phenomena as well. In effect, (81) is simply a more general version of (45).

In sum, if a principle such as (81) is assumed to apply in the case of PRO interpretation, then the ambiguities observed in sentences (75a,c) can be explained. The lack of ambiguity of the other sentences follows in a principled manner from the theory of scope for type II quantifiers elaborated in chapter 4.

Finally, let us reconsider the problems raised in (71) and (72). Chomsky 1981 observes that PRO can be controlled by a pleonastic non-theoretical element like weather-'it', but 'Wh'-Movement is impossible from these positions. To explain this, Chomsky distinguishes between entities and pseudoentities. Weather-'it' denotes a pseudoentity that allows control of PRO but is not sufficient for 'Wh'-Movement. 'Wh'-Movement can only apply to an element that refers to a real entity. Given the above discussion, we need not invoke these sorts of distinctions. If we view PRO interpretation as Reconstruction rather than variable binding, the 'wh' case and the PRO case separate neatly. An operator can only bind an element that has a θ-role. However, PRO is not a variable on the account presented here. In particular, the 'it'-PRO relation in a sentence such as (71) is not a case of variable binding, and the relation indicated there is therefore not suspect.

The distinction between entities and pseudoentities is a murky one, designed to do limited work. Since the basis of the distinction did not extend much beyond the data it was meant to explain, namely, the difference between (71) and (72), its explanatory power was negligible. Fortunately, however, the analysis of PRO interpretation as an instance of Reconstruction allows us to dispense with this quasi-semantical apparatus.

Conclusion

I have considered some apparent problems for any theory that tries to limit the scope of type II quantifiers in the way suggested in chapter 4, arguing that in the case of 'donkey'-sentences there is a well-motivated analysis that confirms the theory of quantifier types I have proposed. That is, if we assume that the phrase 'a donkey' is ambiguous, being glossed in the relevant contexts as either a type I or a type II QP, the full range of properties of such sentences follows. No new assumptions are needed beyond this one, which has considerable independent support. On this analysis, then, 'donkey'-sentences are not anomalous, and their properties are not unexpected.

As for the 'Englishman'-sentences, I have suggested that, correctly analyzed, they too are compatible with the earlier analysis. By assuming a Reconstruction principle like (45) or (81), we can fully account for the properties of such sentences. Moreover, a Reconstruction principle has considerable independent support and can even illuminate the process of PRO interpretation.

This chapter ends the technical elaboration of the theory of quantifier-quantifier and quantifier-pronoun interactions. In following chapters I will discuss the properties of this theory of interpretation more broadly, highlighting its strongly syntactic nature. By *strongly syntactic*, I mean not only that the theory is developed using syntactic notions but also that the principles invoked and the distinctions advocated have no natural semantic analogues. If the above analysis is compelling, then at least for this class of interpretive phenomena a semantical perspective would lead us to expect entirely different groupings of data. I will concentrate on making this point clear in the next chapter.

Chapter 6

Is Interpretation Theory a Semantic Theory?

In the preceding chapters I have argued that a theory of quantifier-quantifier and quantifier-pronoun interactions can be developed that preserves and articulates the central generative claim concerning natural language—the logical problem of language acquisition. A three-way distinction in quantifier types, a generalized version of the binding theory, and some independently motivated extensions and refinements of processes such as Reconstruction and indexing together define a theory from which the salient interpretive features of quantifiers and pronouns can be derived. In this chapter I will examine the nature of this theoretical apparatus. I will assume that I have in general correctly described the operations of the language faculty in the domain of quantifier-quantifier and quantifier-pronoun interactions, and on this basis I will discuss the general properties of the principles and distinctions invoked. In particular, I will argue that the technical machinery necessary to explain the phenomena is syntactic *in a strong sense*. In chapter 7 I will suggest that this is a very desirable property for a theory to have, at least if it wishes to address certain fundamental issues in the theory of meaning.

To say that a theory is "syntactic in the strong sense" means that the theoretical apparatus—the rules, distinctions, and generalizations that constitute the theory—*is* and *must be* framed in terms of a syntactic vocabulary. To see this more clearly, consider for a moment the properties of a logically perfect language, that is, one where syntactic distinctions perfectly mirror semantic ones. A theory of the properties of such a language can be cast in either syntactic or semantic terms. For every semantic distinction there is an analogous syntactic one, and vice versa. For every syntactic generalization concerning the well-formed strings and phrases of the language and their relations to one another there is a trivial semantic analogue invoking notions like "object," "truth," "reference," and "proposition." In typical examples of such languages (e.g., standard versions of the propositional calculus), one proves that syntactic properties of sentences such as derivability are mirrored by semantic properties such as validity. Thus, beginning students of logic typically prove that in standard versions of the propositional calculus the sentence "A" is derivable from the sentence "B" if and only if the proposition expressed by "A" is validly inferred from "B." In short, in such logically perfect languages, it really does not matter whether one approaches its properties from a syntactic vantage point or a semantic one. Whatever distinctions and generalizations can be devised using one vocabulary can be mimicked or duplicated without loss of elegance or explanatory power in the other. For such a language one *can* develop a syntactic theory but one *need* not. In fact, it is natural to consider that the syntactic theory is derivative, simply mimicking the "real" semantic structure.

By claiming that the theory sketched in chapters 2–5 is syntactic, I mean that it has no natural semantic analogue. The distinctions and generalizations that do the explanatory work *must* be cast in a syntactic vocabulary and exploit syntactic notions; moreover, adopting the semantic point of view will be very costly if the goal is a systematic explanation of the discussed phenomena. Natural languages are *not* logically perfect or very nearly logically perfect. Much of what we would pretheoretically call "meaning phenomena" can only be accounted for in terms of a syntactic theory, where laws exploit the grammatical distinctions of language that are arbitrary from any natural semantic point of view.

In the rest of this chapter I will try to substantiate this claim. I will discuss the distinction of quantifier types, the i/i Condition, the θ-Criterion, Reconstruction, indexing, and the binding theory. I will claim that if the proposed theory works as I have indicated, these distinctions and principles have no semantic or interpretive analogues. In fact, for many of the cases a stronger point can be made: the natural distinctions and generalizations that a natural semantic theory of interpretation would make available lead us to expect configurations of data that are simply not attested. In short, such a semantical theory will in many instances lead in the wrong direction. The assumption that a theory of meaning must (or at least can) exploit semantic notions must be dropped as a regulative principle in the study of natural language.[1]

The Quantifier Types

I have argued that there are three types of quantifier expressions. Type I QPs are characterized by their namelike properties; they are not moved by some instance of Move-α in LF to form operator-variable structures. Type II QPs are moved by QR, do not form operator-variable structures in LF, and have the logical syntax of the traditional logical quantifiers.

When QR moves a type II QP, the variables (i.e., null elements) left behind are subject to principle (A) of the extended binding theory. Type III quantifiers are the same as type II, except that in their case, variables left behind by QR are subject to both principle (A) and principle (C). Many facts relating to pronoun binding, quantifier scope, ECP effects, etc., can be explained if this trichotomy is assumed. The question now is, On what specific notions does this trichotomy depend?

The class of type I QPs in English is large and interpretively diverse. 'Any' and 'a certain' fall into this class, as do definite descriptions and generic phrases. Moreover, as far as the proposed theory of quantifiers is concerned, all these expressions form a *natural class* with ordinary names like 'Derek Whittenburg', 'Sidney Lowe', 'Thurl Bailey', and 'Jim Valvano'. It is this last feature of the analysis in particular that should strike a traditional semantical theorist as odd.

Traditional semantical theories make an important interpretive distinction between names and general expressions like quantifiers. At times the line is fuzzy, and some expressions (definite descriptions, for example) have fallen sometimes on one side, sometimes on the other (see chapter 3 and Kaplan 1970 for discussion). However, virtually every theory has recognized that elements like 'every' and 'any' function in ways quite different from ordinary names. Although it is obvious that names denote the individuals that they name (e.g., 'John Wayne' denotes the individual John Wayne), general expressions such as 'everyone' or 'anyone' do not denote something we might call a general object, an Anyone or an Everyone. By traditional interpretive lights, 'anyone' is much more similar in its semantical, and hence interpretive, properties to a general quantified NP like 'everyone' than either is to a name. For this reason, the grouping of NP elements like 'anyone' together with common names is quite unnatural from a standard semantic point of view.[2]

Let me be slightly more precise. A theory of interpretation based squarely on semantical notions leads to certain natural groupings of classes of expressions.[3] On this point of view, expressions form natural classes by having denotational or referential features in common. Names form a semantically coherent interpretive class because all names denote or refer to specific individuals. General expressions (in particular, quantifiers) also form a natural interpretive class, because they do not denote or refer to specific individuals at all. Rather, they are second-order functions that range over sets of individuals but do not specifically denote or refer to any. A semantical theory will therefore naturally classify expressions like 'any' and 'every' together and treat them as interpretively distinct from expressions like 'Dean Smith' and 'James Worthy'. What such a semantical theory cannot do, at least not in a way that exploits the natural semantical distinctions underlying its interpretive theory, is to treat as a natural interpretive class elements as semantically diverse as 'anyone' and 'Bobby Knight'. But according to the theory I have proposed, this is precisely what must be done if the data are to be explained in a non–ad hoc manner, given the logical problem of language acquisition. Whereas this type of syntactic theory of interpretation easily suggests natural interpretive classes that group elements as semantically diverse as 'anyone' and 'Baskerville Holmes', a semantical theory of interpretation does not. At the very least, the distinctions forming the basis of the class of type I QPs invoke notions that cut against the natural interpretive grain of semantical theories. Of course, this does not mean that a similar classification of quantified NPs and names could not be tacked onto a semantical theory of interpretation. But I believe that such a move would ignore, rather than endorse, the natural interpretive categories that a semantical theory suggests.

The degree of artificiality such an addition would induce in a semantical theory of interpretation is further highlighted by considering the contrast between 'personne' and 'anyone' discussed in chapter 2. As noted there, the French 'ne . . . personne' construction is interpretively very close to 'not . . . anyone' constructions in English; in fact, these phrases standardly translate each other. Nonetheless, the two behave quite differently in their respective languages. 'Personne' is a type III QP; 'anyone' is a type I QP. A syntactically based theory can explain this difference in behavior quite naturally by noting that 'personne' belongs to a different LF category (syntactically defined) from 'anyone'. How would a semantical theory describe the same difference? I believe that in fact there is no natural account if one's interpretive theory exploits only semantical resources. The natural distinctions made available by such a theory are just too blunt to accommodate the required treatment.

The proposed interpretive theory of quantifiers provides a vocabulary in which certain classifications of expressions can be naturally stated. In particular, it naturally allows us to view 'anyone' as closely related to 'John' and as quite distinct from 'everyone'. Moreover, it is capable of treating near paraphrases like 'personne' and 'anyone' as structurally quite distinct. A *semantical* theory, on the other hand, is both too weak and too strong. It does not naturally accommodate the interpretive similarities of names with 'anyone' and is too blunt to explain the differences between 'personne' and 'anyone'. This does not mean the requisite distinctions and resulting classifications could not be added to the ones a semantical theory offers; but this could only be done by ignoring the natural interpretive cleavages a semantical theory highlights. If one is prepared to do this, none of the above considerations undermine a semantical approach to the interpretive issues at hand. However, if one is prepared to do this, it is very unclear in what sense the resulting interpretive theory remains semantical.

The Extended Binding Theory

Analogous observations pertain to the version of the binding theory outlined in chapter 4. It is traditional to construe principle (A) of the binding theory as a condition on the indexing of bound anaphors (e.g., 'each other', 'himself'), principle (B) as a condition on the indexing of pronouns, and principle (C) as a condition on the indexing of R-expressions (e.g., names). This can arouse the suspicion that the binding theory is somehow semantically motivated—that is, that the principles apply to interpretive classes clearly demarcated on the basis of semantical considerations. I believe that this is simply incorrect.

Consider first standard versions of the binding theory. In such theories principle (A) applies to bound anaphors such as 'each other' and 'his' in sentences such as 'John lost his way'. It also governs the distribution of reflexives such as 'himself'. Moreover, as has been pointed out since the earliest discussions of such issues, an expression's status vis à vis the binding theory cannot be deduced from a consideration of its interpretive properties. For example, it is well known that although 'each other' is subject to principle (A), constructions involving 'each . . . the others' are not:

(1) a. *The men$_i$ told Harry to kick each other

     b. Each of the men told Harry to kick the others

This would not be a problem were it not for the fact that these phrases are (very often) virtual paraphrases of one another, a fact that motivated earlier transformational treatments to invoke an 'each' movement transformation, illustrated in (2) (Dougherty 1970):

(2) a. The men kissed each other

     b. Each of the men kissed the other(s)

These observations strongly suggest that the categories of the binding theory are not simply determined by, or mere reflections of, interpretive considerations that a semantical stance would simply and naturally suggest.

Similar considerations obtain for reflexives. Many languages have elements that appear to carry reflexive interpretations but do not behave like English reflexives in other respects. Indeed, in English, although phrases such as 'his own' have interpretations very closely related to those of other bound anaphors, they are not subject to the binding theory.

(3) a. *John$_i$ believes that himself$_i$ is handsome

   b. John$_i$ believes himself$_i$ to be handsome

   c. John$_i$ believes that his own$_i$ face is handsome

   d. John$_i$ told Mary to ignore his own$_i$ views

   e. *John$_i$ told Mary to ignore himself$_i$

At the very least, such facts indicate that semantical considerations do not suffice to account for the features of the binding theory (even standard versions; see below). The fact that some expression is an "anaphor" in the sense of having the interpretive properties typically displayed by anaphors (being dependent for its local interpretation on another element, not denoting anything on its own, etc.) does not imply that this expression will fall under the purview of the binding theory. Being an anaphor interpretively does not mean that an element will be an anaphor grammatically. At the very least, an element's semantic anaphoricity does not suffice for considering it as falling under principle (A) of any version of the binding theory.

Is the converse true as well? If an element falls under principle (A), must it be an anaphor? This weaker position might be defensible for standard versions of the binding theory, but it is clearly false for the version adopted in chapter 4. As we saw there, to account for the scope properties of type II QPs, which pattern rather closely with the distribution of standard anaphors, we had to extend the binding theory by introducing the notion "X-binding" into the statement of principle (A) (see Aoun 1981 and chapter 4). This notion enabled us to treat variables left by type II QPs moved by QR as "anaphors" in the sense of falling under principle (A). However, from a purely interpretive point of view, there is no great semantic similarity between the operator-variable relation and the antecedent-anaphor relation. In strictly semantic terms, the first is a case of variable binding, the second a case of anaphorization. A reflexive "picks up" the reference of an element that is independently denotational or referential, i.e., that independently "picks out" an individual. A variable does not do the same thing, because the operator that binds it has no independent reference or denotation. In short, the collapsing of these two semantically distinct cases into the single principle (A) of the extended binding theory is completely unmotivated from a purely semantical point of view. Moreover, the extended version of principle (A) does not support even the weakened conclusion noted above. An element falling under principle (A) need not be an anaphor in the *semantic sense*. In particular, type

II variables are not anaphors in any except a purely *formal* sense, i.e., falling under principle (A). In the extended binding theory, the notion "anaphor" is relieved of any natural semantic import.

Consideration of the rest of the extended binding theory leads to very much the same conclusions. The grouping of both names and type I QPs under principle (C) has no plausible semantic motivation, nor does the bifurcation of variables between those subject only to principle (A) and those subject to both principles (A) and (C). Semantically speaking, the variables behave exactly alike. Consequently, a semantical theory of interpretation leaves their behavioral differences unmotivated and unexplained.

Thus, we see that the principles required (and made available by the extended binding theory) simply ignore the distinctions made available by a semantical theory of interpretation. Indeed, the necessary principles actually run counter to those distinctions. In short, the resources of the extended binding theory are at best completely unanticipated by standard semantical theories, which are inadequate to explain many of the facts currently considered to be the proper subject of a theory of interpretation. At worst, a semantical perspective on interpretation theory leads away from the distinctions and principles that appear to be empirically necessary. At least with regard to the binding theory, the syntactic account presented here has no natural semantic analogue; for this domain of data the correct theory of natural language interpretation appears to be strongly syntactic.

An important theoretical point is involved here. The degeneracy and deficiency of the primary linguistic data are overcome by invoking general innate principles or laws that constrain the options available to the language learner. Consequently, if, as I have argued to be the case, the generalizations and principles needed to solve the acquisition problem are strongly syntactic, then in a very important sense syntactic notions rather than semantic ones are at the heart of an adequate theory of language and of natural language interpretation. As in any theoretical enterprise, the crucial issue is in what terms the laws and principles of the theory should be stated. If my argument is correct, the central laws of linguistics must be seen as applying to syntactic items rather than to the semantic values of such syntactic items. In short, the relevant explanatory level of generalization is syntactic, not semantic. In this strong sense, therefore, syntactic actions and principles have primacy over semantic ones. Language may be used to talk about the world, among other activities, but the *structure* of language should not be seen as a mere reflection of this feature of its use. Nor, for that matter, should logical syntax be seen as the mere reflection of the salient features of any other kinds of uses. If linguistic structures were primarily used for the conveying of semantic information, we would expect the principles of language to be defined over semantic values. They are not. And because of this, the vision of language as *primarily* an instrument of communication or essentially a semantic mechanism should be set aside.

The Other Conditions

In this section, I will argue that the i/i condition and Reconstruction are also strongly syntactic; that is, they are properly seen as defined over syntactic objects and not the semantic values of such objects.

As we have seen, Reconstruction is a principle limiting the interaction of linguistic elements. In particular, it states that two linguistic items X, Y can interact just in case they can do so with X interpreted from any A-position with which it is coindexed. The sentence we have used to illustrate this is (4):

(4)   The woman that every Englishman loves is his mother

In (4) 'his' can be coindexed with 'every Englishman' even though ·it is not c-commanded by it in logical form:

(5)   [the woman$_i$ [that who$_i$ [every Englishman$_j$ [x_j loves t$_i$]]]] is [$_{NP_i}$ his$_i$ mother]

In (5) 'his mother' is coindexed with 't$_i$'. If 'his mother' were interpreted from the position 't$_i$', then 'every Englishman' could legitimately bind it. Reconstruction is the principle that makes this interpretive option available.

Reconstruction states that an NP must be interpreted from a trace position with which it is *coindexed*. It is a principle defined over indices; it invokes indices as explanatorily crucial elements. To understand the nature of Reconstruction, therefore, we must understand how an index is to be construed. In particular, we must consider whether the notion of an index exploited here is primarily syntactic or semantic. As the following discussion will show, the answer seems to be that indices *must* be construed syntactically.

In the theory of grammar, indexing serves several functions. For example, in (5) indexing marks (a) that the head of the relative clause 'the woman' is also the object of the verb 'loves', (b) that 'the woman' is the head of the relative clause NP$_i$, (c) that 't$_i$' is a variable bound by the operator 'who$_i$', (d) that 'the woman that every Englishman loves' and 'his mother' are both satellites of the copula 'is', and (e) that 'his' is bound by the quantified phrase 'every Englishman'. Note that these five functions do not form a natural semantic class in any sense. One might claim that the relation of 'who$_i$' to 't$_i$' is semantically similar to the relation between 'every Englishman$_i$' and 'his$_i$', both being instances of variable binding. However, even here there is really no semantic parallel. 'Who$_i$' is not so much a quantifier semantically as an abstraction operator like λ. Thus, for example, when 'who' acts like a quasi-quantifier, as in questions, it cannot be deleted as it can be in (5), to yield (6a) (see Chomsky 1981).

(6) a. *John wonders John ate

b. John wonders what John ate

However, even if we were to construe these two instances of indexing as marking a semantically similar function, we could not view the other indices in a similar light. There is nothing *semantically* similar between binding a pronoun and being the head of a phrase or being a bound pronoun and being the satellite of a copula. From a purely semantic perspective these functions of indexing do not form a natural class. A purely semantic theory of interpretation would therefore not predict that such an odd array of indexes would form a natural domain for interpretive processes, nor that conditions on possible interpretations should crucially invoke the notion of index as such.

Let us approach this point in another way. Coindexing marks a myriad of relations, some of which can be construed as being semantically natural and as forming semantically natural subclasses. For example, pronoun binding and types of operator binding such as the 'Wh'-Movement in question formation form a semantically natural interpretive class. Other relations marked by coindexing (the relation of a head to its projection or a copula to its satellites, for example) do not form a natural semantical class of relations with each other or with pronoun and variable binding. Consider now a condition on interpretation such as Reconstruction, which is defined over indices. Two cases are logically possible. Case one defines the condition only over indices that form a natural semantical class. Case two defines the condition over indices in general regardless of the grammatical, functional, or semantic roles that the indexed elements may play. Case one is what we should expect if the theory of natural language interpretation is semantical, i.e., cast in terms of and exploiting the natural distinctions made available by a semantic theory. Case two is what we should expect from a strongly syntactic theory of interpretation that simply ignores natural semantical distinctions. In fact, case two should be virtually incoherent from a semantical perspective. From such a point of view indices are not "real." They are at best convenient notations for the marking of real semantical roles.[4] From a syntactic viewpoint, indices are real elements over which laws can be defined. What makes various and sundry functional, semantical, and grammatical roles similar is simply the fact that they involve coindexing. There is, in short, a syntactic level of representation at which these otherwise different relations look alike.

Clearly, then, Reconstruction is a perfect instance of case two. It crucially treats all indices on a par in order to establish the relevant relation between the reconstructed phrase ('his mother' in (5)) and the position from which it is interpreted ('t,' in (5)). For the purposes of this LF principle, it does not matter what roles indices mark; it matters only that they are there in LF. Reconstruction thus demands a strong syntactic interpretation of indices—an interpretation that ignores the distinctions that would be naturally highlighted by a semantical theory of interpretation. In short, just like the extended binding theory, Reconstruction supports a strongly syntactic view of interpretation theory.

The i/i Condition supports this conclusion even more strongly. The i/i Condition rules out structures in which an NP is coindexed with the phrase containing it, such as (7) and (8):

(7)   *[the owner of his$_i$ boat]$_i$

(8)   *John$_i$ is his$_i$ cook

The i/i prohibition has often been viewed in semantical terms. Thus, phrases like (7) are often treated as anomalous because of some sort of referential circularity. The reference of the whole NP seems to depend on the reference of a subpart of the NP, which is in turn dependent on the reference of the whole NP. Seen thus, the unacceptability of phrases like (7) rests on a semantical fact about the interpretation of the indices. The indices are taken to indicate interpretive dependencies that cannot be realized in such cases because of the circularity of the referential dependencies.[5]

The problem with such a view of the i/i Condition is that it rules out using the condition to account for the unacceptability of (8). In (8) there is no referential circularity; the phrase 'his cook' carries the index i, but only because of the process of copular coindexing: 'John$_i$ is [his$_i$ cook]'.

The i/i Condition is best interpreted in formal syntactic terms if it is seen as responsible for the unacceptability of (8). The reason for this is straightforward: the i on NP$_i$ in (9) is not an index marking referentiality—or at least it is not obviously such a marker.

(9)   [John]$_i$ is [$_{NP_i}$ his$_i$ cook]

Seen syntactically, (7) is not ruled unacceptable because of referential circularity but simply because it is an instance of i-within-i coindexing. That the indices mark reference relations is irrelevant for the applicability of the condition; it is the indexing itself that counts, not the coreference.

This syntactic interpretation of the i/i Condition is supported by many other sorts of examples in the literature.[6] Additional evidence is provided by (10):

(10)   [the owner of his$_i$ father's boat]$_i$

(10) is considerably more acceptable than (7). However, this judgment is incomprehensible if the source of the trouble in (7) is some sort of referential circularity.[7] In (10), no less than in (7), "his" is contained within the noun phrase to which it refers. (11) is also acceptable:

(11)   John$_i$ is his$_i$ father's cook

Why should (7) be unacceptable, if (10) and (11) are all right? It seems that the i/i Condition is sensitive to the syntactic depth of the embedded coindexed element. In other words, roughly speaking, it applies only to a phrase that is both coindexed with a containing phrase and of relatively low embedding in that phrase.[8]

Two points are worth making regarding these observations. Although (10) involves as much referential circularity as (7), (10) seems better than (7). That a syntactic condition like depth of embedding should affect *referential* circularity is quite mysterious; that it should restrict a *syntactic* well-formedness condition is not.

Second, it is curious that cases like (11), where referential circularity seems besides the point, are nonetheless acceptable, whereas (7) is not. In short, why do the acceptability judgments on (10) and (11) co-vary in relation to (7) and (8) if the i/i Condition is the principle involved *and* if it is a semantical condition on referential circularity? The answer is clear. The i/i Condition is defined on indices, syntactically construed; and (7) and (8) are structurally parallel, as are (10) and (11). This clearly accounts for the facts.

Thus, the facts surrounding the i/i Condition lead to a familiar conclusion. The conditions and distinctions exploited in chapters 2–5 are strongly syntactic; semantical versions of them simply yield the wrong results. The relevant generalizations needed to account for the data cannot be stated in any natural semantic terms. The theoretical structures and concepts necessary to an empirically adequate theory of linguistic interpretation are strongly syntactic. If the goal is to discover the nature of the linguistic laws that make it possible to solve the logical problem of language acquisition, semantical interpretations seem to lead in the wrong direction, at least in this range of cases.

It is important to see that this is an *empirical* claim. We could imagine theories that exploited the natural distinctions made available by a semantical theory. As we have seen, it would be possible to construct a version of Reconstruction of the i/i Condition that was only well defined over indices that marked out semantically natural relations and distinctions. The fact that these possible semantical theories of interpretation are empirically inadequate indicates that such theories are simply the wrong kinds of theories.

It is also important to note that the syntactical twist to issues in the theory of meaning is not all that novel. In fact, this understanding about theories of interpretation for natural language has been implicit in most work on LF and "semantics" since the earliest papers on these topics within generative grammar. The extent to which issues of structural meaning have been syntactically approached has to some degree been obscured by the technical vocabulary used in presenting the theory. The various accounts have freely used notions like "variable," "scope," "opacity," and "argument," which were first used by logicians and philosophers interested in different, though related, issues (see Chomsky 1981 and references cited there). Nonetheless, the mechanisms actually developed to explain the various interpretive linguistic phenomena have been overwhelmingly syntactic in structure.

One example of this is the θ-Criterion of Chomsky 1981. The θ-Criterion is a well-formedness condition on abstract linguistic structures at the level of LF, according to which NPs must have one and only one θ-role at LF. θ-roles are notions such as "agent of action," "goal of action," "theme," which, it is customarily observed, appear to play an important role in the interpretation of natural language sentences.

It is interesting from our perspective to observe that the θ-Criterion is a condition stated on *NPs*, which are syntactic objects. In fact, not only is it stated on syntactic objects—it cannot be stated on the *semantic values* of these syntactic objects rather than on the syntactic objects themselves. Why not? Consider sentences like (12a,b):

(12) a. *The table nudged e

b. *The ball hit e

These sentences are ruled out by the θ-Criterion. The structure underlying (12a) is (13):

(13) *[the table]$_i$ nudged t$_i$

'The table' was moved by the rule Move-α from the object position of 'nudge' to subject position of the clause. However, since both object and subject positions are θ-positions, NP$_i$ ('the table') has two θ-roles and therefore violates the θ-Criterion. Similar considerations hold for (12b).

Now consider a sentence like (14):

(14) John$_i$ hit himself$_i$

In (14) 'John' and 'himself' are coreferential; they both refer to the same individual, John. Thus, *John himself* has two θ-roles. However, since the NPs 'John' and 'himself' each have one and only one θ-role, the θ-Criterion judges the sentence fully acceptable. If the θ-Criterion were stated on semantic values of NPs rather than on the syntactic object itself, (14) would presumably be unacceptable, like (12a,b). In short, it is precisely a syntactic reading of the θ-Criterion that yields the correct empirical results.

In sum, if the theory presented in chapters 2–5 is correct, then, for a large array of cases, the principles and mechanisms in terms of which meaning is determined have nothing to do with semantic notions like "object" or "truth" or "truth is a model." The key notions are not semantic at all, but syntactic. "Truth," "object," "denotation," etc., turn out to be uninteresting interpretive concepts if the goal is discovering general principles and linguistic laws that address the problem of how meaning functions in natural language.

Truth and Meaning

There are various reasons for the widespread influence of the idea that semantic notions like "truth" are central to a theory of interpretation. They can be classified into three main groups: technical, historical, and philosophical.

Technical Reasons
As noted in chapter 3, earlier theories of the logical syntax of definite descriptions and 'belief'-sentences managed to effect real theoretical economy by viewing certain ambiguities as pertaining to scope mechanisms. The interpretations that such sentences support made it necessary to view quantification as inherently objective if the mechanism of scope was to suffice to yield the appropriate readings. For example, consider (15):

(15)   John believes someone ate petunias

(15) has either a *de re* or a *de dicto* reading. It can be paraphrased as either (16a) or (16b):

(16) a. There is someone such that John believes that he ate petunias

b. John has a someone-ate-petunias belief

Under the first reading, 'someone' is a referential position and we can legitimately infer from (15) that someone ate petunias. We can also infer, trivially, that there exists someone other than John, i.e., the individual of whom he has the belief.

These sorts of inferences are illicit under interpretation (16b). There does not necessarily exist a person "of-whom" John's belief can be predicated. He might be deluded. We can make no existential inferences.

The mechanism of scope can be used to represent the ambiguity of (15) as in (17):

(17) a. someone x [John believes[x ate petunias]]

b. John believes [someone x [x ate petunias]]

(17a) corresponds to the reading (16a); (17b) corresponds to (16b). In (17b), but not (17a) 'someone x' is *in the scope* of 'believe'.

Such an explanation posits that the primary interpretation of quantifiers is objectual; that is, their primary or standard interpretation is to range over real/actual objects, and that nonobjectual interpretations are secondary, being dependent on the scope relations of quantified NPs to a certain class of "opaque" verbs like 'believe'. Thus, if one's concern is to find ways of representing and explaining the range of interpretations of the sentences of natural language, and one considers scope to be the right mechanism for the job, then an objectual interpretation of quantification (and thereby a semantical approach to interpretation theory) follows naturally. Conversely, if one is wedded to a semantical theory of interpretation (and thereby to an objectual interpretation of quantification) because, for example, one sees logic as a theory of "being" in its most general sense, then scope will seem the right way to approach the ambiguity in question. These views are mutually supporting.[9]

Therefore, it is important to see that such phenomena should *not* be accounted for with scope mechanisms. This is what Chapter III tried to demonstrate. Once we are able to divorce the observed phenomena from this particular technical treatment, this reason for a semantical approach to the interpretation of quantification disappears.

Historical Reasons

Other considerations supporting a semantical theory of interpretation can be traced to the concerns of the early developers of quantification theory. Both Frege and Russell were primarily interested in the construction of formal languages for the investigation of science and mathematics. Indeed, until quite recently the belief that natural language had a logic or theory of interpretation of any systematic nature was vigorously disputed. What was not controversial was that formal techniques could illuminate the language of science and mathematics, and it was language as used for these specific purposes to which Frege and

Russell wished their formal work to relate, at least in the first instance. This concern, however, led to their highlighting semantic and ontological issues. It is plausible to suppose that scientists are concerned with objects that exist and mathematicians with objects that could possibly exist. More particularly, their concern is the semantic *values* of their theoretical and mathematical terms. Their goal is to discover what is actually or what logically could be the case—what facts are true, what entities exist or could logically exist. Given such goals, objectual interpretations of quantifiers or semantical theories of interpretation that focus on the relations between terms and their referents are relatively benign.[10] The specific use of language that Frege and Russell investigated does aspire to refer to actual or possible objects. Equally clearly, however, this is just *one* use of language. When the focus of linguistic investigation shifts from scientific and mathematical uses of language to language in general, the interpretations developed with those earlier aims in mind cannot be adopted uncritically. With the shift in perspective, the semantical assumptions are no longer benign. Rather, they constantly impart to language as such ontological and semantic concerns that hardly seem credible. Transferring the formal techniques that earlier philosophers developed to investigate the logic and language of science and mathematics to the investigation of natural language requires rethinking just what the devices mean. And this, as I have argued, should lead to rejecting semantical preconceptions as regulative guides for the theory of natural language interpretation.

Philosophical Reasons
There are two main philosophical views concerning natural language and its acquisition that make semantical theories of interpretation attractive. Both are supported by elaborate considerations. Both, however, also make assumptions that are far from compelling, especially given the framework of assumptions sketched in chapter 1.

One set of considerations can be traced back to the assumption that a radical empiricist theory of language acquisition would advance, e.g., a version of Quine's theory in his *Roots of Reference* or in chapters 1 and 2 of *Word and Object*. On such a view, the way that native speakers develop interpretive abilities (e.g., quantificational competence) is by being trained by the speech community to deal with actual middle-sized objects that impinge on the perceptual apparatus. Such a theory of learning emphasizes the central role of actual objects and the real world in the development of linguistic abilities. Thus, the structure of one's quantificational skills is determined by one's encounters with one's environment. Moreover, it is so determined in a very strong sense. Exposure to the actual world, in conjunction with reinforcement from one's speech community, molds the capacity one actually attains. The picture of learning-as-training that informs this approach makes the actual environment the chief parameter in explaining the nature of one's developed capcities. Given such a view of language acquisition, it is not surprising that semantical theories of interpretation (e.g., objectival interpretations of quantification) would seem natural. Treating truth and its attendant notion of reference to actual objects as central to interpretation theory simply mirrors the specific features of learning that a radical empiricism invokes, i.e., the shaping effects of the learning environment and reinforcement as the key explanatory notions.

The empiricist theory of learning in general and language acquisition in particular has been vigorously questioned in recent years. Especially relevant here is the denial that language acquisition is solely or chiefly a shaping effect of the environment controlled by reinforcement. The environment is not construed as forming or shaping an unstructured mind but as triggering the activity of a largely innate capacity. The structure of the linguistic ability a mature native speaker acquires is not a copy or near copy of the environment in which it develops. In particular, the shape of the grammatical rules of linguistic interpretation do not simply reflect the structure of the environment in which language acquisition takes place. The implications of this for interpretive processes should be clear. For example, the objectival interpretation of quantification need no longer be viewed as simply the interpretation that is intrinsic to the learning process. It may be important to explaining interpretive rules that actual objects can be the values of variables, but it need not be. It is an empirical question. The real world and actual objects do not have the same type of role in nonempiricist theories of language acquisition; therefore, such theories need not enshrine semantical notions like "truth" and "reference" as the key interpretive concepts for natural language.

A second avenue of philosophical speculation that leads to much the same conclusion concerning the centrality of semantical notions to interpretation theory starts from the view that the primary function of language is the communication of information. Such theories fix on the communicative use of language (i.e., assertion, the conveying of true and false information) as its most essential feature and construe the semantics of natural language as in some way derivative of this function.

Of course, no theory of language can deny that language can be used to convey information. (Indeed, how it is possible for language to do this is an interesting question.) However, a communication theory of meaning goes beyond this. It presupposes that the fact that language can be used to convey true information explains or determines the nature of the rules by which this is done; in other words, that this communicative function strongly determines the linguistic structure of natural languages. However, this is an unwarranted assumption. As is well known, function need not strongly determine structure. That language can be used to communicate information may tell us next to nothing about the rules and structural principles by which this can be accomplished.[11]

From the point of view elaborated in chapter 1, this communication theory confuses or conflates what someone knows with how this knowledge is put to use (the competence-performance distinction). The fact that language is used for communication is no more intrinsic to it than its use to tell jokes or fairy tales, to insult or praise, or simply to record one's thoughts. In fact, from the perspective developed in chapter 1 there is nothing particularly central about assertions as opposed to interrogatives or imperatives. Communication (and assertion) is one use of language among many, and there is no reason to believe it has any privileged import for a theory of interpretation. To defend this communication position, evidence is needed that the rules and principles that underlie our interpretive abilities are primarily based on this communicative use and that all other uses derive from this one. But this has not yet been done. Moreover, we have seen that many phenomena traditionally considered to be part of the domain of a theory of meaning are insensitive to considerations that would naturally follow from a theory of comunication. At the very least, therefore, there is a subpart of meaning pretheoretically conceived and the theory of interpretation that is use independent. In sum, there is little reason for believing that the communicative function of natural language is the key to its structural properties or that a theory of natural language interpretation must be semantical because language can be used to talk about the world.

Final Remarks

In this chapter I have argued that the theory presented in chapters 2–5 is strongly syntactic. If this is correct, it implies that part of the theory of natural language interpretation is syntactically based and that semantic notions are irrelevant or even misleading in explaining the range of phenomena I have considered. One might reply, however, that this shows only that the syntax-semantics boundary must be redrawn, not that semantical notions should be ousted from their central explanatory place in a theory of interpretation. In a sense, I agree with this. What I have tried to show is that for many facts whose explanation has been held to be the responsibility of a semantical theory of interpretation, a syntactically based theory is more adequate. However, mightn't semantic notions be important elsewhere? Of course they might, since there can be no a priori conclusion on such an issue; but in my opinion they are not. Moreover, the notions that a semantical theory would invoke are rather unclear. In my opinion the presumption that notions like "truth" and "reference" must play explanatory roles in a theory of meaning is quite ill founded. In the next chapter I will offer some reasons for these opinions.

Chapter 7

Is Semantics Possible?

In the course of this book I have outlined a theory of quantifier-quantifier and quantifier-pronoun interactions. This theory is strongly syntactic in the sense that the theoretical parameters over which the laws and generalizations are defined are syntactic and, more importantly, have no natural semantical analogues. For these aspects of meaning, I have argued, a theory of natural language interpretation fails to be a *semantical* theory in any interesting sense. In other words, semantical notions do not seem important for explaining these kinds of interpretive phenomena.

The style of explanation I have used is reminiscent of earlier approaches to the problem of meaning in natural language, in that it proceeds by postulating internal mental representations of natural language sentences. These internal representations have certain abstract syntactic properties over which linguistic generalizations can be elaborated to account for the attested linguistic judgments. In short, then, the account rests on a theory of *translation*. Natural language sentences, in this case English, are translated into another format, a kind of *mentalese*, whose properties are described by the principles of Universal Grammar, and the ability of native speakers to make various discriminations concerning relative quantifier scope, pronoun binding, etc., in ordinary English sentences is explained by assuming that these judgments are the result of specific computational abilities defined over these "translations" in mentalese. The value of assuming that such a translation in fact takes place lies in the nontrivial explanations we are able to devise. If these explanations are at all convincing, then it appears that *part* of the complex ability that human beings have to use and understand a natural language is due to their (tacit) ability to "translate" natural language strings into the mental language postulated by Universal Grammar. Their judgments concerning particular English sentences are a reflection of the well-formedness conditions on the translations of these same sentences in mentalese.

I have belabored this point because of the suspicion that philosophers have often expressed that such forms of explanation do not contribute much to an explanation of the linguistic phenomena we would pre-theoretically characterize as pertaining to a theory of meaning.[1] The reason they give for this opinion is that such translation theories are not sufficient to explain how competent speakers are able to speak and understand their native language; in other words, that translation theories presuppose that speakers already *understand* mentalese, without explaining what such understanding consists in.

This sort of criticism does not really touch the remarks I have just made. It is perfectly possible that translating a natural language into mentalese is a *necessary* condition for understanding it (in other words, that *one* of the abilities (perhaps tacit) that native speakers have is to make this sort of translation) but that this sort of translation is not *sufficient* to explain the capacity of competent speakers fully. What more must be added? Very roughly, a theory that explains what other abilities competent native speakers must have besides translational ones, on the basis of which they are able to speak and understand a natural language.

The need for this is obvious if we examine translation theories more fully. Consider sentences (1a,b) and their representations in mentalese, (2a,b):

(1)   a. John loves Mary

      b. John hates Mary

(2)   a. $[_S[_{NP}$ John] $[_{VP}$ loves $[_{NP}$ Mary]]]

      b. $[_S[_{NP}$ John] $[_{VP}$ hates $[_{NP}$ Mary]]]

Given that (1a,b) have a common syntactic structure, what explains the difference in meaning between them? One answer might be that (1a) is translated into a sentence of mentalese that uses the concept *love*, whereas (1b) is translated into a sentence of mentalese that uses the concept *hate*. Since the concept *love* is different from the concept *hate*, (1a) and (1b) mean different things. But this is hardly an *explanation*. In asking the original question, we take it for granted that 'loves' does not mean the same as 'hates' and that (1a) therefore does not mean the same as (1b). What we want is an *explanation* of this fact, an account of what it is for a sentence to have the interpretive content we call its meaning. The statement that 'love' and 'hate' are translated into the mentalese concepts *love* and *hate* and that these are different is not so much an explanation as a repetition of the problem: what makes the concepts *love* and *hate* different? What is it for two concepts to have different contents? In particular, what does a native speaker have to know to have mastered a concept? What, is short, is the *fine structure* of this ability? A translation theory does not provide an account of this. In sum, although translation theories are necessary ingredients of a general theory of meaning for natural language, they do not appear sufficient in themselves to answer the crucial questions.

It has been claimed that a theory of meaning must include a traditional semantical theory exploiting notions like "truth," "reference," "model," "object," "predicate," because only this kind of theory provides a nontrivial account of sentential contents and the abilities that native speakers have beyond the translational ones. In what follows, I will examine two versions of this claim. The first version is that semantical theories in fact explain the problems and questions that a theory of translation only begs. The second version is that semantical theories must exist. The first version is by far the more interesting. It essentially claims that semantical theories explain what it is for sentences to have different linguistic contents and what it is for native speakers to be interpretively competent. However, before examining the relative merits of current approaches invoking such a theory, I will discuss the second position briefly.

The central problem to be explained by a theory of meaning is what is often called the *productivity* of language: the fact that competent native speakers have the ability to produce and understand sentences never before encountered, and to do this appropriately.[2] Often when philosophers and linguists insist that semantical theories must exist, they are reaffirming their belief that native speakers have this ability, as well as the belief that notions like "truth," "reference," and "model" will be key ingredients of such a theory.

Now, the fact of language productivity is never seriously contested, certainly not by anyone sharing the assumptions outlined in chapter 1. It is taken for granted by virtually everyone who has written about language. This is as true for advocates of translation theories as it is for proponents of more semantical accounts. The question, then, is not *whether* competent speakers are linguistically productive, but *how*. Given the existence of linguistic productivity, how is it to be explained? What sort of skill is it? What mechanism or subabilities make it possible?

Putting the questions this way, it is clear why translation theories are insufficient as full theories of meaning. They postulate an internal language—mentalese—into which natural languages are translated. They do not, however, explain what it is to understand a concept in mentalese—what subabilities and knowledge are required to explain the complex ability of competent speakers to appropriately use and comprehend an infinite number of novel sentences of mentalese. In effect, a translation theory of this sort presupposes what we want to have explained. It is no less a mystery to say what competent speakers understand when they grasp the concepts of mentalese than it is to say what they understand when they grasp regular words and sentences in a natural language. The ability they are supposed by the theorist to have stands in as much need of explanation (and explanation of exactly the same kind) as the ability we wish to have explained.[3] The demand for explanation is simply pushed one step back; instead of asking what it means to understand a word or a sentence, we ask what it means to grasp a concept. No progress has been made.

Semantical theories of the kind I will discuss supposedly supply what these translation theories presuppose: an articulated theory of what it is for a sentence to have semantic content and what abilities native speakers have that allow them to be linguistically productive. They accomplish this by postulating a set of semantical *rules* that explain a native speaker's ability to produce and understand an unbounded set of sentences. Unlike translation theories, it is claimed that these semantical rules are not trivial. They do not beg the question, as translation theories do, but purport to define the abilities that underlie linguistic productivity.

What is at stake is the nature of the vocabulary that a theory of interpretation should exploit to account for our linguistic abilities. Semantical theories claim that any adequate theory of interpretation will propose that language has certain semantical properties that must be mastered if one is to become a competent native speaker.[4] Moreover, these semantical properties are relatively well defined and can serve as theoretical constructs in an account of interpretive competence. In short, interpretive competence and linguistic productivity in particular have a semantical fine structure. In understanding the meaning of a sentence, for example, we understand what it is for the sentence to be true and for its parts to refer to certain entities, constrain the world, or describe a state of affairs. Such a theory aims to explain our linguistic abilities in terms of our abilities to refer to objects, discern truth conditions, etc. In this chapter I will discuss whether such a semantical theory of meaning deserves recognition as part of a theory of linguistic competence and in particular whether it advances our understanding of the phenomenon of linguistic productivity.

Neo-Fregean Theories

Standard Neo-Fregean theories of meaning are construed as having essentially three parts.[5] The first part, sometimes called a theory of *reference*, attempts to explain what it is for a linguistic expression to have a meaning and why a particular expression has the meaning it does. Unlike translation theories, semantic theories do not consider linguistic expressions to be meaningful by virtue of being related to concepts or other elements of a languagelike mentalese. Rather, meaning arises from the coordination of linguistic expressions with nonlinguistic entities.[6] Semantical theories can differ with respect to the sorts of objects they consider to be coordinated with what sorts of expressions. Thus, for example, theories of the possible worlds variety often assume that names designate individual concepts (i.e., functions from possible worlds to individuals). Situation semantics, on the other hand, construes names as picking out individuals, which are not functions of any sort. For some theorists, sentences denote propositions, which are truth-value bearers; for others, they describe situation types or states of affairs or denote propositional functions, which are not truth-value bearers. All theories, however, agree in this regard: they all coordinate linguistic expressions with nonlinguistic objects, whether these be objects, properties, individuals, propositions, or situation types. This coordination is necessary if the theory is to explain what it is for a linguistic expression to have a meaning; in other words, if it is to avoid the explanatory circularity characteristic of translation theories. At bottom, these non-linguistic entities *interpret* the linguistic expressions they are coordinated with; in fact, it is in virtue of this link to a nonlinguistic entity that a linguistic expression is said to have a meaning.

The basic intuition behind this theoretical stance is that a linguistic expression (like a sentence) pictures, describes, picks out, or denotes a nonlinguistic entity, such as a state of affairs. This is accomplished by coordinating the subsentential elements of the sentence with the objects, individuals, properties, relations, etc., that are the subparts of the states of affairs. When the objects and relations with which the linguistic expressions are coordinated in fact constitute a state of affairs of the kind pictured by the linguistic elements in sentential combination, the sentence is true (otherwise, it is false). In short, according to every account (including translation theory), sentential meaning is compositional. The meaning of the whole is a function of the meaning of the parts. This compositional aspect of semantic entities is necessary if the theory of meaning hopes to account for linguistic productivity. Basically, it must be shown how the meaning or contents of an unbounded set of sentences can be constructed on the basis of a finite number of rules. Semantical theories do this by considering the contents of sentences to be compositionally derived from the contents of the subsentential units. The interpretive rules that determine the meanings of these sub-sentential elements (words) are therefore crucial in accounting for our apparent ability to comprehend an unbounded number of sentences. By coordinating the finite number of words in a language with determinate semantic values—for example, names with objects or transitive verbs with relations—that can be repeatedly combined by a finite number of interpretive operations, we can associate an interpretation with each of the infinitely many sentences while still exploiting only finite resources. In effect, therefore, it is by assuming that the semantic value of a sentence (for example, a state of affairs) is complex and so made up of simpler elements (for example, objects and relations) in particular combinations that linguistic productivity is explained.

It is important to emphasize that compositionality is not a property specific or unique to semantical theories. All theories incorporate it in some way; indeed, it seems to be a virtual precondition of any theory attempting to explain linguistic productivity. What is unique to semantical theories is instead the coordination of expressions with entities via something like the reference relation, which breaks the circularity characteristic of translation theories' explanations of meaning.

The second part of a Neo-Fregean theory is a theory of *sense* which explains what it is for someone to know the meaning of a linguistic expression. It coordinates the competent speaker's abilities and knowledge with the rules in the theory of reference that explicate the meaning of linguistic expressions. In effect, it attempts to say what knowing one or another bit of the theory of reference amounts to, that is, what sorts of cognitive capacities a speaker attains when he comes to know the meaning of a linguistic expression.[7]

The theory of sense is a crucial ingredient in explaining linguistic productivity. Recall that what we wish to explain is *how* people are able to use and understand sentences never before encountered, by articulating the subabilities that underlie this particular competence, the kinds of knowledge it requires. And in fact a theory of sense explains what it is in particular that someone knows when he knows the rules that constitute the theory of reference: How knowledge of the theory of reference manifests itself in articulated subabilities that *together* interact and constitute the complex ability of being a linguistically productive competent speaker.

It is important to see that without a theory of sense we have no account of linguistic productivity. The fact we want explained is *how* competent native speakers can use and understand an unbounded set of sentences. Semantical theories postulate that a competent speaker grasps the rules of meaning, or is attuned to the regularities among situation types, or whatever. It is in virtue of this grasping or attunement that we *explain* the ability to be linguistically productive. However, it is the theory of sense that "breaks down" the complex ability we call linguistic productivity into its subparts so that we can understand what it amounts to. It breaks down the ability to be linguistically productive by mapping parts of the theory of reference onto parts of the complex ability. By doing this, the theory of sense explains how a competent speaker understands a novel sentence by explaining what he knows when he knows the meanings of the parts and what he knows when he knows the rules of combination.

Without such a mapping of subabilities with parts of the theory of reference we do not explain the problem of linguistic productivity. We simply reaffirm it to be a fact. In short, we do not get beyond the explanation offered by a translation theory.

Like the theory of reference, the theory of sense will be compositional. It will both isolate specific abilities and specific bits of cognitive knowledge that explain what we understand when we understand a given interpretive rule and show how these subabilities and basic bits of knowledge combine to yield the total linguistic ability of productivity. Its main tasks will therefore be to isolate basic abilities and knowledge structures and to explain how they combine to yield more and more complex abilities and knowledge structures.

A word of caution. By saying that a theory of sense "breaks down" the complex ability of linguistic productivity, I do not mean to suggest that the explanation must be reductive, but only that the theory of sense must articulate the structure of the complex ability. If the ability is best explained by reducing it to other abilities, the theory of sense says what these are and how they interact. If the ability is best explained holistically, at the level of the language as a whole, then it explains how the ability functions holistically: what its principles of operation are and how they interact. A theory of sense does not require one kind of analysis of the complex ability rather than another. It simply requires *some* account that goes beyond saying that grasping the theory of reference *as a whole* results in the *total* ability to be linguistically productive.

The third part of a Neo-Fregean theory of meaning is a theory of *force*. The complex ability we wish to explain consists of two parts: the ability to speak and comprehend novel sentences, and the ability to do this appropriately. The theory of force deals with the second. It takes as input the meanings of sentences, as determined by the theories of reference and sense, and yields as output particular kinds of linguistic acts: assertions, interrogatives, imperatives, requests, and so forth. If the theory of reference is an account of what it is for a sentence to have a content or meaning and the theory of sense is an account of what sort of abilities it takes to know meanings, then a theory of force is the first part of a theory of language use, its goal being to explain how competent speakers use sentences with particular meanings to execute particular linguistic acts such as asserting, requesting, commanding, and asking.

It is a feature of Neo-Fregean theories that *some* part of the meaning of a sentence (its cognitive content, or the types of situations it describes, or the proposition it expresses) is determined in a context independent manner. In other words, the rules of the theory of meaning are *in part* context insensitive. If they were not, we could not explain how competent speakers could use an unbounded number of sentences *appropriately*. The reason is that no general *rules* could be devised if all of the content of a sentence were contextually determined. As such, the division between a theory of meaning and a theory of use is a virtual prerequisite of any account wishing to explain linguistic productivity. Context-insensitive rules of some kind must be assumed in terms of which the content of a sentence is provided. If the *rules* of content are themselves determined in the context of use, then there is no way of explaining, as opposed to repeating, the fact of linguistic productivity.

This briefly describes the internal structure of a Neo-Fregean theory of meaning (abstracting away from the differences among the several versions of such a theory, as I have noted). As a whole, such a theory of meaning (semantics) itself fits into a larger structure; that is, it is one of three parts of a general theory of language, the other two being a theory of form (syntax) and a theory of use (pragmatics). Both a theory of reference and a theory of sense deal with linguistic expressions. The theory of syntax (including syntax, morphology, phonology, etc.) deals with the formal properties of such linguistic expressions (*syntactic objects* such as sentences, names, verbs, or noun phrases) in isolation from the entities they refer to or how this reference is determined. The theory of pragmatics is the theory of language use. Its goal is to elucidate how the general properties we associate with the meaning of an utterance follow from the propositional content of the utterance (determined by the theories of reference and sense) along with its context of use. In short, a pragmatic theory takes as input propositions or linguistic meanings suitably defined and yields as output utterance meanings. (As noted, the theory of force can be seen as the front end of such a theory. However, mood is probably just a small part of pragmatics.)

These three parts of the traditional theory of language interact in the following ways. The outputs of the syntax are uninterpreted strings. These are given a meaning by semantical rules of reference and sense. The interpreted linguistic items that result are then input to the pragmatics. This component determines the meaning of the utterance (proposition-in-use) by rules defined over propositional contents and contextual parameters. Importantly, propositional contents remain fixed across contexts of use. Indeed it is in terms of such fixed contents that the contextual appropriateness of utterances are explained. In a Neo-

Fregean theory, notions like truth, reference, situation type, object, property, possible world, etc. are not themselves context dependent notions. The rules determining the meaning of a linguistic expression are not context sensitive rules, or at least are not sensitive to exactly the same parameters used in explaining use, i.e. utterance meaning. In effect, therefore, the theory of meaning in a Neo-Fregean theory occupies a position halfway between syntax and pragmatics. Like syntactic rules, rules of meaning (particularly the rules of sense and reference) are context insensitive rules. The interpretation of semantic content a linguistic item possesses is largely determinable independently of pragmatic factors of context. What the reference of an expression is and how it is fixed by its sense are not features that are dependent on the pragmatic particulars of a context of utterance. Rather, they are independent of contextual parameters and in conjunction with the contextual features of an utterance determine the import of a particular linguistic act.

This, then, is what a standard semantical theory of meaning looks like in outline. In what follows, I will concentrate on two of its central features. First, the feature that knowing the meaning of a linguistic item is knowing what sort of entity it refers to. To have any explanatory power (i.e., to explain the phenomenon of linguistic productivity) a Neo-Fregean theory must explain what it is for a native speaker to know that some linguistic item refers to some nonlinguistic entity. This, in turn, requires explicating the reference relation. After all, it is in virtue of a reference relation between a linguistic expression and a nonlinguistic object that a linguistic entity has a meaning. If a theory of sense is to explain how we understand linguistic expressions by claiming that we come to see, or mentally grasp, or are attuned to certain regularities between expressions and entities as expressed in a theory of reference, then we must have some general nontrivial account of what this mental grasping consists in and, in particular, some account of what, in general, is grasped. I stress "general" here. The problem facing a theory of meaning is *not* to explain this or that sentence used in this or that circumstance. As native speakers, we understand what a sentence means when it is used. This we take for granted. What we want from a theory of meaning is an explanation of *how* we do this, not a justification *that* we do it. To have such an explanation demands providing certain general concepts and an articulated set of rules in terms of which the ability is explained. Moreover, if a Neo-Fregean theory of meaning is not to suffer the same inadequacies as a translational theory of meaning, the rules it postulates must not be trivial in the sense of presupposing abilities no less opaque than (actually not very different from) the ability to be explained, i.e., linguistic productivity.

A Neo-Fregean theory claims to be such a positive theory. Its central features are its claims that (a) there exists a general relation of reference between words and things and it is in virtue of such a relation that we get meaning, and (b) it is this relation that we grasp when we understand the meaning of a linguistic item.

Problems with Neo-Fregean Theories

The stress points in a Neo-Fregean theory of meaning can be described in terms of the following questions: (1) *What* is it that we grasp when we grasp the meaning of a linguistic item? That is, what is the nature of the rules of reference? and (2) *How* do we grasp the meaning of a linguistic item? That is, what is it to know these rules and to use them? The first of these questions focuses on the theory of reference. The second probes the connection between the theory of reference and the theory of sense. Let us consider them one at a time.

As we have seen, in a Neo-Fregean theory of meaning linguistic expressions are meaningful *in virtue of* their referring to nonlinguistic objects. The latter "interpret" the former. Moreover, to understand the meaning of a linguistic expression is simply to understand how the referent is determined, that is, what it is for a certain linguistic item to be referentially related to its referent. But what is it that is known? What is this reference relation that someone who understands the meaning of a linguistic expression comes to know? For example, if I know the meaning of 'dog', I know that 'dog' refers to dogs. What is it to know this?

One answer might be that to know the meaning of 'dog' is to know that 'dog' *names* those objects that are dogs, i.e., the set of dogs. But this sort of answer simply repeats the problem. What is it to know that 'dog' *names* the set of dogs? Surely 'dog' names the set of dogs if and only if 'dog' refers to dogs. What then is it to know the naming (i.e., reference) relation? To say that the reference relation is just like the naming relation hardly explains the former; both are equally obscure and in exactly the same ways.

Another answer might be that knowing the meaning of a linguistic item is knowing what part of the world it pictures. For example, take a sentence like 'Jim Valvano was born in Brooklyn'. To know the meaning of this sentence is to know its truth conditions, i.e., the circumstances under which it is true or perhaps the constraints its situation type places on the world or the sorts of situations it describes. The sentence 'Jim Valvano was born in Brooklyn' is true if and only if Jim Valvano was born in Brooklyn. Similarly, we can say that the sentence describes a state of affairs or situation in which the individual named 'Jim Valvano' has the property of having been born in Brooklyn. But what is it to know what the biconditional above expresses? Or that a state of affairs has certain objects and properties in some combination? In particular, what ability does knowing the biconditional afford someone who knows it? What sort of ability or knowledge is it to recognize that a type of situation or state of affairs is being described? How is saying that what someone knows is that the biconditional obtains or that a certain kind of situation is described any more informative than the statement that all agree is trivial: namely, that what one understands is the concept associated with 'Jim Valvano was born in Brooklyn'? Since it is quite clear that the only hold we have on concepts is via their sentential or linguistic proxies, this type of explanation is inadequate. But is it any less the case for the semantical notions deployed?

Perhaps the ability (tacitly) invoked by a semantical theory that allows it to avoid triviality is the ability to *compare* the sentence 'Jim Valvano was born in Brooklyn' with the state of affairs of Jim Valvano being born in Brooklyn. But what is it to compare a linguistic item like a sentence with a state of affairs? Do we do this directly: holding the sentence in one hand, so to speak, and the state of affairs in the other? Since Kant, at least, such an answer has been untenable. The problem lies with comparing. Like translation, comparing is an activity that involves language-like processes, namely, representing the items compared. However, if this is so, then we only understand what it is to compare if we already understand what it is to represent those things we are comparing. But is representing really any different from picturing or referring? If 'X' represents X, then doesn't 'X' refer to X, and doesn't 'X' picture X? It seems so. But if so, how can an explanation of referring or picturing proceed in terms of comparing? Not without evident circularity. Both are obscure, and in the same ways. So we return to the question: what is it that we know when we know the meaning of a linguistic item? What is it to know that a certain linguistic expression refers to an object, or describes a state of affairs, or constrains reality to be a certain way?

Yet another approach might be that knowing the meaning of a linguistic expression 'X' is to know what property of Xness it picks out. For example, to know the meaning of 'dog' is to know that it picks out all those things that have the property of being a dog. But is this any different or less obscure than the ability to name dogs 'dog'? Saying that knowledge of the meaning of 'X' is the ability to identify Xness is no help unless we already know what it is to identify Xness. In other words, Platonic maneuvers like this are no help unless we can say what it is to "see" Platonic objects. One possibility is to say that being able to identify Xness is having a definition that applies to Xs and only to Xs.[8] However, as is well known, most linguistic items appear to have no definitions at all. What are the definitions of 'table', 'chair', 'lap', 'dog', 'game'? Are there necessary and sufficient conditions that would pick out these and only these? Not that anyone has been able to provide. In fact, if Wittgenstein is correct (and his examples are rather persuasive) that the various uses of linguistic items are bound together by nothing more than "family resemblance," then the belief in the existence of *definitions* is really utopian. Rather than there being objective properties or definitions that we already understand and in virtue of which we explain our ability to name Xs 'X', it seems more likely that the causality is reversed: because we call Xs 'X', we assume that they all have the property of Xness in common. But if this is so, then invoking properties does not in the least explain reference or the ability to refer. We have little understanding of these properties or definitions of common linguistic items except that they appear to be necessary to "explain" our abilities. However, unless we develop a theory of definitions or an account of what it is to know properties (e.g., Xness) in virtue of which individuals are called what they are called (e.g., 'X'), what we have is less an explanation of how we mean what we mean than a commitment that such an explanation must exist. This may well be true. But faith is no substitute for the actual account. We are saying nothing more than that what all Xs have in common is that they are called 'X', and this cannot explain what the meaning of 'X' is. It is unilluminating to say that the meaning of 'X' is that all Xs are called 'X' and that to know the meaning of 'X' is to know that Xs are called 'X'. Once one dispenses with the metaphysics of properties or gives up on the possibility of definitions, then one must concede that there is nothing illuminating in saying that 'X' refers to Xs in virtue of picking out the property of Xness; no more illuminating than saying that 'dog' translates into the concept *dog*.[9]

I would like to dwell on this point for a while because its importance is often overlooked, for example, by various approaches to meaning in natural language. Take current versions of the Davidsonian approach as a case in point. The basic intuition of this program is close to that of a Neo-Fregean approach. The goal of a theory of meaning for a language is to provide a recursive truth definition of a language L, that is, to provide a theory such that, given L, one can derive from the theory, for every sentence of L, an instance of the Tarski biconditional (e.g., ' "Snow is white" is true if and only if snow is white'). Let us assume we can do this. What have we accomplished? In particular, if this theory of truth-for-L is the meaning theory of L, then presumably what it is to know the meaning of a sentence S is both to know how to derive the biconditional ' "S" is true if and only if S', and to understand what it is for the right side of the biconditional to obtain. In other words, it is because one understands that the right side of a biconditional specifies the truth conditions that one understands the meaning of the quoted expression on the left side. In terms of the example, if one understands what truth is and that 'Snow is white' is true, then one will understand that 'Snow is white' means that snow is white. To be picturesque, the Tarski biconditional and its derivation mirror the knowledge a speaker has of the reference relations of the parts of a sentence and the truth condition of a sentence.

To explain what it is to know the meaning of a sentence S, one must *explain* what it is to have the semantic abilities that the theory implicitly attributes to a speaker who understands the language. If one gives an account of what it is to know truth conditions, states of affairs, reference, or indeed any of these semantical relations, then a truth theory can explain what it is that speakers, know when they know the meaning of a sentence. The problem is that the theory on its own *presupposes* that we understand the notion of truth and attendant notions like "object" and "reference." It does not explain what it is for an arbitrary sentence to be true or what it is to have this sort of knowledge.[10] As we shall see, there is little reason to believe that we do have the necessary understanding of truth. Lacking this understanding, the approach to a theory of meaning via a theory of truth will leave most of the difficult questions concerning meaning untouched. Of course, once we have an account of truth and what it is for someone to know that a given sentence is true, then we can dress the answers to the problem of meaning in terms of a theory of truth. However, once we have this, then we can probably rehabilitate the translational theory of meaning as well. "Having a concept" will be no worse (nor better) than "under-standing the truth conditions." The problem is that both accounts are lacking. There must be some further explication of what it is for a sentence in general to be true—of the notion of truth—if we are to attain an explanation of semantic competence in terms of knowing how to derive a Tarski biconditional for every sentence of the language.

Seeing this leads one to appreciate the motivation behind meta-physical maneuvers that invoke objects, properties, states of affairs, situation types, events, etc., as the referents of linguistic items. These entities are invoked to explain what sort of property truth is—hence, to explicate that in virtue of which linguistic items have a meaning and what it is in general for a sentence to be true. Furthermore, it is a knowledge of the relation between nonlinguistic objects and the corresponding linguistic expressions that allegedly underlies our linguistic abilities.

The trouble with this metaphysical maneuver, however, is that it appears to be impossible to give a general explanation of truth, reference, describing, etc., that does not have all the difficulties of the original notion. For example, it seems unilluminating to explain truth by some notion of correspondence to reality, for the latter notion is as opaque as the former and in exactly the same ways. If one of them is puzzling, the other one will be equally so. The same is true for the other notions surveyed above.[11]

We thus appear to have no independent purchase on notions like "truth" or "correspondence," or what it is to know that names refer to objects and that sentences picture states of affairs or correspond to reality—no independent notions that do not invoke exactly the same relations, powers, and abilities that this apparatus is intended to explain. What power or ability or knowledge does one acquire when one knows the meaning of a linguistic item? The theorist answers: one knows its truth or reference conditions, or the situation type it describes, or the state of affairs denoted. But what is it to know this? The theorist replies: it is to know that certain terms pick out certain objects, or that sentences describe types of states of affairs or correspond to reality. But what sorts of relations are these and what is it to be able to discern that the putative relation obtains? Is this really saying anything different from that it is the ability to understand the meaning? Is our understanding of referential abilities any different from—in particular, any clearer than—our understanding of our ability to use expressions meaningfully? Isn't our understanding of each equally murky, and murky in exactly the same way? If so, we can hardly expect that reworking semantical relations without a further explication of what these are will do much to explain our abilities to use expressions meaningfully or to be linguistically productive.

The move to metaphysics is motivated by explanatory desires; but such a move seems to bring us no closer to an explanation of what meaning is or what we know when we know the meaning of a linguistic term. Might we then not question these desires: why isn't a purely disquotational theory of truth enough? Perhaps we should forget the metaphysics and accept that a truth theory of meaning can be perfectly explanatory on the basis of a very modest[12] notion of truth. Something like a redundancy theory might suffice: to assert that 'X' is true is just to assert X. In other words, 'true' is essentially a disquotation operator; what it means is that if one appends 'is true' to a quoted sentence, then whenever one can assert the sentence one can assert its quoted counterpart with 'is true' appended. But what sort of explanation is this? We want a theory of meaning to *explain* what we are doing when we assert a sentence—to explain what the content of the assertion is. The content is supposedly related to the meaning of the sentence that the utterance uses. A truth theory of meaning like the one above that invokes a redundancy notion of truth tells us that what we do when we assert 'S' is just the same as what we do when we assert ' "S" is true'. This is simply unilluminating—indeed trivial, redolent of Voltaire's dormitive powers. If a truth theory of meaning is to explain our interpretive abilities, then it must do better than this.

As it stands, then, the discussion seems to have come to the following point: Neo-Fregean theories attribute to linguistic items certain interpretive properties explicated in terms of reference to nonlinguistic entities, and to speakers of a language certain semantical capacities to "detect" these properties in virtue of which competent speakers' interpretive abilities are explained. The problem is to explain what having these semantical capacities consists in, which in turn means explaining what it is for a term to refer, or for a sentence to be true, or for a situation type to hold in a noncircular and nontrivial manner. Unfortunately, the proposals we have examined seem to give answers that invoke relations and capacities no better understood than the ones we want explained. As the nature of the interpretive capacities of competent speakers is the problem we started with, in what sense do such truth theories explain what meaning is and what it is that speakers grasp that underlies their ability to be linguistically productive?

Must the Reference Relation Be Explained?

We have asked what it is for a person to understand the reference relation, and we have concluded that the natural replies fail to illuminate the issue. However, how serious a problem is this for a Neo-Fregean program? The objections presuppose that the reference relation is some vague, mysterious thing and that what it is to "know" it has to be explicated. But isn't this simply being skeptical? Isn't it perfectly clear what truth, reference, situations, individuals, objects, properties, and states of affairs are? After all, we claim, for example, that certain sentences are true all the time. What's the big mystery? Truth is truth, and reference is reference. There is no further explanation, and there needn't be one.

Such a rejoinder to the demands for explanation in the previous section is presupposed (at least tacitly) by many researchers into the theory of meaning.[13] Semantical notions such as "reference" or "truth" are taken to be tolerably unproblematic and clear. Examples are given—for instance, of the referential use of names: 'Jim Valvano is that guy (pointing) next to Thurl Bailey'. Concurrently, it is implied that the example is a typical instance of the reference relation at work. The claim tacitly made is that when we invoke the notion of reference in the context of a theory of meaning, that is the sort of thing we have in mind. In short, such a reply goes, such notions as truth or the reference relation cannot be further explained not because they are deep and mysterious but because they are mundane and obvious. Thus, skepticism of the sort displayed in the previous section is really out of place. Typical examples of true sentences and referring phrases abound, so why the fuss?

It is always hard to argue that a certain skeptical attitude is appropriate. What is there to say to someone who simply doesn't feel the lack of clarity? Still, I think this sort of rejoinder can be shown to be slightly disingenuous. The skeptical position does not deny that the word 'reference', the verb 'refers', and the notion 'true' have perfectly reasonable uses and that we understand what they mean when so used. Rather, it questions their legitimacy as theoretical concepts within a general explanatory theory of meaning. Granted, the skeptic might say, that we understand what reference and referring are in certain contexts, or what it means to say of a particular sentence that it is true—what do these instances have to do with the theoretical use of the notion, i.e., the notion exploited by a theory of meaning? "They're just the same," the theorist might reply. How can we determine whether this is so? In particular, what considerations, if any, can the skeptic advance to undermine our confidence that the theorist is right? It is important to understand from the outset that, concerning disputes such as this, conclusive arguments are never forthcoming. For all of that, however, the discussion need not be unpersuasive. Recall that semantical theorists make invidious comparisons between their theories and translation theories. In criticizing the latter, Neo-Fregean theorists do not intend to deny that words like 'concept' have perfectly respectable uses in common parlance. Rather, they deny that such notions can be used as the basis of an explanatory theory of linguistic productivity. What they claim for their own theoretical vocabulary is precisely what they deny the translation theorist. Namely, they claim not only that their own terms of art are clear and intuitive common sense, but also that, unlike the theoretical terms of the translation theorist, they beg none of the questions at issue.

Note, first, that the theorist's reply is little more than an injunction to consult our intuitions as we look at examples of reference. Reference/referring is what is going on here (pointing): 'Jim' refers to Jim Valvano. The theorist then says that *this* is what is meant by reference: the theoretical term invokes this same relation, but in a slightly more general form. One way to reply to the semantical theorist, therefore, is to review more fully the cases where the theoretical notion of reference is invoked. If it is intended to be just the same as the commonplace relation the theorist urges us to consider, then presumably we should recognize it. More important, if it is *not* recognizably the same relation, then why should we unproblematically assume it to be?

Semantical theory denies that its theoretical vocabulary stands in need of explication, because it does not invoke any problematic notions. By 'reference', 'truth', 'property', 'situation', etc., the semantical theorist intends no more than what we intend when we use the word in ordinary contexts. In a sense, this is the best kind of theoretical vocabulary: entirely intuitive, because the theoretical uses of the terms are so closely linked to their ordinary uses. The question then becomes: do we in fact have a clear understanding of the ordinary uses of the relevant terms *and* are these really all the semantical theorist requires? For the reply to be affirmative, the fit must be rather tight. The greater the distance between our ordinary uses of terms like 'refers', 'object', or 'true' and what the theorist needs, the greater will be the relevance of the skeptic's demands for clarification.

With this in mind, consider different *ordinary* cases of referring: 'Pegasus' refers to the winged horse captured by Bellerophon, 'Jim Valvano is that guy over there'. Do 'Pegasus' and 'Jim Valvano' refer in the same way? Do these two cases really exhibit only one kind of relation— reference—as the theorist suggests? One refers to a fictional entity while the other does not. Does this matter? Does the meaning theorist wish us to treat reference to Pegasus the same as reference to Jim Valvano? There are clearly differences between them. But for that matter, there are similarities as well. Should we focus on the similarities or the differences? If we focus on the similarities, i.e., assume some common reference relation they both invoke, where in the theory will we explain their different uses? After all, 'Pegasus' is used differently from 'Jim Valvano'. We can point to the latter but not the former, for example. We recognize that Pegasus is not a real winged horse but a mythical creature. Not so Jim Valvano.

If we do decide to focus on the similarities, we might relegate the differences to pragmatic factors: 'Pegasus' refers to Pegasus in just the way 'Jim Valvano' refers to Jim Valvano, but for pragmatic reasons their use is different. But for *what* reasons? To simply say this is just to repeat that the terms 'Pegasus' and 'Jim Valvano' are different. If they act differently, why should we assume that they nonetheless instantiate the very *same* kind of reference relation? Is this intuitively clear, open to common-sense inspection, as the semantical theorist is suggesting?[14]

The names 'Jim Valvano' and 'Thurl Bailey' are used differently, the theorist might reply, but would we want to say they refer differently? The first can be used to pick out the coach of the 1983 N.C. State basketball team, the second to pick out the center. In such a case the names refer *in the same way*, and the differences are accommodated by pointing out that they refer to *different objects*. Why not say the same thing about 'Jim Valvano' and 'Pegasus'?

Surely we can see a difference. Both 'Jim Valvano' and 'Thurl Bailey' pick out real individuals, but 'Pegasus' refers to a fictional creature. Are we then saying that the *same* relation of reference obtains between names and *real* entities that obtains between names and *fictional* entities? Is the ability to refer to fictional entities just the same as the ability to pick out real ones? Moreover, do all differences between the use of referring expressions and the use of fictional ones *follow* from the different entitities referred to? If so, how? Does this seem obvious? Do we recognize all this when we consider the theorist's simple example? Would we wish to say this if we were not committed in advance to the position that there is a general semantical relation between linguistic expressions and nonlinguistic entities that underlies our ability to be linguistically productive? Of course, if we already believe that there is a general reference relation, then this is what we would say. However, what is at issue is precisely the nature of such a relation, and what the skeptic wants us to see is that there is no difficulty in generating reasonable grounds for doubting that we have an intuitive understanding of it.

The fictional/nonfictional issue is just the tip of the iceberg. The reference relation is presumably more general still. Standard semantical accounts provide lists stating, for example, that names *refer* to individuals or individual concepts, that intransitive verbs and adjectives *refer* to sets of individuals or properties, that transitive verbs *refer* to sets of ordered pairs or relations in intension, etc. Given this, consider common nouns like 'chair', 'table', 'strikeout', 'lap', 'gold', 'fist'. Do these all refer to their referents in the same way that 'Jim Valvano' refers to Jim Valvano? Is referring to a property of chairness or the set of chairs just like referring to an object like Jim Valvano? Is it even clear that all of these common nouns refer in the same way? The ontological grounds of these expressions seem different: chairs and tables are artifacts, gold is a natural kind, fists and laps are things at all only in a tenuous sense. And what about strikeouts? They owe their "existence" to the institution of baseball. Are they "in the world" the way gold is or the way chairs are? Does this make no difference to the reference relation that obtains between 'gold' and gold as opposed to the one that obtains between 'strikeout' and strikeouts? Why not?

Once again, if we do not assume in advance that a semantical relation underlies our linguistic abilities, we have good reason to doubt that there is one. As far as some general relation of reference or correlation between expressions and nonlinguistic entitites is concerned, it simply seems false to suppose that its existence is intuitively obvious once we inspect the various cases that seem relevant. If behavior is our guide, or if we ask whether all these cases of reference presuppose the same ability, we have good reason for denying the existence of a general reference relation that extends to all parts of language. It is not intuitively obvious, nor does common sense dictate, that referring to electrons is the same as referring to chairs, which is the same as referring to fictional creatures, which is the same as referring to Jim Valvano, which is the same as referring to beauty. In short, it is not clear that 'refers' in the previous sentence is being used in the same way throughout; therefore, it is not even clear that a *single* relationship is being invoked, let alone that we have a clear understanding of what that relationship is. If nothing else, the grounds we adduce in concluding that we have referred successfully in each case are quite different, and this alone should shake our faith that we have any common-sense grasp of reference in the theoretical sense that an account of linguistic productivity requires.

The same is true of other semantical terms. 'True', 'corresponds', or 'situation' are virtually parallel to 'refer' in their behavior. For example, is it so reasonable to believe that there is a property—truth—that all true sentences share? Consider sentences (3)–(6):

(3) Bellerophon captured Pegasus

(4) There are six kinds of quarks

(5) Turner was the first English painter to understand the reality of color

(6) Jim Valvano coached a smart game against Houston in the NCAA finals

Is (3) true in the same way as (4), or (5), or (6)? Are the situations described by (3)–(6) similar in any interesting sense except that they can all be "depicted" or "expressed" linguistically? It is often conceded that the first sentence is only "fictionally" true—in other words, that it is different from the other three. But why say this? Does (3) "feel" all that different from (5)? Do (4) and (5) seem that much like (6)? Why believe that sentences (4), (5), (6) are all true in some way that is similar to but different from the way in which (3) is true? What, except a commitment to a Neo-Fregean theory of meaning, hangs in the balance? Do we use, defend, or understand these sentences in the same ways? What reason do we have for treating them differently or alike? At this point, given the skeptical question of the previous section, it will not do to point to the *theoretical* intent of these semantical notions. We are trying to see the point of these notions, and we have been told that it can be intuitively appreciated by considering cases. We cannot now be told that the cases only bear on a notion of truth, for example, considered as a theoretical notion within a total theory of meaning. To say this would require an *explication* of the theoretical notion. But this, as we have seen, is not forthcoming.

When pressed to explicate their theoretical terms, semantical theorists reply, as in the previous section, that no further explication can be given, since the notions are just those of rock bottom common sense. When common sense is shown to be more equivocal than initially supposed, they reply that this is not surprising, since they intend the notions to be construed as part of a theoretical vocabulary, not in their common-sense uses. But clearly they cannot have it both ways. If 'refers', etc., are used as technical notions, then demands for explication are perfectly appropriate. If common sense is the basis, then it must be conceded that from this vantage point, these notions are anything but clear.

The skeptical point then stands. Whatever our ordinary understanding is of terms such as 'refers' or 'true', it does not support an understanding of the sort these notions require within a Neo-Fregean theory of meaning. Even a brief survey of how different words are used leads quickly to doubts of whether there is one relation called 'reference' in which all meaningful expressions stand to nonlinguistic entities and of which we have a tolerably clear understanding. The same holds for truth and the other semantical notions; it is not at all obvious that whenever we say that a certain sentence is true, we mean that it has the same property shared by all the other sentences we consider true. There is no obvious reason for believing that there is much in common among all the sentences we call true, at least if normal use is our guide. The fact seems to be that a simple inspection of the way words normally function will not serve to put off a skeptic's reasonable qualms. Further, depending on the context of use and the words we are focusing on, 'refers', is true', 'is an object', 'describes a situation' appear to function differently. Therefore, the semantical theorist's simple reply seems quite unsupported.

In short, there is little reason to believe that we already have an understanding of reference, truth, or any other semantical notion that could be invoked through examples as an intuitive basis for a Neo-Fregean theory of meaning. Different terms "refer" (in the ordinary sense of the word) in different ways: nouns are neither like verbs nor like names. Indeed, in the ordinary sense of the word, most words do not refer or correspond to nonlinguistic entitites at all. As we normally use the words, for example, verbs do not "refer" or "correspond" to properties or relations.

Even within a syntactic category there are important differences. For example, intuitively fictional names are not like names of actual individuals, nor are natural kind terms intuitively similar to the names of artifacts like chairs or institutional "objects" like strikeouts. If all these kinds of words really function in the same way at bottom, the only difference being the entities they pick out or refer to, then semantical theorists must present a rather elaborate story to motivate this claim, a story that is responsive to the kinds of demands made in the previous section. Neo-Fregean semantical theorists hold that notions like "truth" and "reference" have a firm intuitive basis. This is because they consider very simple cases—for example, proper names of nonfictional entities. They then proceed on the assumption that all of language works in this way. For example: 'Abe Lincoln' and 'George Washington' refer to their respective referents in the same way. They differ in meaning not because they refer differently, but because they refer to different things—Abe Lincoln and George Washington, respectively. They then generalize the account. *All* linguistic items refer in the same way. All of the differences they exhibit are the result of their referring to different referents: individuals, sets, properties, truth values, fictional entities, or whatever. The problem with this sort of generalization is that it loosens the intuitive grip on the notion of reference that the original examples were intended to have us focus on. There is no intuitive "reference"-similarity of any robustness that all such items share. Therefore, if such a similarity is to be invoked, semantical theorists cannot simply direct our attention back once again to the simple case of 'Lincoln' and 'Washington'. Their theory demands more of us than such examples can sustain. To understand what Neo-Fregeans intend by their theoretical vocabulary, we need an account of 'reference', 'true', 'object', 'situation', etc., not simply a list of examples. As yet we surely have no such account, and in my opinion we have little reason to think that one is imminently forthcoming. Moreover, unless one is developed an account of linguistic productivity has not been provided.

Context Sensitivity

A possible retort to the point just made is that the critic of a Neo-Fregean semantical theory has been demanding too much. The critic has been asking for an elucidation of the *general* notion of truth, reference, object, etc. However, why insist on general accounts? Why not rehabilitate the theorist's reply by conceding that there is no *single* general notion like "truth" (for example) but rather a series of indexical notions. This sort of reply is suggested by model theorists who wish to substitute the notion "truth-in-a-model" for the simple notion of truth as the central interpretive predicate. Such theories end up relativizing the notion of truth. In addition, it is customary to specify the model relative to a collection of indices whose values are, among other things, the time, place, and persons of the utterance situation. Some theories include further contextual indices as well: beliefs of the discourse participants, their hopes, knowledge, prior discourse, and more. All of this results in highly contextualized semantical notions rather than the more context-insensitive notions discussed here. On this view, 'true', 'refers', etc., would be terms whose exact meaning or import could only be contextually determined. However, in any given context of use, the sense of these terms is set and they then enter into a theory of meaning.

This sort of approach is motivated by the suspicion that the extreme generality of a Neo-Fregean theory is probably unattainable. The theoretical notions are opaque because they are really not one notion but a series of them whose import can only be settled contextually. What counts as a property or as the referent of a name (e.g., an individual), or what it is for a sentence to be true or for a state of affairs to obtain or be described cannot be settled except in a context of use. It is for this reason that the demands of the skeptic could not be met. The obvious solution is to construe these notions as hidden indexicals and thereby to (tacitly) concede that a single, unified nonindexical approach is unattainable.

There are serious problems with such an account, however. The first is to specify the contextual indices that are relevant to fixing the meaning of these terms. As noted, the contextual parameters of time, place, and person are not enough; they surely do not suffice to explain all that we intend by contextual difference. What more must be added?

A current influential theory suggests that relevant context parameters may include those objects perceived or imagined by persons in the context, the shared common knowledge, previous contexts, beliefs, hopes, desires, etc., of the speakers, and more—in short, whatever is needed.[15] The obvious danger is that we want to avoid the outcome in which linguistic items—for example, sentences—are correlated one to one with different contexts. Why do we want to avoid this? Recall that a theory of meaning is supposed to explain why sentences mean what they mean and what it is that native speakers know about meaning that enables them to be linguistically productive. The explanation offered here is that we identify the meaning of a sentence with the state of affairs it depicts, the notion "state of affairs" itself being determined by the context. In short, we can identify the meaning of a sentence on any given occasion of use with the contextual indices that determine its meaning. But what are these indices, and how do they go about determining the meaning of a sentence? There needs to be some *general* account of how they do this. Otherwise, we have not so much said *how* linguistic items have meaning as *that* they have it. If all we do is assign an interpretation for a sentence once given a context, then we have not explained how a native speaker is able to use sentences appropriately until we explain what it is for a native speaker in general to be "given a context." The capacity to use sentences appropriately presupposes abilities that cut across contexts of use. All we do when we assign a sentence an interpretation given a context (but have no context-insensitive rules on which to base these interpretations) is reaffirm that sentences have meanings and that native speakers are linguistically productive.

To repeat, the problem is not to *justify* our beliefs that particular sentences mean what they do but to *explain* how they mean what they do and how knowing this enables speakers to be linguistically productive. This is, in effect, a request for the general rules that determine meaning in the particular case. Correlating sentences to contexts does not advance this enterprise any more than correlating sentences with states of affairs or truth conditions, unless a general theory of how contextual indices operate is forthcoming. To accomplish this, one must elaborate a finite set of relevant indices and then a finite set of rules that say when and how they are relevant. It will not do to simply cite context as an *explanatory* parameter. "Context" is the name of the problem, not a solution. If there are as many different rules of context as there are sentences and contexts, then nothing has been gained by simply correlating linguistic items with contexts. For the theory of meaning, the important elements are the general rules, not the correlation with context. The set of indices and the rules for their use cannot be themselves contextually sensitive. Otherwise, we would see neither how a sentence means what it does nor how a speaker could come to know the meaning of a linguistic item. If the rules determining the meaning of an expression were themselves context sensitive, they would be rules in only the most degenerate sense. There would be nothing general about them, and they could do no more than reiterate that a sentence means what it means and not something else, and that people know what they know, and that this is what underlies their capacity to be linguistically productive. Clearly, this will not advance our understanding. If context is to be invoked, there must be *general* contextual parameters that are relevant across different occasions of use and *general* rules governing their function. In effect, therefore, a reply such as this simply moves the problem back one stage. We still need general rules. Once we have them—though as yet we have not even begun to develop them, except most impressionistically—we can use semantical notions like "object," "true," "referent," etc. However, at that point the explanatory burden of the theory of meaning will be carried by the theory of contextual indices and rules. The semantical notions will be theoretically secondary and will only come into their own once the indices fix their interpretations. We can speculate about what such a revised semantical theory might look like—though not fruitfully, in my opinion, since a general theory of contextual indices and rules does not now exist. Unfortunately, there is no theory (i.e., a set of rules) such that for every sentence this one theory determines its meaning. More usual is the case where the quantifier order is reversed: for every sentence a (different) indexical account is provided; different contextual parameters are invoked in accounting for the relevant phenomena. Again, this does not help to explain how it is that sentences or linguistic items mean what they do or how linguistic productivity is possible. It simply reiterates the fact that speakers somehow have this capacity.

It will not be easy to develop such a theory of context. Consider the notion "context" itself. The hope of model theorists rests on the assumption that this notion can be unpacked to form the foundation of a general theory of interpretation. However, the notion of context is beset by many of the same problems characteristic of the other semantical notions considered. So, for example, the notion "context" is as "context dependent" for its import as are notions like "truth," "reference," "object," etc. Moreover, it seems likely that the crucial notion will not be "context," but "*relevant* context." Do we really have reason to think that the notion of relevance can be fixed once and for all, or that we can discover an algorithmic or rule-based procedure for determining it? What is contextually relevant seems to switch from context to context and is not something that appears to be given ahead of time. Indeed, I believe that this is Wittgenstein's keenest observation and the foundation of his attack against Neo-Fregean theories of meaning. Let me explain.

In the *Philosophical Investigations*, Wittgenstein tried to suggest that the idealization concerning language that logicians and semantical theorists make in order to develop their theories begs most of the important issues. He did this by describing the variety of language, its myriad uses, and, in particular, the crucial role that contextual parameters play in determining the "meaning" of a linguistic expression like a sentence. He noted that these contextual parameters do not themselves appear to be liable to precontextual elaboration. At the very least, Wittgenstein can be read as making the accurate observation that, as yet, there is no general theory about what must or will count as a significant or relevant context that is itself context insensitive. But without such account we have no general theory of interpretation or linguistic productivity. Given this view, the real trouble with semantical theories is that they *presuppose* that there is something fixed that is nonlinguistic and that acts as the backdrop against which rules of interpretation are constructed. It is the existence of such a fixed backdrop that a semantical theory couched in terms of a vocabulary of "properties," "object," "reference," "correspondence," etc., needs if it is to have explanatory clout. Unfortunately, it is unclear what the properties of this fixed backdrop are. Semantical theorists presuppose that it has all the properties needed to account for linguistic productivity, but they never say what those properties are. The formalism then tends to obscure the fact that the hard problems have not been solved but instead have been presupposed out of existence in the act of assuming the fixed backdrop against which interpretation rules and procedures are then given.

There is another way to put this. Semantical theorists seem to think that the weakness of translation theories is that they postulate a mentalistic language of thought. But this is not the real problem with translation theories. The real problem is that what it is to know mentalese is as opaque as what it is to know a natural language. In other words, translation theories *assume* the existence of a fixed, already interpreted background without saying what such a fixed background is or what properties it has. All we know about it is that it appears to have exactly the same complexity as natural language and therefore appears to raise exactly the same sorts of problems as the original issue of linguistic productivity.

To avoid what they perceive as the translation theorists' circularity, semantical theorists postulate that a reference relation between linguistic expressions and nonlinguistic entities lies at the core of a theory of meaning. Thus, semanticists also postulate a fixed background, but they claim it is not linguistic like mentalese. However, on inspection it appears to have all the complexity of linguistic expressions. The nonlinguistic entities that interpret a linguistic expression look very language-like. And this is the problem. We seem to require an explanation of what it is to have such a fixed background that is virtually identical to explaining what it is for a linguistic expression to be meaningful. Moreover, knowing that the fixed background has one or another property seems to invoke the same capacities and abilities that it takes to explain linguistic productivity. In short, we seem to be "explaining" the problem by assuming it is solved. In effect, therefore, the semanticists misconstrue the source of the translation theorists' explanatory inadequacies. The problem lies in postulating a fixed background. Whether it is a mentalistic language of thought, or an external world, or fixed confirmation or verification procedures is secondary. The trouble with semantical and indexical pragmatic theories of meaning is that their idealizations presuppose what must be explained, by taking as given the existence of a fixed, already interpreted background against which interpretation theory proceeds.

Conclusion

As I remarked at the outset, late Wittgensteinian considerations such as these cannot in general be conclusive. They are meant to undermine the reasonableness of a particular kind of idealization. They ask one to consider the point of the enterprise, the problem it means to deal with, and, in light of this, the adequacy of the theoretical stance assumed. The aim of this chapter was not to settle once and for all whether some variant of a Neo-Fregean theory might succeed (I do not believe such a general sort of argument can ever be given), but to cast a jaundiced eye on the complacent assumption that semantical theories have already basically explained linguistic productivity or that any theory of meaning that does not exploit notions like "truth," "reference," "object," etc., is for that reason less explanatory than interpretation theories. Such attitudes are only warranted if we take semantical notions as clearly understood. In my opinion, no such assumption is warranted. Semantical theorists have proceeded as if the objections noted above had already been met, or at least could be easily answered. In effect, they have simply assumed that semantical notions are crucial rather than showing what they come to and how they explain linguistic productivity. The goal of their research has been to determine which semantical account is most adequate, which semantical notions are basic and which derived, which refinements these notions require, etc. In short, most theoreticians have simply assumed that a theory of natural language interpretation must invoke semantical notions, without asking whether such notions are appropriate vehicles for explaining the problem of linguistic productivity.

One last point. Doesn't this criticism vitiate the account of structural meaning outlined in chapters 2 through 5? I believe that the answer is no. As I argued in chapter 6, the proposed theory of quantifier-quantifier and quantifier-pronoun interactions is strongly syntactic. It is basically a translation theory. It is defined over syntactic entities, that is, the shape a string has. Its rules seem to be use insensitive and to hold regardless of context. In fact, they appear to hold even when the sentences considered are quite uninterpretable:

(1) a.   That it$_i$ is both round and square characterizes the$_i$ round square

   b.   *That it$_i$ is both round and square characterizes every$_i$ round square

The fact that (1b) is far less acceptable than (1a) despite the "meaning" of both being opaque (if not gibberish) was used as evidence that the rules presented in chapters 2 through 5 should not be construed semantically. What is nice about syntactic notions is that they concern only the linguistic elements of a string. We need not assume any "reference" relations that must be explicated or context effects that must be faced. In fact, it was the robustness of the phenomena and the judgments—their contextual insensitivity—that first led me to the view that these types of data should be dealt with in *purely* syntactic terms. Why didn't it matter whether the sentences were sensible or gibberish (i.e., without truth conditions), if semantical notions were really the key to understanding these phenomena? At any rate, the syntactic nature of the account enables it to ward off the objections cited above.

Let me put this one more way. Quantifier-quantifier and quantifier-pronoun interactions involve the relations of linguistic entities to one another. Two basic kinds of approaches to such data are conceivable. One would view them as cross-reference relations, the other as reference relations. The latter approach would try to explain cross-reference relations—i.e., when and how cross-reference works—in terms of a theory of reference. The former approach would see these as two different issues. The rules determining the scope of the interaction of linguistic items are independent of questions of the relation of linguistic items to nonlinguistic objects. This approach essentially divorces the analysis of cross-reference or coreference from an analysis of reference. A syntactic approach to these phenomena is a reflection of seeing the issues concerning reference as being irrelevant to issues concerning cross-reference, at least for this range of cases. An account of quantifier-quantifier and quantifier-pronoun interactions need not proceed via a theory of reference. In effect, the theory in chapters 2 through 5 proceeds on the assumption that cross-reference is a syntactic phenomenon whose properties can be explicated without basing them in a semantical theory of reference. In my view, given the Wittgensteinian shortcomings of current semantical approaches, it is precisely when a translational approach can be adopted that nontrivial accounts of some linguistic phenomena can be provided.

If this line of reasoning is correct, then to explain linguistic productivity we may have to start questioning the apparent cogency of certain kinds of questions, or at least the informativeness of the answers they usually elicit. Certain kinds of questions invite certain kinds of answers. For example, when one asks for the meaning of a sentence or inquires what speakers know when they know the meaning of a sentence, there is a temptation to give a single, all-encompassing answer: the proposition it expresses, its truth conditions, the state of affairs it pictures, etc. This sort of answer presupposes that all sentences have a certain property *in common* that is crucial to their meaning and that a competent native speaker knows. Indeed, it is in virtue of knowing this feature of a sentence that a native speaker is considered competent. In short, the question seems to require an answer that states in effect, that meaning is *one* thing and that what one grasps when one grasps the meaning of a sentence is *one thing*, regardless of the sentence being discussed. In a word, there is something that all sentences have that accounts for (or is a necessary part of any account of) their meaningfulness.

The remarks earlier in the chapter, derived essentially from the later Wittgenstein, are meant to shake our faith that the question above has the sort of answer it invites or that such answers address, rather than beg, the relevant issues. At the very least, there may not be any single answer. What meaning is and what is grasped may depend on the specific kind of sentence under consideration. If so, language is not a unified whole, but a crazy quilt. Different parts have different properties, with the result that no unified account of meaning will be forthcoming. This is surely a coherent possibility. Keeping it squarely in mind can serve as an important antidote to the view that there *must* be a single, unified account of what meaning is and how it operates in natural language or that we already understand what making such an assumption amounts to. More specifically, accounts of meaning will have to be quite sensitive to the kinds of sentences involved. There may not be a general account of what it is to know the meaning of an arbitrary sentence.

In fact, it often appears that things are even worse than this. Wittgenstein gives myriads of examples that appear to indicate that meaning is even more sensitive to context or subject matter than already suggested. It often seems that each sentence must be taken on its own terms. Modes of classification will themselves be context sensitive and will carry no general implications. In short, whether a sentence is fictitious seems to be a property not of the sentence but of the sentence in context. Thus, the same sentence often seems to have a different interpretation depending on its use. What sentences are literal appears to change across contexts, as does what sentences are theoretical, observational, etc. Moreover, in the worst cases, the criteria for these various categorizations themselves appears to shift with context. If both the categories and what falls under them shift with change of context, no theory of meaning of any sort will be forthcoming. The fact of linguistic productivity will remain a mystery. Given the state of current research, this possibility cannot be lightly dismissed. We have no general theory of meaning or context effects. We do not know what features of a context are, *in general*, relevant. We have no finite set of context parameters and no theory of how these parameters affect sentence meaning in general. At present, we *de facto* take each sentence as it comes and construct an account for it. The hope seems to be that eventually we will have isolated all the relevant parameters. As yet, there is no end in sight. At the very least, these sorts of cases are the appearances that an account of linguistic productivity will have to explain away. What is needed is tolerably clear. How to achieve it remains a mystery.

Thus, I have suggested that semantical theories have not been able to give us what we want from a theory of interpretation and that more context-sensitive pragmatic theories cannot give us what we need: *general* rules of interpretation. In my opinion, semantic and pragmatic approaches to meaning will not get beyond formal pyrotechnics unless they find some way of dealing with the sorts of issues raised above.

Syntactic approaches to meaning can sidestep these sorts of worries. In fact, it has been my goal in this chapter to suggest that supplementing the syntactic account presented in chapters 2 through 5 with a semantics may not advance the cause very much. Whether semantical or pragmatic theories are capable of carrying any explanatory weight, in light of the problems I have discussed, is a question that interpretation theorists must squarely face. Realizing the extreme modesty of the contribution that current approaches to meaning make to solving the problem of linguistic productivity is, in my opinion, an important first step.

In this book I have considered how to approach meaning in natural language. What are the theoretically necessary basic concepts? What is the nature of the interpretive rules for specific types of data that we pretheoretically think of as pertaining to meaning? What do native speakers learn and what do they tacitly know about the interpretive procedures of their native languages?

These questions are not really novel. The contribution of this book lies, I believe, in how I have pursued these issues and the emphasis I have placed on syntactic translation theories in particular. I have proposed that questions that philosophers and logicians often ask about meaning can be fruitfully carried on within a framework of assumptions characteristic of work in generative grammar. I have tried to redeem this assumption by arguing in detail that rather subtle and interesting

insights can be achieved concerning the interpretive structures underlying our abilities to make judgments about sentences involving quantifier-quantifier and quantifier-pronoun interactions.

The results of these efforts are, to my mind, quite surprising. I have
argued, for example, that for this range of "meaning" data the correct
theory of interpretation should not be seen as a semantical theory but
as a syntactic one. Moreover, I have noted that it is not at all clear
what a semantical theory is supposed to add to the admittedly partial
accounts that translation theories provide. The debate between meaning
theorists who advocate translational approaches and those who advocate
semantical approaches appears more and more like an idle controversy.
The problem is not whether there is a language of thought or a reference
relation but rather what it is to have a fixed, already interpreted backdrop
against which interpretation is supposed to proceed. Whether one sees
this background as mentalistic, as an external world, or as basic verification procedures appears to be of secondary importance. This conclusion, I believe, reiterates the nub of the late Wittgensteinian critique
of meaning theories. The problem is that once one has gotten beyond
the issues that a translation theory readily, indeed happily, accom-
modates, one is at sea. I have tried to show that this does not mean
that theories of meaning that stop here are trivial or uninteresting, as
many critics seem to suggest. But it does seem clear that much remains
to be done and no one has any very good idea of how to go about
doing it. Further progress awaits, I believe, a more penetrating analysis
of the fact that all agree is central to any theory of meaning: the fact
of linguistic productivity.

To date, three basic intuitions have been exploited in theorizing
about meaning: translation, communication, and representation. Translation theorists have construed the basic features of meaning as whatever
it is that we do when we translate. According to this theory, what it
means to understand a sentence can be explained in terms of what
sort of language it is translated into. If the "translation" is tacit, this
simply requires a language of thought. This language of thought also
conveniently mediates communication. For others, communication deserves primary emphasis. It determines what the basic notion of meaning
is and what we understand when understanding meaning. Still others
consider representation to be the central notion, one that is tied to
some conception of acquisition or learnability.

It may be, however, that these three notions ought not to be linked
very tightly. Perhaps none deserves greatest emphasis. The theory of
language as an instrument of communication, for example, may not
illuminate what it is that goes on "internally" when a speaker is being
linguistically productive. How one acquires a language may not be

trivially extendable into an account of communication. Translation and understanding are not the same under a normal conception of these notions, given that one can translate what one may not be able to understand. Furthermore, the problem of linguistic productivity may not be specific to *linguistic* systems but may be a reflex of behavioral productivity, creativity, or originality more generally. For example, organisms to which we might wish to ascribe some sorts of behavioral creativity do not all appear to have overt languagelike communication systems. The ability to represent and the ability to communicate may just not be the same. Perhaps the former rather than the latter is what is crucial to the kind of behavioral originality that linguistic productivity highlights. In short, after one abstracts from purely grammatical abilities, maybe the problem of linguistic productivity is not really a specifically linguistic issue at all.

These sorts of speculations deserve further reflection if the logjam in interpretation theory is ever to be broken. However this may be accomplished, two things are relatively clear. First, that *part* of the story of linguistic productivity will include an account of grammar and logical form of the kind outlined here. And second, that the remaining problems will not be substantially illuminated by the sorts of discussions characteristic of current work in formal semantical approaches to meaning. What will eventuate is a topic for future research.

Notes

Chapter 1

1. I will in particular be concentrating on generative theories of the Extended Standard Theory (EST) variety, among which the Government-Binding (GB) version developed in Chomsky 1981 is standard. In what follows, I will assume that a version of this theory is roughly correct.
2. This approach follows Dummett's 1976 account of the relation of theories of meaning and theories of understanding. Also see Davidson 1965.
3. For a general critique of innateness theories that concentrates on assumptions (a) and (b), see Putnam 1971. For an elaborated criticism of many of Putnam's points, see the introduction of Hornstein and Lightfoot 1981. Also see Wexler and Culicover 1980 on degree II learnability.
4. The fact that one need not worry about (a) and (b) too much seems all to the good. The counterarguments have been convincing only because they have been vague. At any rate, the issue is really moot, since it is deficiency (c) that lies at the heart of generative grammar's nativist approach.
5. See Chomsky 1965 and Lasnik 1980 for further discussion, and Berwick and Weinberg 1982 for an examination of the difference in linguistic importance between weak and strong generative capacity.
6. Much work in the theory of meaning takes entailment relations among sentences to be the subject of any reasonable theory of meaning. Furthermore, whether two sentences stand in an entailment relation is taken to be relatively unproblematic. This, unfortunately, is far from true. Entailment will be important to a theory of meaning just in case truth is. Whether truth is a core explanatory notion should be kept an open question. However, whether this notion comes to be seen as indispensable or not, one cannot assume that one can, by simple inspection, tell which sentences entail each another and which are related in different ways, e.g., via Gricean implicatures. In sum, whether entailment relations ought to be a central focus of a theory of meaning and, if so, which sentences stand in this relation are both open questions.
7. Consider, for example, Lewis's 1972 critique of Katz-Fodor theories of meaning. The assumption seems to be that unless one gives a model, one has done nothing that pertains to the issue of meaning in natural language. This is *not* to say that a Katz-Fodor theory is the right way to proceed. However, the fact that "markerese" is syntactic rather than semantic (i.e., no mapping to a model has been provided) is not in and of itself sufficient reason for questioning its adequacy. For more relevant reasons, see Fodor 1981. Criticisms of Procedural Semantics similar to Lewis's are offered by Fodor 1978. Once again, it is assumed that a theory of meaning must be a semantical theory, in this case a Tarskian theory of truth. Why, however, is not made clear. As in the case above, this does not mean that procedural theories are

either reasonable or interesting. However, the fact that they stay clear of semantical notions is not a sufficient reason for believing that they are inadequate. For further discussion of these issues, see chapters 6 and 7. For a critique of computer-based approaches to language such as Procedural Semantics, see Dresher and Hornstein 1976.

8. Whether highly context-sensitive rules are "rules" in any but a degenerate sense is open to question. See chapter 7 for a fuller discussion.

Chapter 2

1. Too much should not be made of this use of words. *Logical form*, in this context, is not intended to carry any of the metaphysical or ontological import that the term carries in the philosophical literature.

2. Variables in EST are defined as empty NP categories, i.e., [$_{NP}$ e], which are coindexed with operators. Variables are found in argument positions (A-positions). These positions include subject, object, indirect object, and object of a preposition. Operators are found in Ā-positions, e.g., in complementizer position or adjoined positions. For a full discussion, see Chomsky 1981.

3. QR, see Chomsky 1976 and May 1977. On the local nature of QR—i.e., that type II QPs are adjoined to the most proximate S-node—see chapter 4 and Aoun and Hornstein (forthcoming).

4. An element A c-commands an element B if and only if the first branching category dominating A also dominates B. For example, consider structure (i):

(i)

In (i) the first category dominating A is E. However, the first *branching* category dominating A is D. D in turn dominates B. Thus, A c-commands B. A also c-commands G, F, H, and J. Of these, only F c-commands A. See Reinhart 1976 for a full discussion of c-command.

5. 'Someone' is a type II QP, as are 'somewhere', 'something', 'somebody', 'sometime', etc. However, quantified NPs whose quantifier is 'some', such as 'some woman', 'some man', are not type II QPs. The latter expressions appear to function in some dialects more like type I QPs than type II QPs. In fact, 'some N' seems to function in such dialects quite similarly to 'a certain N'. I will discuss this later in the text.

6. The 'a' to be discussed here is the nongeneric, existential 'a'. Isolating this 'a' can be tricky. One way to make sure one is dealing with the existential 'a' is to embed it in the scope of a universal quantifier. For a discussion of generics, see chapter 5.

7. See Chomsky 1976 and Higginbotham 1980 for discussion of pronoun binding.

8. The judgments indicated here are for the existential 'a', not the generic 'a'. See note 6.

9. Stressed names—indeed, stressed elements in general—are subject to a rule of Focus. This rule moves the stressed element, by QR, to an Ā-position. In effect, stress creates structures of operator-variable form. See Chomsky 1976 for discussion, as well as note 23.

10. The Leftness Condition has recently been analyzed as a special instance of the Bijection

Principle in Koopman and Sportiche 1981. I consider their analysis and its relationship to the issues discussed here in chapter 4.

11. I say "relatively" insensitive because it appears that unstressed 'any' may interact with other operators in certain complex constructions. See Hintikka 1976a,b for discussion of some of these issues, as well as note 16.

12. In standard semantical approaches, the noninteraction of names with quantifiers is attributed to a uniqueness condition on names. In the account given here, a focus on the termlike nature of names is what allows the explanation for names to be extended to operators more generally, even those whose interpretation is not subject to uniqueness conditions. This does not mean that uniqueness is not sufficient to allow free scope permutations without affecting interpretation. Rather, it is not necessary. Operators that do not form operator-variable structures, but are not subject to uniqueness conditions, can nonetheless be regarded as branching, or freely permutable with respect to all other operators. The point made here is that this is true for all terms (elements not forming operator-variable structures), and not just names or definite descriptions. See chapter 3 for further discussion of the relationship between uniqueness and termhood in definite descriptions.

13. There is one kind of sentence that appears to require an existential treatment of 'any':

> (i) Is anyone home?

(i) is roughly paraphrased as (ii) rather than (iii), where '?' is the operator involved in yes/no questions:

> (ii) ? $\exists x$ (x home)

> (iii) $\forall x$? (x home)

One way around such cases is to note that '?' is a trigger for a negative polarity item (Linebarger 1980). For regular negations like 'not', 'not $\exists x$' is equivalent to '$\forall x$ not'. What if we extended such equivalence to '?'? We could then treat 'any' as having wide scope and explain its existential import by noting that 'any ?' is equivalent to '? $\exists x$'. In short, the yes/no question operator decomposes into two parts: a question operator and a hidden negation. The latter, like negation in general, permits the above equivalences and hence the existential reading in (i).

14. Similar data are discussed in Linebarger 1980.

15. This presentation of the Immediate Scope Condition (ISC) is adapted from Linebarger 1980. Her account treats the ISC as a condition on logical form rather than interpretation procedures. She thus interprets the scope part of the ISC syntactically. As I have argued, this notion cannot apply to 'any'-phrases, since they do not have operator-variable form in LF. I have therefore reinterpreted the ISC as a condition on interpretation procedures rather than LF.

16. If a branching account were to be pursued, the standard accounts would have to be altered in important ways. For example, branching would not be symmetrical. In standard accounts, if a quantifier A branches with respect to B, then B also branches with respect to A (see (34)). However, in English, if a branching account of 'any' is correct, then this is not the case.

> (i) John didn't give anyone a present

Here the existential phrase is conditioned by the interpretation of 'anyone'; thus, its interpretation cannot branch with respect to 'anyone'. In (ii), however, 'anyone' does not condition the interpretation of the existential.

> (ii) Someone doesn't like anyone

Note that in (ii), but not (i), the existential c-commands 'any'. Perhaps, then, A branches with respect to a type I QP B if and only if A c-commands B. This would account for the examples above.

17. For other examples of acceptable, yet ungrammatical, sentences, see Hornstein and Weinberg 1981.

18. Both types of 'any' are also immune to ECP violations, as discussed in the next section. Note that if different interpretive procedures are required to account for these two kinds of 'any', the main point will still be valid: the different interpretive procedures for 'any' do not correspond to different representations at LF. Interpretive interaction, if it is found to be necessary, is not due to QR or other mechanisms of syntactic scope. Also see note 23.

19. The ECP is defined as follows:

   (i) An empty category $[_\alpha$ e] must be properly governed.

   (ii) An element α properly governs an element β iff α governs β and
      a. β is a variable bound by an operator or
      b. α is adjacent to β.

   (iii) α governs β iff
      a. α is a lexical category and
      b. α and β c-command each other.

   For further discussion and details, see Chomsky 1981:250ff.

20. As noted in Chomsky 1981:234, Kayne 1979 gives some plausible English violations of the ECP. See Aoun, Hornstein, and Sportiche 1980 for a more elaborate discussion of the ECP and the case of multiple questions.

21. Sentences like (42a,b) are discussed in chapter 4 of Chomsky 1981. The difficulties he notes are eliminated if 'any' is treated as a type I QP.

22. What appears to be pronoun binding can occur even if binding is not involved. These sorts of cases are discussed in Evans 1977. As Evans points out, there are important differences between his cases of E-type pronouns and regular binding. Most overtly, there are complex conditions on pronoun agreement in the case of E-type pronouns that do not exist in the case of binding:

   (i)   Everyone$_i$ saw his$_i$ mother

   (ii) *If everyone$_i$ comes he$_i$ will have a good time

   (iii) If everyone comes they will have a good time

(i) is a regular case of pronoun binding. In (ii), since 'everyone' is a type II QP, the indicated coindexing is disallowed. (iii), however, is fine with 'everyone' and 'they' coreferential; it is an instance of E-type binding. In this book, I have tried to control for E-type effects by concentrating on examples such as (i) and (ii).

As Evans notes, pronoun binding and E-type binding exhibit other differences as well, of an interpretive variety. The cases he discusses and the ones considered here appear to be interpretively and structurally distinct. To take one example:

   (iv) Mary danced with many boys$_i$ and they$_i$ found her interesting.

(iv) does not mean 'Mary danced with many boys who found her interesting', which a bound pronoun approach would require. Similarly for (v):

   (v) John likes $\begin{cases} \text{just any dog}_i \\ \text{every dog}_i \end{cases}$ and $\begin{cases} \text{*it}_i \\ \text{they}_i \end{cases}$ like(s) him

23. Consider one more case. The proposed theory predicts dependencies among the five properties discussed in the text. Thus, for example, if an NP obeys the Leftness Condition, it will act like a type II quantified expression more generally. Consider the case of 'any' found in "insult" sentences:

(i) If anybody can do it, John can.

(ii) John won't talk to (just) anybody.

In these cases 'any' carries intonational stress. Therefore, by the rule of Focus, discussed in Chomsky 1976, it is moved by QR; that is, it is treated like a type II QP. Note that in (i) 'any' is *within* the scope of the conditional. Similarly, in (ii) it is in the scope of the negation. This case of 'any' (call it *insult-'any'*) is not interpretively independent in the sense discussed earlier. Moreover, it does not allow cross-sentence or cross-discourse coindexing, and it obeys the Leftness Condition:

(iii) *His$_i$ being sent home didn't worry (just) anybody$_i$

(iv) *If (just) anybody$_i$ can win, he$_i$ can.

(v) *John likes any dog$_i$ (stressed intonation). He$_i$ only likes Sam.

Here, sentences with insult-'any' do not act like the sentences with 'any' discussed in the text. The rule of Focus, plus the distinction between type I and type II QPs, explains why this is so and predicts the properties in (i)–(v).

Note as well that insult-'any' has the import of a universal quantifier. This adds some weight to the account of 'any' as a *single* interpretive element, i.e., a universal quantifier. The unstressed counterparts of (i) and (ii) would require the existential reading of 'any'. Stress appears to change these to universal 'any'. Why stress should be able to do this if there are in fact two types of 'any' is unclear. However, the assumption that 'any' is always universal accounts straightforwardly for these sorts of examples.

24. These sorts of semantical notions will be discussed in chapter 7.

Chapter 3

1. The coindexing indicated here between 'every peach' and 'them' is a case of E-type coreference, discussed briefly in note 22 of chapter 20. For what follows I will abstract away from the effects of such coindexing. This causes no significant difficulties, I believe, if we accept Evans's 1977 analysis. The cases of E-type binding are interpretively and syntactically distinguishable from the cases I discuss here. I mention this, because despite their being distinguishable, in the case of plural quantifiers such as 'all', 'many', and 'few', the simple test (checking whether the pronoun is plural or singular) does not work. Thus, a more subtle investigation is necessary.

2. For a clear elaboration of the two positions, see Kaplan 1970.

3. This approach interprets the Russellian analysis of definite descriptions to be claiming that they are parallel to regular quantifiers like 'every'. Strictly speaking, however, this was not Russell's analysis. There, definite descriptions were adjoined to predicates to yield terms. Here, they are treated as simple sentential operators, i.e., moved by QR just like other QPs. As it turns out, I believe, this approach is incorrect. However, it is a natural way of viewing Russell's proposal within the context of the assumptions made here.

4. The terms 'marked' and 'unmarked' are related to the salience that a particular value of a parameter has among the options made available by Universal Grammar. Some parametric values may be more "favored" than others in the sense that Universal Grammar assumes that a given parameter has a given value unless the primary linguistic data provide evidence that this is *not* the case. Such a parametric value is said to be *unmarked*. It is possible to have "degrees of markedness"; that is, a value *a* may be more marked than *b*, which is more marked than *c*.

5. The analysis presented here makes a rather strong prediction: namely, that whereas the logical form of quantified NPs may vary from language to language, the logical

form of definite descriptions may not. In *all* languages definite descriptions should pattern as in (A)–(E).

6. In suggesting a three-level theory, Barwise and Perry follow Kaplan. Where they part company with him is over whether to flesh out such a three-level theory in terms of a possible-worlds approach or, as they prefer, a model theory employing what they call "situations." I find neither situation semantics nor possible-worlds semantics particularly enlightening. However, this issue seems largely separable from the three-level hypothesis. See chapter 7 for further discussion of current model theoretical approaches to meaning.

7. Burge 1977 can, I believe, be read as making a very similar point. Beliefs do not dichotomize neatly for Burge any more than they do for Scheffler.

8. The conclusions relating to scope in propositional attitudes agree in substance with those of Jackendoff 1977. He also argues against traditional approaches and suggests a theory close in spirit to Kaplan's. His arguments against a scope analysis are acute and very convincing. Also see Jackendoff 1980.

Chapter 4

1. This chapter is based on work carried out with Joseph Aoun. For a more technical and fuller elaboration of the issues discussed here, as well as further applications, see Aoun and Hornstein (forthcoming). An earlier version of this material was presented at Northeast Linguistic Society, Montreal, 1982.

2. See Chomsky 1981 for the standard version of the binding theory and Aoun 1981 for the version adopted here.

3. Recall that we are only dealing with quantifier-quantifier interactions. Issues relating to opacity are not dealt with in terms of scope (see chapter 3).

4. This analysis of multiple questions was first proposed in Chomsky (1973). For an elaboration and extension of this proposal to 'wh'-in-situ constructions more generally, see Aoun, Hornstein, and Sportiche 1980.

5. This was suggested in Freidin 1978. The idea of construing Subjacency as a condition on structures rather than on rule application is supported by arguments in Aoun 1982. Aoun argues against derivational theories that postulate a level of D-structure. If these are no derivations in the theory of grammar, there can be no conditions on derivations or rule applications, e.g., the version of Subjacency noted above.

6. That variables are anaphoric was first suggested by Chomsky 1980, who subsequently rejected this view. Aoun 1981 revived this approach and showed how to incorporate an anaphoric view of variables with a version of the binding theory. This theory was then extended to apply to quantifier variables in Aoun and Hornstein (forthcoming), on which the present account is based.

7. *R-expressions* are elements such as names, variables, etc. "R" stands for 'referential'. This, however, should not be taken too seriously. See below in the text and chapter 6 for discussion.

8. Projections are defined in terms of the $\bar{X}$ system. Thus, for example, a VP (verb phrase) is a *projection* of the lexical category V (verb), which in turn is the head of this projection. VP $= V^n$ for some n. The *maximal projection* is the V^n with greatest n. Examples of maximal projections are the phrasal categories NP, VP, PP, S, $\bar{S}$.

To understand what the *minimal maximal projection* is, consider the following example:

(i) $[_S [_S NP_1 [_{VP} V NP_2 [_{PP} P NP_3]]]]$

NP_3 is in the projections PP, VP, S, and $\bar{S}$; its minimal maximal projection is PP. For NP_2 it is VP, and for NP_1 it is S.

α is a *governor* of β iff α is a lexical category (i.e., X^0) and subcategorizes β or α is an operator and binds β (e.g., a *wh*-element).

AGR is that part of *Inflection* (i.e., the auxiliary) responsible for subject-verb agreement phenomena. In English AGR co-varies with tense. In other languages, however (e.g., Portuguese and Turkish), infinitives may have AGR.

[NP,S] means 'subject of S'.

9. In Aoun 1981, (19) continues: "and the indexing does not violate the *i/i* condition." For our purposes, this addition is not necessary. See chapter 5 for a discussion of the *i/i* (*i-within-i*) Condition and Aoun and Hornstein (forthcoming) for further discussion of accessibility and QPs.

10. To be A-bound, an element must be coindexed with an element in an A-position, e.g., subject, object, indirect object. Ā-positions are peripheral adjoined positions (e.g., complementizer position) and are associated with no grammatical functions.

11. The second $\bar{S}_1$ category is formed by Chomsky-adjoining the operator via QR. Under standard assumptions, such adjunction does not create an independent governing category; that is, S_1 and $\bar{S}_1$ are in the same governing category.

12. (32b) is an instance of the Leftness Condition cases discussed in chapter 2.

13. The subject and the AGR element are co*super*scripted. However, for our purposes, what sort of coindexing pertains is unimportant. For a discussion of coindexing in general and cosuperscripting more particularly, see Chomsky 1981 and Aoun 1981.

14. A root sentence, in this case, is the matrix sentence.

15. Note that the same assumptions will suffice to explain the central cases of the scope of quantifiers in complex NPs:

   (i) Someone bought a picture of everyone

   (ii) Someone bought John's picture of everyone

(i) has interpretations with 'everyone' either wider than, or within the scope of, 'someone'. The first scope order corresponds to the case in which there are a number of pictures, one of each person, and every picture has a buyer. In the second case, there is a single group picture of everyone and a single buyer. In the second case, 'everyone' has scope *internal* to the NP.

Now consider sentence (ii). Here the first reading does not exist. Only the second (group) reading is available. Why? The structure of (ii) is (iii):

   (iii) someone bought $[_{NP}$ John's $[_{\bar{N}}[_N$ picture] of everyone]]]

In (iii) the first reading above would correspond to (iv):

   (iv) $[_S$ everyone$_x$ $[_S$ someone$_y$ $[y$ bought $[_{NP}$ John's picture of $x]]]]$

'x', however, must be X-bound in its governing category. In this case, NP is the governing category. 'John' is the accessible subject. Therefore, 'x' is X-free in NP and (iv) is an illicit structure. The only possibility is that 'everyone' remains internal to the NP:

   (v) $[_S$ someone$_y$ $[_S y$ bought $[_{NP}$ John's $[_{\bar{N}}$ everyone$_x$ $[_{\bar{N}}[_N$ picture] of $x]]]]]$

The structure of the internal reading is discussed in Fiengo and Higginbotham 1982. See Aoun 1981 for discussion of anaphors in NPs with subjects.

16. For 'wh'-in-situ, there is an optional +WH in matrix COMP position (Aoun, Hornstein, and Sportiche 1980). This +WH must appear in matrix clauses; in other words, the evidence for its existence can be provided by simple Ss.

Kayne, cited in Chomsky (1981), observes that certain negative elements like 'nobody' can act like type III QPs. Such cases parallel the 'ne...personne' cases where negations act as scope indicators.

Chapter 5

1. That is, the 'donkey'-phrase is interpretively independent of the QP. Strictly speaking, such phrases are scopeless (see chapter 2).

2. This is the main idea behind the analysis in Haïk 1982. In 'donkey'-sentences, 'everyone' and the 'donkey'-phrase form a single quantifier for the purposes of pronoun binding. In effect, the scope of the 'donkey'-phrase derives from the scope of the head of the relative clause. This yields the result that the 'donkey'-phrase has the scope of the entire relative. In short, if 'everyone' and 'a donkey' are treated as a single operator, the 'donkey'-phrase receives the entire sentence as its scope domain.

3. This example is not a problem for Haïk's approach but mainly because it is stipulated that indirect binding is possible only with a universal QP in the head of the relative clause and a noninherent QP like 'a' in the relative clause itself. There are some similarities between Haïk's analysis and mine. Both distinguish different kinds of QPs. However, whereas Haïk 1982 construes the pronoun binding and relative quantifier scope as both being due to the same mechanism, my analysis divorces the two. I would like to thank I. Haïk for useful discussion of these issues.

   An approach similar to that of Haïk 1982 is presented in both Kamp 1982 and Heim 1982. Unlike Haïk's, this approach is more semantical than syntactic. In Kamp's theory, for example (Heim's is virtually identical), Discourse Representations (DR) are derived. 'A donkey' in 'donkey'-sentences is in an accessible DR, but not so 'every donkey' in (5). According to Kamp, the reason is that universal QPs are really hidden conditionals. But if this is so, why is 'A man who owns any donkey beats it' acceptable? If 'any' is a universal QP, as suggested in chapter 2, (cf. note 23, chapter 2 as well), it should also be ruled out. Kamp's DRs, in effect, mimic scope relations by whether or not a DR box is or is not accessible to some other DR box. However, to go beyond simple stipulation, it must be explained *why* 'any' is in an accessible DR box but 'every' is not and why 'a' patterns like 'any' rather than 'every'. This is what the theory I present attempts to do. I do not see that either Kamp's or Heim's account succeeds.

   One last point. Kamp 1982 crucially assumes that universal QPs have DRs of conditional form. However, it is quite well known that this analysis of universal QPs does not generalize very well to other quantifiers; see Wiggins 1980. If this analysis of universal QPs is revised, then Kamp's theory cannot explain the unacceptability of (5) at all. A key issue, therefore, is to what degree the analysis of 'Every man runs', for example, as '$\forall x(M(x) \rightarrow R(x))$' is linguistically well motivated. Other QPs cannot be treated as unrestricted. Why, then, believe that 'every' should be so treated?

4. It is interesting to consider whether 'a'-phrases can ever have a dual structural description except in 'donkey'-sentences. It seems that they can:

   (i) a. Everyone dissected a frog's heart$_i$ while Fred described its$_i$ peculiar physiology

   b. Everyone drew a beaver$_i$ and Bill described its$_i$ typical habitat

   In these cases the 'it' seems to be coindexed with the 'a'-phrase, but it carries generic import. The 'a'-phrase itself is behaving like a regular existentially quantified NP; that is, more than one frog's heart was dissected and several beaver pictures were drawn.

   I am grateful to Ruth Kempson for bringing this possibility to my attention.

5. Haïk 1982 dispenses with the rule of QR but obtains its effects through a more complex process of indexing. This appears to be a notational variant of a QR analysis, the more complex indexing procedure taking the place of the regular indexing procedures plus the rule QR. Suitably modified, the remarks here apply to this theory as well.

6. Though this is necessary for the other examples noted above as well, in particular, the 'easy-to-please'-constructions.

7. The problem is not to give an interpretation for these kinds of sentences but to explain, on general grounds, how they get the interpretations they have. Both Kamp 1982 and Heim 1982 give a model theoretic account that represents the interpretation of such sentences. However, it is not clear how this interpretation is obtained, i.e., what general interpretive principles underlie it. In fact, as we shall see, the structures underlying 'donkey'-sentences can support two alternative interpretations, only one of which is realized in the case of the sentences themselves. The problem is to explain why the other interpretation is not available.

A version of this section on 'donkey'-sentences was presented to the University of Massachusetts Linguistics Colloquium. I would like to thank its participants, especially Mats Rooth and Ruth Kempson, for helping me clarify these issues. Of course, they are not responsible for the conclusions I have drawn from their helpful discussion.

8. See Carlson and Hintikka 1979, for example. It is also well known that generics are not identical to universally quantified phrases. I will assume that the standard assumption that generics and universal quantifiers are related is correct.

9. In short, I agree with Kamp's and Heim's interpretation of these sentences and with Haïk's analytic approach to them. With Haïk, I advocate a syntactic rather than a semantical analysis. With Kamp and Heim, I agree that the 'donkey'-phrase-'it' relation is analogous to a universal quantifier–pronoun relation.

Note, further, that an approach exploiting E-type binding will not work in these cases. (i) would be the form of an E-type 'donkey'-sentence.

(i) Everyone who owns a donkey beats *them*

It parallels examples such as (ii):

(ii) If everyone kissed someone, John kissed them too

The fact that a singular pronoun can be the bindee indicates that this is not a case of E-type binding.

10. Taraldsen 1979 points out an apparent counterexample to a Reconstruction analysis. He notes the following sentences:

(i) *Which picture of John$_i$ did he $_i$ buy

(ii) Which picture that John$_i$ liked did he$_i$ buy

Why is it that (ii) is acceptable, whereas (i) is not? (i) is unacceptable because of Reconstruction. With the 'wh'-phrase interpreted from object position (it is coindexed with the trace in object position; cf. (iii)), 'he' c-commands 'John'; thus, coindexing is prohibited by principle (C) of the binding theory:

(iii) $[_S[_{NP_i}$ which picture of John$]$ $[_S$ he buy t$_i]]$

On this reasoning, though, shouldn't (ii) be ruled out as well? Its LF is (iv):

(iv) $[_S[_{NP_i}$ which picture $[_S$ that John$_i$ liked$]]$ $[_S$ he$_i$ buy t$_i]]$

With the 'wh'-phrase interpreted from 't$_i$', 'he$_i$' c-commands 'John$_i$'; the structure should be ill formed, since it violates principle (C). Nonetheless, it seems fine.

One way of dealing with the problem is to say that (iv) is indeed ill formed. The *grammar* prohibits the indicated binding in both (i) and (ii). However, there is a nongrammatical principle that allows the coreference of 'John' and 'he' in (ii) but not in (i). Let us assume that this is a discourse principle, based on the fact that the unit of discourse analysis is the S. According to this principle, NPs that one names can be the referents of pronouns in a discourse, and these NPs are stored on leaving the S that contains them. Being a processing principle, this discourse principle is sensitive to left-right asymmetries. Thus, (v) is more acceptable than (vi) and (vii)—'John' is available for referential duties for pronouns later in the discourse in (v).

(v)   John$_i$ played baseball. He$_i$ went home. He$_i$ drank a beer.

(vi)   *He$_i$ played baseball. John$_i$ went home. He$_i$ drank a beer.

(vii) *He$_i$ played baseball. He$_i$ went home. John$_i$ drank a beer.

If some such principle is assumed, the acceptability of (ii) can be traced to it. Note that in (ii), but not (i), 'John' is located in an S—i.e., the relative clause. Therefore, it can be picked up by the discourse principle for use later on as a referent for a "free" pronoun. The discourse principle thus allows the interpretation in (ii), not the grammar.

What sort of evidence can we find to support the existence of such a discourse principle? Since it is sensitive to left-right asymmetries, names that occur earlier (to the left) can be used as referents for pronouns that occur later (to the right). Consider (viii):

(viii)   *Which picture did he$_i$ buy that John$_i$ liked

(viii) is the extraposed version of (ii); the relative clause is moved to the right. The analysis predicts that (viii) should be unacceptable, as it is. The grammar prohibits coindexing between 'he' and 'John', because of Reconstruction. Moreover, the discourse principle cannot operate in this case, because 'John' is to the right of the pronoun 'he' and is therefore not available for discourse reference. All that extraposition does is to alter the left-right relations of the pronoun and name in (ii) and (viii). This, however, is enough to render the sentence unacceptable, given Reconstruction and the discourse principle.

Consider one more set of cases.

(ix) a.   *After John$_i$'s run, he$_i$ drank a beer

    b.   *He$_i$ drank a beer after John$_i$'s run

    c.   After John$_i$ ran, he$_i$ drank a beer

    d.   *He$_i$ drank a beer after John$_i$ ran

Regardless of whether or not the 'after'-phrase is preposed, 'he', the subject, c-commands the elements in that phrase. This accounts for the unacceptability of (ixa) and (ixb). However, (ixc) is fine. The discourse principle would explain why. 'John' is in an S in (ixc), but in an NP in (ixa,b). Therefore, in (ixc), but not in (ixa,b), it can be picked up for later referential use by the discourse principle. Note also that (ixd) is predicted to be unacceptable, as it in fact is, since 'John' is now to the right of 'he'.

In the case of preposed PPs, Reconstruction does not obtain, as can be seen by considering (x):

(x)   *After his$_i$ long speech, everyone$_i$ fell asleep

(x) is far less acceptable than (xi):

(xi)   Which of his$_i$ pictures did every artist$_i$ refuse to sell

This is easily accounted for if (xi), but not (x), involves Reconstruction. If (x) is not reconstructed, then its unacceptability follows from the Leftness Condition.

Note one last feature of this principle. As observed, it picks up *names* for later discourse reference:

(xii) a.   Which picture that $\begin{Bmatrix} \text{a certain man}_i \\ \text{anyone}_i \end{Bmatrix}$ can get cheap will he$_i$ buy

b. *Which picture will he$_i$ buy that $\begin{Bmatrix} \text{a certain man}_i \\ \text{anyone}_i \end{Bmatrix}$ can get cheap

These sentences parallel (ii) and (viii). In short, once again type I QPs like 'any' and 'a certain' are acting like names. This, I believe, further corroborates the analysis presented in chapter 2. Contrast (xii) with (xiii):

(xiii) *Which picture that everyone$_i$ got cheap did he$_i$ buy

'Everyone' is a type II QP (hence, not syntactically namelike). The discourse principle therefore does not pick it up, and the unacceptability of (xiii) results.

In sum, if we assume the existence of a discourse principle that picks up syntactic namelike expressions for later discourse reference, the full range of data above can be explained. In particular, it explains the acceptability of (ii), and it is independently motivated for other constructions.

I would like to thank Amy Weinberg for helpful discussion of these issues.

11. Reconstruction is an LF phenomenon. If, following Aoun 1981, we assume that only a case-marked trace or PRO is "visible" in LF, then the relevant trace position will exclude traces left by raising and passivization. The examples to be discussed do involve 'Wh'-Movement and PRO interpretation, as Aoun's principle would suggest.

12. This well-formedness condition was first proposed by Vergnaud 1974. For discussion, see Chomsky (1981), Aoun 1981, Williams 1982, and chapter 6 of this book.

13. Dominique Sportiche has pointed out that similar judgments appear to arise in the following sentences:

(i) *Sally considers John$_i$ his$_i$ cook

(ii) *Sally sees John$_i$ as his$_i$ cook

In such cases there must be agreement in number between the predicative phrase, 'his cook', and the predicated phrase, 'John', as shown in (iii):

(iii) a.   John considers the men idiots

b. *John considers the men idiot

c.   John sees the men as idiots

d. *John sees the men as idiot

Since agreement is signaled by coindexing, the predicative phrase is coindexed with the phrase it predicates. Thus, the structure of (i) is (iv):

(iv) Sally considers [$_{NP_i}$ John] [$_{NP_i}$ his cook]

Consequently, 'his' cannot bear the index 'i' without violating the i/i Condition; similar considerations hold for (ii). This would explain the above data.

Note also that the relation between 'John' and 'his cook' in (i) is virtually identical to their relation in (57). Indeed, (i) was once thought to be derived transformationally by a deletion rule from (v):

(v) Sally considers John to be his cook

I mention this because it provides independent support for the assumption that 'John' and 'his cook' are coindexed in (57). Such cases also exhibit number agreement:

(vi) a.   John is the cook at the Ritz

b. *John is the cooks at the Ritz

c.   John and Fred are the cooks at the Ritz

d. *John and Fred are the cook at the Ritz

If such agreement generally involves coindexing, then this is further evidence that copular coindexing takes place in these cases.

14. Chomsky notes (personal communication) that this approach would claim that sentences like (i) are ill formed:

    (i) The owner of his$_i$ boat is John$_i$

Chomsky is correct. However, I am not sure that this is a problem. Chomsky claims that (i) is much more acceptable than (ii):

    (ii) [$_{NP_i}$ the owner of his$_i$ boat] left yesterday

However, these judgments do not receive universal agreement. If there is a difference between the two sentences, many do not see it as a sharp one. In fact, most people I asked found both examples rather unacceptable. Certainly they are judged far less acceptable than (iii) and (iv):

    (iii) a. The owner of his$_i$ own boat is John$_i$

         b. The captain of his$_i$ father's boat is John$_i$

    (iv) a. [$_{NP_i}$ The owner of his$_i$ own boat] left yesterday

         b. [$_{NP_i}$ The captain of his$_i$ father's boat] left yesterday

I discuss the reasons for such relative acceptability judgments in chapter 6.

Finally, there are some examples, structurally identical to (i), that seem to favor the disjoint reading quite strongly:

    (v) *The biographer of his$_i$ life is John$_i$

As for Chomsky's judgments, there may be some confounding pragmatic effects at work here. The intonation contour on which 'John' can be understood as the same as 'his' in (v) seems different from the regular one. The former has a slight rising intonation on 'life'. In any event, Chomsky's judgments do not seem very robust. The relative acceptability judgments seem far sturdier. In what follows, I will assume, perhaps incorrectly, that Chomsky's observations do not undermine the main lines of this analysis.

15. 'Himself' cannot be coindexed with AGR either, since AGR and the subject are coindexed. See chapter 4.

16. Bouchard 1982 and Sportiche 1982 both advocate a 'PRO-self' analysis for Fodor's examples. In effect, PRO in this position is analyzed as an anaphor, in which case (70a) can be treated as parallel to (i):

    (i) Only Churchill remembers himself giving the blood, sweat, and tears speech

In this way, they explain the parallelism in meaning between the two sentences.

Actually, Bouchard's and Sportiche's analyses exploit the same theoretical intuition being pursued here. Reconstruction makes PRO sentences look very much like earlier transformational theories did. In those theories, the structures underlying Reflexivization and Equi had *identical* NPs in the related positions. Thus, both my analysis of PRO and Bouchard's and Sportiche's advocate returning to an earlier account that divorced PRO interpretation from pronoun binding.

Despite these similarities, however, it appears that the cases of Reflexivization and Equi, collapsed to PRO interpretation in current accounts, differ. Thus, consider (73e), which does not appear to have the same ambiguity as (73b) and (73c). Perhaps these two instances of PRO are simply different. Still, given these observations it would be nice if the two sets of data could be unified.

17. This represents a change from the analysis of Chomsky and Lasnik 1977, where

(74a) was treated as an instance of 'self'-deletion and (74a) and (74b) therefore had different structures.

18. Note that in the version of Reconstruction developed here, 'someone' does not actually move to the embedded position of 'PRO' in (76). This is important, for if it were moved, how would the matrix variable (the subject position) be bound? As presented here, Reconstruction allows us to bypass certain restrictions on interpretation that a tree structure would impose. Essentially, it allows us to relate pairs of phrase markers. Thus, although the existential QP in (76) is interpreted as within the scope of the embedded universal QP, it does not follow that the subject variable in the matrix is unbound. Reconstruction "opens up" a third dimension so that the relevant phrase marker for interpretation is three-dimensional, not two-dimensional as in a tree structure. Viewing Reconstruction in this way thus explains how the matrix QP can be within the scope of the embedded QP and still bind the matrix variable. The only assumption that must be dropped to make this possible is that the relations mentioned must be specifiable in a two-dimensional tree format.

I am indebted to Edwin Williams for a discussion of this point.

19. The order of the variables X, Y, 't_i' is irrelevant.

Chapter 6

1. The term *regulative principle* is being used in the sense of Elster 1979. A principle is regulative if it is assumed to be characteristic of a certain domain and does in fact obtain in a large number of the central cases.

2. Montague grammarians have treated names in ways akin to quantified NPs, following the treatment in Montague 1973. Note, however, that for Montague *all* quantifiers were assimilated to names. There is no reason why 'any' but not 'every' should be so classified. Moreover, this treatment holds for the intensional logic, not for the final output, which was a translation in standard first-order terms. As subsequent authors have emphasized, this intermediate level can in principle be eliminated (Dowty, Wall, and Peters 1981). Therefore, it is not clear whether Montague "really" thought it natural to group names and quantifiers semantically. Certainly, in this regard, he departed from the mainstream.

3. A semantical theory is not identical to an interpretive theory. Rather, it is one instance of an interpretive theory, one that exploits semantical notions primitively in its theoretical structure. See chapter 7 for further discussion.

4. In fact, Higginbotham 1982 has advanced such an argument.

5. Such an explanation requires a tacit commitment to compositionality. If the interpretation of a phrase is constructed "from the bottom up," then 'his' in (7) cannot be interpreted until the phrase containing it has been interpreted. But the whole phrase cannot be interpreted until its subparts have been interpreted—in this case 'his'. This circularity allegedly leads to the unacceptability of (7).

6. See Williams 1982, for example.

Examples such as (i) are also relevant:

(i) John$_i$ saw that a picture of $\begin{Bmatrix} \text{*him}_i \\ \text{himself}_i \end{Bmatrix}$ was on the wall

(i) appears to violate the binding theory, since 'himself' is not bound in its minimal governing category. It is also unclear why 'him' cannot be coindexed with 'John'.

Chomsky 1981 has advanced an explanation of these facts in terms of the i/i Condition. Recall that the subject phrase of a tensed sentence must agree with the verb. To mark this, the grammar coindexes the subject NP with the AGR marker:

(ii) $[_{S_2}$ John saw that $[_{S_1}[_{NP_i}$ a picture of himself$_i]$ AGR^i be on the wall$]]$

However, in (ii) neither NP_i nor AGR is an accessible subject for 'himself', because coindexing 'himself' with either would violate the i/i Condition. Therefore, 'John' is the accessible subject and 'himself' has S_2 as its governing category. Hence the judgments in (i).

In this case, the i/i Condition does not involve any semantic circularity. The index on NP marks "agreement" and the index on 'himself' marks "accessibility of subject." The i/i Condition in this case "means" that an element α is not accessible to an element β if α agrees with β. But this hardly seems to be a case of interpretive circularity. From an interpretive point of view, the i's do not mark the same sort of relation; thus, if the i/i Condition is construed semantically, it should not apply. That it does apply is a reason for construing it in a strongly syntactic way.

Incidentally, this explanation of (i) suggests that the i/i Condition does not hold for QPs:

(iii) Someone saw that a picture of everyone was on display

(iii) does not have an interpretation in which 'everyone' has widest sentential scope, indicating that the variable it leaves behind is not subject to the i/i Condition. This further suggests that the condition does not apply to anaphors in general; at most, it applies to A-anaphors. In fact, I believe that a possible interpretation of the i/i Condition is that it is a principle regulating the indexing of "pronouns"—be they bound anaphors or regular anaphors. This requires construing 'each other' as a pronoun, but this is not very counterintuitive anyhow. In any event, construing the i/i Condition in this way leads to the correct results with respect to its applicability.

7. In fact, if compositionality is what is being violated here (cf. note 5), then examples such as (10) and (11) should be worse than (7). The items causing the referential circularity are even more deeply embedded here than in (7); hence, compositionality is violated to a greater extent.

8. Note that the cases of predication (chapter 5, note 13) behave in the same way:

(i) a. *Sheila considers $John_i$ his_i cook

b. Sheila considers $John_i$ his_i father's cook

Note, as well, that on this analysis 'his own' is not an anaphor:

(ii) $John_i$ is his_i own cook

For this to be acceptable, 'his' must be construed as "too deep" to be affected by the i/i Condition because of the presence of 'own'. This result should not be seen as disturbing. 'His own' is not *grammatically* an anaphor. It acts more like 'each . . . the others' than 'each other'. For example, it can stand alone:

(iii) a. *Each other's are in the yard

b. His own is in the yard

It can be "bound" across a discourse:

(iv) $John_i$ gave me Sheila's car. His_i own is in the shop.

Finally, it can be bound outside its governing category:

(v) $John_i$ told Sheila that she could borrow his_i own car

9. The shift in perspective regarding the interpretation of natural language interpretive processes recapitulates a shift made earlier in mathematical logic. As Goldfarb 1980:353 put it:

Our view of logic carries with it the notion that logical truths are completely general, not in the sense of being the most general truths about logical furniture, but rather in the sense of having no subject matter in particular, of talking of no entities or sorts of entities in particular, and of being applicable no matter what things we wish to investigate.

10. The qualifier 'relatively' is important. The methodology of science is not greatly illuminated by realist assumptions characteristic of such semantic theorizing. See Morgenbesser 1969, Putnam 1983, and Rorty 1979.

11. See Brandon and Hornstein 1982. Semantical notions are often taken to be obviously central to interpretation theory because language can be used to make assertions and convey information. Communication is further taken to be the essential feature of language on tacit evolutionary grounds. For the sake of argument, let us assume that this was so—that language developed because it could carry information, that is, because it was a vehicle for semantic properties. This does *not* mean that semantical notions are the essential features of the structure of language, viewed synchronically, or indeed that they are central to the organization of the language faculty. The semantical capacity of natural languages may well be the by-product of essentially nonsemantical structures. All that evolutionary considerations allow us to conclude is that, if language indeed was selected for because it could convey true and false information, then, whatever the structure of the language faculty, it must be able to do this. However, whether the means at its disposal directly reflect this semantical capacity is an open question from such a point of view. It can only be resolved by showing that the principles of the language faculty—the "laws" that describe its structure and operation—are *best* cast in a semantical vocabulary. But I have shown that this is not the case for certain large domains of data, and I will suggest that casting such principles in a semantical vocabulary is not as important or explanatory as it is often taken to be.

Chapter 7

1. For a critique of translational theories along these lines, see Lewis 1972, Fodor 1978, and the introduction to Evans and McDowell 1976. These papers not only criticize translation theories but also suggest that a semantical approach can fill the gap left by such theories.

2. This fact has been noted by, among others, Barwise and Perry, Chomsky, Davidson, Dummett, Montague, Quine, the early Wittgenstein, and, on at least some readings, the late Wittgenstein—in short, by virtually everyone who has written on the topic. To my knowledge, the only dissenting opinion is that of Baker and Hacker 1982, who appear to deny that there is anything like linguistic productivity, under any interpretation of productivity.

This consensus does not mean that the notion of productivity is at all clear. However, there does seem to be rather wide agreement on the abilities mentioned in the text, namely, that speakers of natural languages are routinely able to understand an unbounded number of sentences never before encountered, and to do this appropriately.

3. This is not a problem for a syntactic theory, that is, the part of the total ability that can be fully characterized in terms of a translation theory. As long as the information processing analogy can be maintained, such an approach seems satisfactory. It is when this analogy breaks down that the problem begins. For discussion, see Fodor 1975.

4. Semantical theories may have other aims as well, such as explaining why certain scientific theories succeed and what it is for them to succeed. For some discussion of this, see Putnam 1978, Rorty 1979, and the introduction to Rorty 1982.

5. Under the heading *Neo-Fregean* I will include numerous theories that differ among themselves in important ways: standard possible worlds accounts, situation semantics, some versions of the Davidsonian program, and current versions of Montague grammar.

6. In what follows I will use the term 'reference' for this general relation between linguistic expressions and nonlinguistic entities.

7. The analysis can be pitched at various levels of specificity. Thus, for example, the theory of reference might be coordinated with abilities and knowledge at the level of the axioms of the theory, yielding what Dummett 1976 calls an *atomistic theory*. Or it might be coordinated with them at the level of the theorems, e.g., the T sentences of a theory of truth, yielding what Dummett has called a *molecular theory*. Davidson 1973 argues for this approach. Theories of sense coordinated at yet higher levels could easily be imagined. None of these possibilities should be ruled out a priori. See note 9 for further discussion.

8. See Fodor 1981 for a discussion of the attempts to achieve a theory of definitions. The classical locus of arguments against this program remains Wittgenstein's *Philosophical Investigations*.

9. Kripke 1980 makes this point, as does Davidson 1967. The latter, however, thinks that it is confined to a theory of sense. A theory of reference or of truth does not seem to be similarly vulnerable to these sorts of objections. Harman 1974 makes some very important observations on this point. Davidson tries to answer Harman's objections, the gist of which is repeated above in the text, but I am not certain how his remarks bear on Harman's points. In Davidson's sense a theory of translation is not meant to be a theory of meaning dealing with the problem of linguistic productivity. Rather, it is an account of when it is legitimate to ascribe beliefs and other attitudes to a language user. This problem may be addressable without explicating the notion of truth. At any rate, it is not the problem being addressed here, nor is it the problem that Davidson appeared to be addressing in his original papers.

As Dummett 1976 has observed, there is another move that semantical theorists attracted by this approach to meaning make when confronted with such difficulties: they adopt a holistic account. Words have meanings, but only in the context of language as a whole or behavior as a whole. It is often quite unclear what sort of notion of meaning is left after this move has been made (see Putnam 1983 a and b). Dummett points out, correctly in my opinion, that such holistic retorts, often backed up by an analogy to the practice of science, often beg the issues. What is needed is an account of the ability. Holism in language or science is not itself such an account but a further specification of the problem. We still require an account of what it is to make holistic evaluations of meaning.

Note that this does not mean that meaning may not be best described by taking the language as a whole as the unit of meaning. In such a case the principles will be stated at the level of the language as a whole. Although no one has yet provided such principles, the possibility that they exist should not be ruled out a priori, as Dummett appears to do in the appendix of Dummett 1975.

10. Since Tarski is interested in the notion of truth rather than meaning, this process is reversed in his theory. Tarski takes meaning for granted in the guise of a list of translations for the relevant linguistic terms. Given these translations/meanings of the basic components of the language L, a recursive definition of L is constructed. In sum, if one assumes either the notion of meaning or the notion of truth, one can explain the notion not assumed. The problem is to fix one or the other notion. Davidson's approach appears to take the notion of truth for granted, asserting that if this is done a Tarski-like theory of meaning can be constructed. Harman 1974 points out that this may not get us what we want out of a theory of meaning, since what we want is an account of what it is for an arbitrary sentence to be true. Davidson

1973 appears to answer that this is not necessary, since we can all make judgments concerning whether or not a speaker holds a sentence to be true, and suggests that this is all we need. This may be so, if all we want is a theory of translation. However, for a theory of meaning we appear to need an account of truth if we are to explain the practical ability of linguistic productivity. Here we cannot *assume* that a speaker knows what it is for a sentence to be true; we want to explain it. This is essentially Dummett's point in his critique of Davidson's program. I believe it is also the point that Field 1972 makes. The introduction to Putnam 1983b contains relevant observations as well.

11. Part of the reason that such notions are not considered opaque may lie with the belief that notions like "object," "property," etc., can be physicalistically explicated. Science in the limit will provide us with the precise referents of such notions. However, even if we concede that this might be so (and it is a very large concession), it seems unlikely that this will throw much light on the issues of linguistic meaning. Whatever underlies a native speaker's competence, it is hard to believe that it involves some incipient or inchoate conception of what the true physical theory will look like when science indeed has provided us with all the referents. Nor do we understand what such conceptions amount to.

12. This term is Dummett's; see Dummett 1975.

13. This view is quite explicit in Barwise and Perry 1980, 1983. They assert that their theory of situations is just the "common-sense view." For them the world is made up of objects, individuals, properties, relations, etc., which combine to form situations and situation types. Sentences signify situation types and do this in virtue of their linguistic meanings. Linguistic meanings are regularities across discourse events. However, the nature of these regularities is left totally unexplained.

It is clear from their discussion that Barwise and Perry think that these notions need no further explication. In some sense they are correct. The words have perfectly ordinary uses. However, it is not at all clear that the notions in their ordinary senses can carry the sort of explanatory burden that Barwise and Perry place on them.

I might be mistaken in ascribing to Barwise and Perry the view that the notions they invoke do not need further explication. I am not mistaken in believing that they provide none. Until they do, their view seems no different from the one, widely held, that recognizes linguistic productivity as a problem to be explained.

14. Searle 1974 seems to think that the use of fictional names involves pretending to use them as if they referred to real entities. For this suggestion to carry any explanatory force, Searle must explain what such pretending consists in. It seems possible to use fictional names without believing that they refer to real individuals and without intending to get anyone else to believe this. But then is pretending anything more than using the fictional names in ways similar to real names, except for believing that the fictional names are fictional? The problem is explaining what holding this sort of belief amounts to. For some discussion of these and related issues, see Rorty 1981.

15. Some theorists propose taking the notion of context as a primitive index; see Dowty, Wall, and Peters 1981 and their reference to Creswell. Others, such as Barwise and Perry 1983, note that context can affect the interpretation of a statement by making available "resource situations" that can be used to get secondary interpretations. The problem with this theory is that it fails to account for where resource situations come from and how they are *in general* made available. This is not to say that Barwise and Perry give no examples. However, as far as I can tell, no general pattern emerges. What a possible resource situation is and how it can be used to get secondary interpretations seems to be decided on a case-by-case basis. But this does not explain how context affects meaning, so much as repeat that it does affect it. This, however,

is not really controversial. What may be novel in Barwise and Perry's approach is that they regard context as far more important than did earlier theorists. However, until they give an account of linguistic meaning and specify what they take the rules of context to be, this impression cannot be firmly evaluated. The secondary interpretations are distinguished from those that we get simply from a theory of linguistic meaning. As the latter notion has not been explicated, however, the degree of Barwise and Perry's departure from earlier accounts cannot be easily estimated.

References

Aoun, J. (1981). On the formal nature of anaphoric relations. Doctoral dissertation, Massachusetts Institute of Technology.

Aoun, J. (1982). On derivations. Ms., University of Massachusetts, Amherst.

Aoun, J., and N. Hornstein (forthcoming). A theory of quantifier types.

Aoun, J., N. Hornstein, and D. Sportiche (1980). On some aspects of wide scope quantification. *Journal of Linguistic Research* 1.3.

Baker, G. P., and P. M. S. Hacker (1980). *Wittgenstein: Understanding and Meaning*. University of Chicago Press, Chicago, Ill.

Barwise, J., and J. Perry (1980). The situation underground. In J. Barwise and I. Sag, eds., *Stanford Working Papers in Semantics*, vol. 1. Stanford University, Stanford, Calif.

Berwick, R. C., and A. S. Weinberg (1982). Parsing efficiency, computational complexity, and the evaluation of grammatical theories. *Linguistic Inquiry* 13.

Bouchard, D. (1982). On the content of empty categories. Doctoral dissertation, Massachusetts Institute of Technology.

Brandon, R., and N. Hornstein (1982). From icons to symbols: Some speculations on the evolution of language. Ms., Duke University and Columbia University.

Burge, T. (1977). Belief de re. *Journal of Philosophy* LXXIV.6.

Carlson, L., and J. Hintikka (1979). Conditionals, generic quantifiers, and other applications of subgames. In Saarinen (1979).

Chomsky, N. (1965). *Aspects of the Theory of Syntax*. MIT Press, Cambridge, Mass.

Chomsky, N. (1973). Conditions on transformations. In Chomsky (1977a).

Chomsky, N. (1975). *Reflections on Language*. Pantheon, New York.

Chomsky, N. (1976). Conditions on rules of grammar. In Chomsky (1977a).

Chomsky, N. (1977a). *Essays on Form and Interpretation*. North Holland, Amsterdam.

Chomsky, N. (1977b). On wh-movement. In P. Culicover, T. Wasow, and A. Akmajian, eds., *Formal Syntax*. Academic Press, New York.

Chomsky, N. (1980). On binding. *Linguistic Inquiry* 11.1.

Chomsky, N. (1981). *Lectures on Government and Binding*. Foris, Dordrecht.

Chomsky, N. (1982). *Some Concepts and Consequences of the Theory of Government and Binding*. MIT Press, Cambridge, Mass.

Chomsky, N., and H. Lasnik (1977). Filters and control. *Linguistic Inquiry* 8.3.

Davidson, D. (1965). Theories of meaning and learnable languages. In Y. Bar-Hillel, ed. *Logic, Methodology, and Philosophy of Science. Proceedings of the 1964 International Congress*. Amsterdam.

Davidson, D. (1967). Truth and meaning. *Synthese* XVII.3.

Davidson, D. (1973). Radical interpretation. *Dialectica* 27.

Davidson, D. (1977). Reality without reference. In Platts (1980).

Davidson, D., and G. Harman (1975). *The Logic of Grammar*. Dickenson Publishing, Encino, Calif.

Dresher, B. E., and N. Hornstein (1976). On some supposed contributions of artificial intelligence to the scientific theory of language. *Cognition* 4.

Dougherty, R. (1970). A grammar of coordinate conjoined structures: I. *Language* 46.4.

Dowty, D., R. Wall, and S. Peters (1981). *Introduction to Montague Semantics*. D. Reidel, Dordrecht.

Dummett, M. (1975). What is a theory of meaning (I). In S. Guttenplan, ed., *Meaning and Language*. Oxford University Press, Oxford.

Dummett, M. (1976). What is a theory of meaning (II). In Evans and McDowell (1976).

Elster, J. (1979). *Ulysses and the Sirens*. Cambridge University Press, Cambridge.

Evans, G. (1977). Pronouns, quantifiers, and relative clauses (I). In Platts (1980).

Evans, G., and J. McDowell (1976). *Truth and Meaning*. Oxford University Press, Oxford.

Field, H. (1972). Tarski's theory of truth. In Platts (1980).

Fiengo, R., and J. Higginbotham (1982). Opacity in NP. *Linguistic Analysis* 7.

Fodor, J. (1975). *The Language of Thought*. T. Y. Crowell, New York.

Fodor, J. (1978). Tom Swift and his procedural grandmother. In Fodor (1982).

Fodor, J. (1981). The current status of the innateness controversy. In Fodor (1982).

Fodor, J. (1982). *Representations*. Bradford Books/MIT Press, Cambridge, Mass.

Freidin, R. (1978). Cyclicity and the theory of grammar. *Linguistic Inquiry* 9.4.

Geach, P. (1962). *Reference and Generality*. Cornell University Press, Ithaca, N.Y.

Goldfarb, W. (1980). Logic in the twenties. *Journal of Symbolic Logic* XLIV.

Haïk, I. (1982). Indirect binding. Ms., Massachusetts Institute of Technology.

Harman, G. (1974). Meaning and semantics. In M. Munitz and P. Unger, eds., *Semantics and Philosophy*. New York University Press, New York.

Heim, I. (1982). The semantics of definite and indefinite noun phrases. Doctoral dissertation, University of Massachusetts, Amherst.

Higginbotham, J. (1980). Pronouns and bound variables. *Linguistic Inquiry* 11.4.

Higginbotham, J. (1982). Sense and syntax. Paper delivered at NELS 1982, Montreal.

Hintikka, J. (1974). Quantifiers vs. quantification theory. In Saarinen (1979).

Hintikka, J. (1976a). Language games. In Saarinen (1979).

Hintikka, J. (1976b). Quantifiers in logic and quantifiers in natural language. In Saarinen (1979).

Hornstein, N. (1981). Two ways of interpreting quantifiers. Ms., Columbia University.

Hornstein, N., and D. Lightfoot (1981). *Explanations in Linguistics* Longman, London.

Hornstein, N., and A. Weinberg (1981). Case theory and preposition stranding. *Linguistic Inquiry* 12.1.

Jackendoff, R. (1977). On belief contexts. *Linguistic Inquiry* 8.

Jackendoff, R. (1980). Belief contexts revisited. *Linguistic Inquiry* 11.

Kamp, H. (1982). A theory of truth and semantic representation. In J. Groenendijk et al., eds., *Formal Methods in the Study of Language*. Amsterdam.

Kaplan, D. (1970). What is Russell's theory of descriptions? In Davidson and Harman (1975).

Kayne, R. (1979). Two notes on the NIC. In A. Belletti et al., *Theory of Markedness in Generative Grammar. Proceedings of the 1979 GLOW Conference*. Scuola Normale Superiore, Pisa.

Koopman, H., and D. Sportiche (1981). Variables and the Bijection Principle. Paper presented at the GLOW Conference, Göttingen.

Kripke, S. (1980). *Naming and Necessity*. Harvard University Press, Cambridge, Mass.

Kupin, J., and H. Lasnik (1977). A restrictive theory of transformational grammar. *Theoretical Linguistics* 4.3.

Lasnik, H. (1980). Learnability, restrictiveness, and the evaluation metric.

Lewis, D. (1972). General semantics. In D. Davidson and G. Harman, eds., *Semantics of Natural Language*. D. Reidel, Dordrecht.

Linebarger, M. (1980). The grammar of negative polarity. Doctoral dissertation, Massachusetts Institute of Technology.

McDowell, J. (1976). Truth conditions, bivalence, and verificationism. In Evans and McDowell (1976).

May, R. (1977). The grammar of quantification. Doctoral dissertation, Massachusetts Institute of Technology.

Montague, R. (1973). The proper treatment of quantification. In R. Thomason, ed., *Formal Philosophy*. Yale University Press, New Haven, Conn.

Morgenbesser, S. (1969). The realist-instrumentalist controversy. In S. Morgenbesser et al., eds., *Philosophy, Science, and Method: Essays in Honor of Ernest Nagel*. St. Martins Press, Inc., New York.

Newport, E., and H. Gleitman, and L. Gleitman (1977). Mother, I'd rather do it myself: Some effects and noneffects of maternal speech style. In Snow and Ferguson (1977).

Platts, M. (1980). *Reference, Truth and Reality*. Routledge and Kegan Paul, London.

Postal, P. (1974). *On Raising*. MIT Press, Cambridge, Mass.

Putnam, H. (1971). The "innateness hypothesis" and explanatory models in linguistics. In J. Searle, ed., *The Philosophy of Language*. Oxford University Press, Oxford.

Putnam, H. (1975a). The meaning of "meaning." In Putnam (1975b).

Putnam, H. (1975b). *Mind, Language, and Reality*. Cambridge University Press, Cambridge.

Putnam, H. (1978). Reference and understanding. In *Meaning and the Moral Sciences*. Routledge and Kegan Paul, London.

Putnam, H. (1983a). Meaning holism. Ms., Harvard University, Cambridge, Mass.

Putnam, H. (1983b). *Realism and Reason*. Cambridge University Press, Cambridge.

Quine, W. V. O. (1960). *Word and Object*. MIT Press, Cambridge, Mass.

Quine, W. V. O. (1974). *The Roots of Reference*. Open Court Publishing, La Salle, Ill.

Reinhart, T. (1976). The syntactic domain of anaphora. Doctoral dissertation, Massachusetts Institute of Technology.

Rizzi, L. (1978). A restructuring rule. In Rizzi (1982).

Rizzi, L. (1980). Violations of the wh-island constraint and the subjacency condition. In Rizzi (1982).

Rizzi, L. (1982). *Issues in Italian Syntax*. Foris, Dordrecht.

Rorty, R. (1979). *Philosophy and the Mirror of Nature*. Princeton University Press, Princeton, N.J.

Rorty, R. (1981). Is there a problem about fiction in discourse? In Rorty (1982).

Rorty, R. (1982). *Consequences of Pragmatism*. University of Minnesota Press, Minneapolis, Minn.

Saarinen, E. (1979). *Game Theoretical Semantics*. D. Reidel, Dordrecht.

Scheffler, I. (1955). On synonymy and indirect discourse. *Philosophy of Science* 22.

Searle, J. (1974). The logical status of fictional discourse. *New Literary History* V.

Snow, C., and C. Ferguson (1977). *Talking to Children*. Cambridge University Press, Cambridge.

Sportiche, D. (1979). On binding nodes in French. Ms., Massachusetts Institute of Technology.

Sportiche, D. (1982). Some speculations on the binding of PRO. Paper delivered at NELS 1982, Montreal.

Taraldsen, T. (1979). The theoretical interpretation of a class of marked extractions. In A. Belletti et al., eds., *Theory of Markedness in Generative Grammar. Proceedings of the 1979 GLOW Conference*. Scuola Normale Superiore, Pisa.

Vergnaud, J.-R. (1974). French relative clauses. Doctoral dissertation, Massachusetts Institute of Technology.

Wexler, K., and P. Culicover (1980). *Formal Principles of Language Acquisition*. MIT Press, Cambridge, Mass.

Wiggins, D. (1980). "Most" and "all": Some comments on a familiar programme, and on the logical form of quantified sentences. In Platts (1980).

Williams, E. (1982). The NP cycle. *Linguistic Inquiry* 13.2.

Wittgenstein, L. (1953). *Philosophical Investigations*. Oxford University Press, Oxford.

Index